INTO THE MIST
Tales of Death and Disaster, Mishaps and Misdeeds, Misfortune and Mayhem in Great Smoky Mountains National Park

VOLUME 1

Written by David Brill
Edited by Steve Kemp and Kent Cave
Editorial Assistance by Julie Brown, Cyn Slaughter,
Bob Wightman, and Dana Soehn
Design and Production by Karen Key
Cover Photograph by Bill Lea

5 6 7 8 9 10 11 12 13 14 15

Published by Great Smoky Mountains Association
ISBN 978-0-937207-87-1
Printed in the U.S.A.

Great Smoky Mountains Association is a nonprofit organization
which supports the educational, scientific, and historical programs
of Great Smoky Mountains National Park. Our publications are
an educational service intended to enhance the public's under-
standing and enjoyment of the national park. If you would like to
know more about our publications, memberships, and projects,
please contact:
Great Smoky Mountains Association
P.O. Box 130
Gatlinburg, TN 37738
865.436.7318
SmokiesInformation.org

*This book is dedicated to the rangers and staff of
Great Smoky Mountains National Park, who tirelessly devote
their time, skills, and energy to preserving America's
best-loved park and protecting the millions of people who visit it each year.*

CONTENTS

NOTE: This book was in production in November 2016 when fires swept through Gatlinburg, leaving 14 people dead. The firestorm disaster may be included in the next volume of the *Into the Mist* series.

INTRODUCTION

The book you now hold in your hands explores a diverse range of subjects unified by two important aspects: all involve events and circumstances that directly threatened—and in many cases, claimed—human lives, and all took place within Great Smoky Mountains National Park (GSMNP).

Many of these stories are undeniably sad, but all are also engaging because they depict human beings in extreme situations, struggling to survive against brutal and unrelenting adversity. That struggle, as represented by the three varieties of conflict essential to nearly every compelling tale—human against nature, human against human, human against him or her self—is also a central element in this book's chapters.

There is reward in the telling—and, the author hopes, in the reading—of narrative stories steeped in tension and compelled by the intentional suspension of details that reveal the outcome, but that reward is diminished considerably by the reality that, in the case of this book, these are stories about human beings—fathers, mothers, children, friends—who suffered mightily before they succumbed in some cases, or were rescued in others.

In researching and writing about these events, the author took to heart his responsibility to the victims, their families, and their friends to present the details accurately. In this regard, the extensive incident reports produced by GSMNP's staff of rangers and law-enforcement personnel were invaluable. These reports reflect favorably on park rangers in their commitment to investigate thoroughly, and often in minute detail, the circumstances surrounding all untimely deaths that occur in GSMNP.

The events portrayed in the book's chapters have been selected from a list of all known fatalities that occurred in the park between 1931 and

2013. The list, which appears in the book's appendix, presents each fatality by date, location, and victim name and hometown (where such details are known) and includes a textual description of the cause and circumstances of the death.

The author compiled the list over many months of research and gleaned information from a number of sources, including GSMNP monthly superintendents' reports (1931-67) and later annual reports, files of official documents and correspondence stored at the National Archives in College Park Maryland and at GSMNP archives, official incident reports provided by GSMNP, press releases issued by GSMNP, published newspaper and magazine reports, and internet searches (primarily for incidents dating from 2000 onward).

Ancestry.com and Newspapers.com provided details that were, in some cases, lacking or contradictory in the source reports, including full names, ages and dates of birth, hometowns, official dates of death, and, in a few cases, coroners' reports confirming cause of death.

The fatalities list represents one of the first comprehensive databases of all known fatalities created for any of the national parks.

There's no doubt that researching death and disaster is a morbid pursuit, and through the research process, the author endeavored never to lose sight of the enormous pain and suffering these deaths caused for the family members and friends of the deceased. But a study of the deaths that have occurred in the park can also be instructive, allowing GSMNP managers to assess the relative risks associated with various activities and specific locations within the park and thereby enhance their visitor safety and education efforts. It will also serve park visitors in a similar way.

There's no disputing the fact that individuals die in GSMNP. Between 1931 and 2013, 468 documented deaths occurred in the park, an average of about five or six per year. People continue to die in other national parks as well. An August 12, 2015, *Washington Post* article[1] puts the annual death toll at between 120 and 140 people across the entire National Park Service system, not counting suicides.

But as the article points out, 280 million people visit the parks each year. "That means that if you go to a national park, your odds of dying there are roughly 1 in 2 million," the article reports. "For comparison, that's simi-

1   "Forget bears: Here's what really kills people at national parks": www.washingtonpost.com/news/wonk/wp/2015/08/12/forget-bears-heres-what-really-kills-people-at-national-parks/

lar to the likelihood that you'll die of ebola at some point in your life."

It's a bit ironic that some of the threats most feared by park visitors—chiefly venomous snake bites and bear attacks—are, in fact, statistically very rare. Reflecting that reality, the *Post* article is titled "Forget bears: Here's what really kills people at national parks."

The park is home to populations of Northern Copperheads (*Agkistrodon contortrix mokasen*) and Timber Rattlesnakes (*Crotalus horridus*), both venomous, and visitors should be mindful of their presence and aware of their preferred habitats, but bites are uncommon, and no one has died from a snake bite in the park's history.

The park is also home to 1,600 or so black bears (*Ursus americanus*). These powerful alpha predators (also known as apex predators because they're at the top of the food chain) should be respected more than feared, and park wildlife specialists are vigilant in implementing and rigid in enforcing a strict science-based strategy for managing the bear population.

Ultimately, that strategy focuses as much or more on controlling human behavior—particularly feeding bears, drawing too close to them, or careless food preparation and storage in the park—than on the conduct of the animals. It surprises many visitors to learn that only one fatality has resulted from a human-bear encounter since the park's founding. On May 21, 2000, hiker Glenda Bradley was killed by two bears near Elkmont. On page 149, the chapter titled "When Bears Attack" details the circumstances surrounding Bradley's death.

Violent crime is also exceedingly rare in the national park, particularly relative to that occurring in major US cities. Fourteen murders have taken place within GSMNP since 1931. But to put that into perspective, in recent years, the park logs an average of more than 30,000 visits per day, establishing GSMNP as the 24th and 29th "largest cities" in Tennessee and North Carolina, respectively, and making the park statistically one of the safer places in the nation. And, further, nearly all of the slain persons were acquainted with—and entered the park with—their assailants and, thus, were not random victims.

Despite the rarity of violent crime in GSMNP, three incidents involving murder—only one of which actually occurred in the park—are included in this book largely because they detail the meticulous process the park's law-enforcement personnel pursue—often in cooperation with other federal, state, and local jurisdictions—in investigating and solving crime. These details reflect park rangers' extensive training and exemplary conduct and should inspire confidence among GSMNP visitors and give pause to anyone considering commission of a criminal act within the park.

On page 43, "A Murdered Jane Doe in a Smokies Creek Leads to a Cross-country Hunt for Her Killer" recounts one such crime, which occurred in August 1976 and where victim and murderer arrived together. The chapter provides valuable insight into the police work required to solve crimes and apprehend perpetrators in the days before computers and national crime databases.

"Armed, Dangerous, Ready to Kill Cops (and Headed to the National Park)," on page 77, tells the story of John Peck, who in June 2004 began a planned killing spree with the alleged shooting death of his former girlfriend in Wilmington, North Carolina, before entering the park. The courageous and disciplined response of GSMNP's law enforcement personnel, along with partners from the Cherokee, North Carolina, police department, brought Peck's murderous rampage to an end, and in so doing, ensured the safety and protection of park visitors.

And, beginning on page 139, "A Suspected Mass Murderer Arrives in the National Park, but Does He Leave?" explores the case of William Bradford Bishop, a mid-level US State Department employee, who in 1976 allegedly killed five members of his family in Maryland, later abandoned his car in GSMNP, and then disappeared without a trace, becoming one of the longest sought-after fugitives in US history.

While violent crime is rare in the park, more routine activities can, in fact, pose significant risk. Nearly 33 percent (153) of all known park fatalities resulted from motor vehicle accidents (autos and motorcycles), which remain the leading cause of death in the park as well as in the nation. That statistic also establishes GSMNP's roadways as by far the most dangerous places within the half-million-acre park. On page 25, "The Deadliest Night in the Smokies' Deadliest Place" details the events that led to the March 2005 deaths of five senior adults, all riding in one car, on the Gatlinburg-Pigeon Forge Spur.

Drownings have claimed 59 lives and rank as the third leading cause of death in the park, behind aircraft crashes, which have caused 73 fatalities. "Taken Under," on page 53, details some of the tragic deaths by drowning that have occurred in GSMNP, one of which involved a honeymooning groom whose young wife witnessed his death in October 1950.

Millions of cubic feet of water crash and cascade along the park's waterways—particularly during and after storm events—and can overwhelm even the strongest swimmers. Compounding the danger are the silt and algae-covered stones that line the creek beds and create treacherous footing. One could argue that drowning deaths are entirely preventable—don't enter the water, and you won't drown—but the allure of cool water on a hot summer day is a powerful one. Those who succumb to that allure would be well advised to settle on tranquil pools rather than churning rapids.

Meanwhile, fatal falls, often from exposed ledges or the tops of slippery, moss-covered waterfalls, have killed 18 park visitors and rank as the seventh leading cause of death. Like drowning, these accidental deaths are largely preventable through caution and vigilance.

Trekkers who enter GSMNP's backcountry should be fully prepared to contend with the violent forces of nature that occasionally ravage the park. Beginning on page 33, "In an Encounter with Nature's Deadly Force, 'Under Shelter' Does Not Mean 'Out of Harm's Way,'" recounts the fatal lightning strike that killed two hikers inside the Double Spring Gap Shelter in July 1980.

Lightning remains one of the leading weather-related causes of death in the United States, and North Carolina and Tennessee are fourth and seventh, respectively, in a national ranking by state for lightning-strike fatalities between 1959 and 2014.

Hypothermia, a critical loss of body heat from exposure to cold, wet conditions, has killed 14 park visitors. Among them was John Mink, a 25-year-old graduate student from Indiana, who entered the backcountry alone in February of 1984 and walked straight into the teeth of a blizzard.

"The Chill of Death," on page 17, recounts Mink's desperate—but in the end, futile—struggle to survive and the difficulties encountered by the search crew in locating and recovering his body.

Other chapters detail the often heroic responses of the park's ranger staff in the face of brutal weather events and their successful efforts to rescue stranded visitors and ultimately prevent loss of life. "Storm of the Century," on page 113, tells the story of the epic storm of March 1993, widely regarded as the "Storm of the Century," and its lingering impact on the park.

"A Mother's Mission of Thanks," on page 65, about two young backpackers trapped for five days by drifted chest-deep snow, presents a similarly favorable outcome brought about by the park's ranger staff.

"Deadly Derecho," on page 175, describes the July 2012 storm that slammed the park's extreme western region, knocking out radios, toppling thousands of trees, choking off roads, and killing two park visitors and injuring many others.

Among the more heart-rending deaths that occur in the park are those brought about by the victims' own hands. Between 1931 and 2013, suicide has claimed 37 lives and ranks as the fifth leading cause of death in the park. These deaths are particularly tragic because the victims often suffered months or even years of crippling emotional pain and anguish before they sought the ultimate means of escape, and medical science suggests that the vast majority of these deaths could have been averted had the victims sought effective professional help.

Recent years have seen a dramatic improvement in the efficacy of modern antidepressant medications and psychological counseling. And the suicide deaths of public figures, most recently that of Robin Williams, have helped remove the stigma and prompt open discussions about mental illness.

Nevertheless, suicide rates in the United States are increasing. According to a 2016 study by the National Center for Health Statistics, from 1999 through 2014, the age-adjusted suicide rate in the United States increased 24 percent, and the increase was seen for men and women alike and across all age groups.

Though most suicides (roughly 70 percent) take place at home, many occur in public places, including national parks. Based on a review of the notes left by suicide victims who died in GSMNP, for many of the deceased, the park was chosen as the place of death with considerable forethought. For some, the park's vast tracts of wilderness would provide a measure of privacy for executing the final act, while others imagined that the wilderness would ensure that their bodies would never be found. By contrast, one of the suicide victims picked a high-traffic area of the park to ensure that she *would* be found.

For others, the park represented a peaceful environment in which to end things. And a few had spent happier times with family and friends in the park and wanted to return to a place of cherished memories to die.

According to "Suicides in National Parks: United States, 2003-2009," a 2010 article that appeared in *Morbidity and Mortality Weekly Report*[2], 84 national parks reported 286 suicide events (including attempts) during the

---

2   A publication of the Centers for Disease Control and Prevention.

study period. Of those, 194 (or 68 percent) were fatal. Leading the list for suicide deaths were Blue Ridge Parkway, Grand Canyon, and Natchez Trace, while GSMNP ranked 18th.

Suicides traumatize the grieving family members and friends of the victims, but they also place an undue emotional strain on visitors who discover victims' bodies and park personnel who must deal with the aftermath, an especially gruesome task in the case of death by firearm, which accounts for 68 percent of the suicides in GSMNP.

Suicide deaths are often costly in terms of staff time and resources, particularly when the park mobilizes extensive search operations—in many cases involving teams of on-the-ground trackers as well as helicopters and fixed-wing aircraft—to find missing persons thought to be suicidal.

Nearly all of these operations succeed in recovering victims' bodies. "Star-crossed Lovers Part Ways on a Remote Mountain Ridge," which begins on page 103, recounts the intensive search to locate and recover the body of 19-year-old John Rudd, who had entered the park with his wife of less than a month to execute a joint suicide pact. The wife ultimately reneged and arrived at the Abrams Creek Ranger Station dazed, confused, and unwilling—or unable—to lead rangers to her deceased husband. The account of efforts to locate and recover Rudd's body illustrates the methodical approach park rangers apply in searching for missing persons.

In a few cases, potential suicide victims are never found. A week-long search, involving as many as 60 individuals, failed to locate Derek Lueking, whose abandoned car was found at the Newfound Gap parking area on March 17, 2012. Lueking, who was reportedly distraught over the death of a family member, is still missing.

Each of the chapters contained in this book offers a degree of instructive value, despite the often grim subject matter. In some cases, that value derives from a chapter's detailed presentation of how GSMNP administrators and rangers execute their duties, whether those duties involve enforcing the law, investigating or thwarting crime, searching for lost persons, or mounting rescue operations for individuals stranded in the backcountry. There's also value in examining the decisions and choices made by park visitors that, in the end, compromised their safety and survival.

But it would be disingenuous to claim that this book's chapters are intended solely to educate and inform, to inspire prudence and caution, to identify risks lurking within the park, and to allow readers to benefit from others' mistakes.

Indeed, we humans are all bound by the certainty that we will die, but few of us, except perhaps those diagnosed with terminal diseases, have any idea of how or when our deaths will occur. As a consequence, many of us retain a natural curiosity regarding the deaths of others.

That curiosity is reflected in our tendency to slow as we pass the scene of an automobile accident along the highway. It's reflected in the popularity of such true-crime TV series as *48 Hours* and *Dateline*. Likewise, it's reflected in the best-selling books that chronicle tragedies, including Sebastian Junger's *The Perfect Storm* (about the 1991 sinking of the *Andrea Gail* off the coast of Nova Scotia), Jon Krakauer's *Into Thin Air* (about the 1996 Everest disaster), Piers Paul Read's *Alive* (about a 1972 plane crash that stranded a team of young rugby players high in the Andes), Walter Lord's *A Night to Remember* (about the sinking of the Titanic in 1912), and many other popular titles of the disaster genre. The same applies to the many books that depict the horrific experience of war.

Through the researching and writing process, the author endeavored to respect legal protections for certain types of information—including health records of the living[3] and details protected by copyright—and consulted with professors in the University of Tennessee College of Law whenever questions of fair and legal use arose.

This book addresses only a few of the many fatal incidents that have occurred in the park through its history, and as the book goes to press, new events continue to happen that imperil visitors' lives and engage park rangers in rescue or recovery operations. The author will relate some of those events in subsequent volumes of the *Into the Mist* series.

All those who read these stories and who plan to visit the park should recognize that GSMNP remains a place of exquisite beauty and mystery, of biological and geological riches, of vast tracts of untrammeled wilderness, of clear-running streams and dense old-growth arbors. But beneath the spectacle and beauty lurks a degree of risk for those who fail to properly prepare or who neglect to adequately respect the dominion of nature and her occasionally unrelenting harshness.

---

3   Most information pertaining to fatalities is considered part of the public record.

CHAPTER 1
The Chill of Death

"Well, he was bound to freeze anyway, and he might as well take it decently. With this new-found peace of mind came the first glimmerings of drowsiness. A good idea, he thought, to sleep off to death. It was like taking an anaesthetic. Freezing was not so bad as people thought. There were lots worse ways to die."
—Jack London, "To Build a Fire"

Many American readers gained their first intimate glimpse into the process of dying from exposure to extreme cold, or hypothermia, from Jack London's "To Build a Fire." The short story, about the final hours of a lone Yukon prospector's life, graphically depicts the violent shivering, the numbing that begins in the extremities and creeps relentlessly toward the body's core, the panic that succumbs to stupor, and the stupor that yields to death.

There's no disputing the potential brutality of Smoky Mountain winters (consider, for instance, that Mount Le Conte reached a record low of -32° F, on January 13, 1986) or the mountains' capacity to kill or maim hikers who arrive unprepared or who make fundamental errors in judgment. But in other cases, clouds heavy with snow, buoyed by fierce winds and chilled by dropping temperatures, have slammed the mountains—in some cases, with little warning—creating conditions sufficient to overwhelm even experienced and well-equipped hikers.

Such were the circumstances that led to the death from exposure of John Mink, a 25-year-old graduate student from Indiana who arrived in the park in the winter of 1984. On February 28, Mink set out on what he intended to be a three-day, two-night, 12-mile hike, from the Jakes Creek trailhead near Elkmont to the Fork Ridge trailhead near Mount Collins. Under ideal conditions, covering 12 miles in three days would have been hardly challenging for a guy like Mink, a fit, skilled backpacker who had tramped in the Smokies before.

In terms of planning and packing, Mink had done everything right, or nearly so. He carried plenty of water, a reliable stove, and an ample supply of food, including ham and cheese sandwiches and zucchini bread lovingly prepared by his mother. His goose-down sleeping bag was rated to zero. He carried wool hat, mittens, gloves, and sweater and wore a down parka. His stout leather boots featured Vibram® soles, and Mink had strapped a pair of wooden Sherpa® snowshoes onto his pack, just in case.

If the young hiker was guilty of any degree of negligence, it arose from three questionable decisions: First, he opted not to carry a tent, but, then, he had planned to spend his two nights in park shelters at Silers Bald and Mount Collins. Second, he wore blue jeans, despite the old cautionary adage "cotton kills." And, third, Mink, like Jack London's doomed prospector, traveled alone.

Sadly Mink's considerable complement of gear would prove inadequate; as he humped his heavy load up the trail toward Silers Bald, a major blizzard was bearing down on him. Before the storm had dumped its frozen load, drifted snow would reach heights of more than six feet along the hiker's intended route.

Though no one could begin to imagine the precise cascade of events that led to Mink's demise, clues left in the snow later allowed rangers to partially piece together what likely occurred over Mink's final desperate hours. The GSMNP folder on the incident includes a report by Ranger William Acree that tells the story.

Mink's father dropped his son off at the Jakes Creek trailhead at about 10 a.m. on February 28. Two hours later, as Mink reached Jakes Creek Gap, he encountered Ranger Dwight McCarter. McCarter checked Mink's backcountry permit and mentioned to the young man that it was unusual to see a hiker traveling alone during winter months. McCarter advised Mink of the highly changeable weather of the Great Smoky Mountains in winter, particularly at higher elevations, and noted in particular the importance of avoiding becoming drenched in sweat as he labored up the trail.

Dwight McCarter (right).

McCarter's admonishment was well advised. Dampness, from precipitation or from sweat, is a primary killer in the mountains. Sodden clothes, if they're lying next to the skin, can cause rapid chilling of the body, particularly in the presence of wind, which triggers evaporative cooling. Synthetic fabrics tend to dry faster and retain less moisture than cotton—notably among the worst fabric choices for hikers. Consider, for instance, that denim can absorb nearly 30 times its weight in water and can take hours, even days, to dry.

But even synthetic fabrics can prompt rapid cooling if they're not incorporated into a system of layers and shielded by a wind-proof outer shell, ideally a breathable/waterproof fabric like Gore-Tex®.

Wool is an excellent insulator and retains its insulating qualities even while wet. Mink's wool hat, sweater, gloves, and mittens would have continued to warm him, even after they had been dampened by melting snow. The same is true of the synthetic insulating materials used in jackets and sleeping bags (among them, Quallofill®, Hollofil®, PolarGuard®, Thinsulate®, and PrimaLoft®). But, instead, Mink's sleeping bag and parka were insulated with goose down.

Ounce for ounce, down remains one of the best—if not *the* best—insulation sources available, but when water penetrates the nylon baffles of a jacket or sleeping bag, it reduces the once wispy, air-trapping fluff to a useless clump of wet feathers.[1]

After his brief encounter with Ranger McCarter, Mink continued on up the Miry Ridge Trail, en route to Silers Bald. He would never make it, and McCarter would be the last person to see the young college student alive.

At about 2 p.m., as Mink reached 4,000 feet, near backcountry camp-

---

1   Modern manufacturers of down clothing and sleeping bags have begun to treat down feathers so they repel moisture and retain their insulating qualities even when wet.

site 26, he likely encountered a light dusting of snow on the trail. Just over
an hour later, when he reached 4,800 feet, yet a mile from the junction with
the Appalachian Trail (AT), the snow had accumulated to six inches. Here
Mink stopped to put on his snowshoes. By 5 p.m., near dark, he reached the
AT and followed the trail east toward Silers Bald. By then, the snow lay 10
inches deep on the trail. Less than an hour later, he passed Buckeye Gap at
4,800 feet and continued to climb. As Mink ascended, the temperature fell
as the snow piled ever deeper.

Less than a half-mile from Buckeye Gap, at about 6:30 p.m., Mink
was enveloped in swirling snow and darkness. Here, for unknown reasons,
Mink shed his down parka and dropped his emergency whistle. By this time,
the hiker was likely experiencing the first surge of panic and the clouded
judgment that often accompanies it. He may also have been suffering the
first symptoms of hypothermia.

The human body is a marvel at thermoregulation, initiating adaptive
measures to retain temperature within a few degrees of normal. When the
body starts to overheat, for instance, sweat glands release perspiration onto
the surface of the skin, which, in turn, causes evaporative cooling. In Mink's
case, as his core temperature dropped below 95°F, his body initiated a
number of adaptive measures. Canadian trauma nurse Dorothy A. Cochrane
describes them in her article "Hypothermia."[2]

Mink would have begun to shiver to generate internal heat. Other manifestations would have related primarily to Mink's central nervous
system. With mild hypothermia, Cochrane writes, "the patient appears
lethargic and apathetic and has an ataxic [i.e., unsteady] gait, decreased coor-
dination, and difficulty in performing tasks." Mink's respiration, heart rate,
and blood pressure initially would have increased. As Cochrane notes, at
this early stage of hypothermia, the "risk of death is minimal"—provided, of
course, that the patient manages to stem any further loss of body heat.

Now, without his down parka to insulate him and with his sodden
blue jeans beginning to stiffen and freeze, Mink apparently stumbled about
300 yards farther down the AT. As he did, he likely began to lapse into a
state of moderate hypothermia, with his core body temperature falling to
between 89.6°F to 82.4°F. which, as Cochrane notes, is marked by "odd behavior, impaired judgment, confusion, and decreased level of consciousness."

Errant snowshoe prints detected later by search crews suggested that

Mink had strayed from the trail at three separate points before stopping, unshouldering his pack, and pulling out a flashlight. The golden beam cutting through the darkness must have provided some relief, even hope, and he followed it for another 100 feet before his left snowshoe fell off. Mink tucked the detached snowshoe under his arm and kept moving through snow that was a foot deep and still accumulating. Remarkably, he covered more than a mile before his right snowshoe detached.

As Mink struggled with his snowshoes, it's likely that his fingers and feet were beginning to freeze, as his body's autonomic nervous system began to shunt blood flow away from his extremities to preserve the vital organs in his core—heart, lungs, brain—through a process known as thermoregulatory vasoconstriction. At this stage, hypothermia sufferers often respond to this sudden feeling of warmth by what Cochrane terms "paradoxical undressing." This phenomenon explains the numerous photos that depict deceased Himalayan mountaineers in various stages of undress.

Mink stopped here, plunged the left snowshoe upright in the snow, and with freezing, unresponsive fingers, tried but failed to reattach his right snowshoe.

Mink then abandoned both snowshoes and dropped the flashlight before continuing another 100 feet to where a large downed beech tree crossed the trail. Blinded by darkness and unable to negotiate around the obstacle, Mink withdrew his sleeping bag from his pack and prepared an emergency bivouac. It was now 10:30 p.m., and nearly 8 eight hours of darkness and biting cold separated him from the light of dawn.

Miraculously, Mink survived the night and at daybreak on February 29 (1984 was a leap year) fumbled to stow his sleeping bag back in his pack. The morning brought little relief. The snow had reached a depth of three feet—drifting to six—and continued to fall. Mink, in his confused mental state, abandoned his pack at the tree and began to retrace his steps from the night before. He had gone only five feet when he veered off the trail, stumbled downhill 15 feet, and fell face first into the snow.

By then, he had lost his right mitten and clenched his bare hand against the cold. As he did, his breathing became shallow, and his blood flow slowed as he succumbed to the final, deadly phase of hypothermia. His body temperature had dropped below 82°F. Had rescuers reached him at this point, Mink would have appeared lifeless, with a gray or pale complexion, fixed and dilated pupils, and no measurable pulse or respiration. But

hypothermic patients at this stage can revive, if their core temperature can
be raised above 95 degrees, but many suffer extensive and irreversible tissue
damage. Sadly, though, the search team would not locate Mink for more
than 24 hours, and by then it would be too late.

Mink's mother called the park on the evening of March 1, what would
have been Mink's third day in the mountains, to report her son overdue.
The following morning, at 8:30 a.m., the park mounted a search. Air National Guard helicopters were dispatched to comb the area from the sky. The
ground search proved a bit more problematic: Two to three feet of snow,
with deeper drifts, blanketed the search area, much of which was above
5,000 feet in elevation. For assistance, GSMNP called on its neighbors at the
ski area of Ober Gatlinburg and requested the loan of the resort's Sno-Cat®.

By 12:40 p.m., the tracked vehicle had deposited a four-person search
and rescue team atop Clingmans Dome. From there, the rangers started
punching steps in the snow, heading west along the AT. A second team
arrived via the Sno-Cat® at the Mount Collins trailhead a short time later.

At 3:20 p.m., an Air National Guard pilot made a discovery that
appeared to shift the mission from a rescue to a recovery. A few hundred
feet below, less than two miles from the Silers Bald Shelter, the pilot spotted

Snowy Smokies.

what appeared to be a lifeless body, lying face down in the snow.

Just over an hour later, searchers on the ground reached John Mink, whose core body temperature had plunged to 36°F. A later examination of the body established the time of death sometime on the morning of Wednesday, February 29, Mink's second day in the mountains.

The recovery team placed Mink's body on a litter and carried it 1.2 miles through the waist-deep snow to Silers Bald Shelter, the victim's intended destination. From there, an Air National Guard chopper transported the body to the University of Tennessee Medical Center, where Mink's bereaved parents soon arrived to take their son home to Indiana for burial.

Since 1934, hypothermia has claimed 14 victims in GSMNP. The first occurred just a few years after the park was established. The body of Sue Grace Ingraham of Knoxville was found atop Mount Le Conte in April of 1938; she had been missing since the previous November.

But one could argue that the deaths of Ingraham, Mink, and the other victims of exposure might all have been averted. Indeed, in Mink's case, had any one of a number of factors that contributed to his death been altered, the young man's fate might have been different. Had the arrival of the blizzard been delayed by even half a day, Mink might have managed to reach the shelter on the first night of his outing. There, he would have slumbered, out of the weather, in a dry down sleeping bag, feasted on the ample supply of food in his pack, and warmed himself with hot cocoa heated on his camp stove. The rangers were aware of his location from the backcountry permit Mink had filled out at the ranger station before setting out, and they would have reached and rescued him in due time.

Had the path of the blizzard shifted north or south sufficiently to miss the Smokies entirely, Mink would have trod on dry trail. And, most important, had Mink been accompanied by a companion, each of them would likely have possessed the mental acuity to identify the early stages of hypothermia in the other and to take the necessary life-saving measures.

If there's any degree of comfort in this tale, it's found in Mink's experience of his final hours, relative to the 24 hours of profound suffering that preceded them. After Mink's face-first topple into the snow, as his respiration slowed, the sting and stab of relentless cold likely had given way to blessed numbness as he succumbed to oblivion.

CHAPTER 2
The Deadliest Night in the Smokies' Deadliest Place

On an evening in March 2005, a lethal combination of youthful exuberance, powerful cars, and an appetite for speed left five elderly adults dead on the scene along the Gatlinburg Spur, mile for mile, the most dangerous location in GSMNP.

Motorized-vehicle crashes are among the leading causes of accidental deaths in the United States, claiming 32,675 lives in 2014 alone, according to the National Highway Traffic Safety Administration (NHTSA).

In GSMNP, such accidents are, by far, *the* single leading cause of death. Accidents involving automobiles, motorcycles, and mopeds account for 153 deaths, nearly 33 percent of the more than 400 deaths occurring in the park since 1931. To put that into perspective, the next highest causes of death in the park—plane crashes and drownings—resulted in 73 and 60 fatalities, respectively.

Though fatal accidents have occurred along nearly all of the roads that course through the park, a single 4.3-mile stretch of U.S. 441 has proven particularly lethal. In fact, mile-for-mile, the Gatlinburg Spur, a four-lane divided highway linking Gatlinburg to Pigeon Forge, ranks as the single deadliest place in GSMNP's entire half-million acres, accounting for 43 fatalities that have occurred in the park.

Of the 43 deaths claimed along the Spur, one involved 80-year-old Alvin N. McCarter, who drowned in 1987 while fishing along the stretch

This vehicle was involved in a fatal accident on the Spur in July of 1984. The car was towed to Virgil's Texaco in Gatlinburg.

of the Little Pigeon River that parallels the road. But all the others resulted from motor-vehicle accidents, and alcohol was allegedly involved in 16—or 37 percent—of those fatalities.

The Spur was completed between 1953 and 1961, and the Spur's first recorded death occurred on July 27, 1960, when Princella Gale Effler, 18, of Maryville, died as a result of injuries sustained in an accident on a section of the newly opened roadway. Between 1960 and 2014, an average of 1.3 auto-related fatalities has occurred each year on the Spur. But averages fail utterly to convey the scope of the calamity that occurred on that dangerous section of road on the night of March 26, 2005, leaving five senior adults— all passengers in one car—dead on the scene.

John M. Hall, 18, and Steven A. Williams, 19, were certainly not the first to punch the accelerator along the Spur, despite the roadway's notorious twists and turns. Over the years GSMNP rangers have issued hundreds of citations to drivers who were less than respectful of the Spur's posted 35- or 45-miles-per-hour speed limits.

But in a tragedy tinged with irony, these two teenagers, from different Tennessee towns—Hall from Lebanon and Williams from Murfreesboro— and who had never met face to face, became co-catalysts in precipitating what remains the deadliest single automobile accident in GSMNP history.

Though the two men were unknown to each other, both had arrived in Gatlinburg over the Easter weekend eager to engage in the same activities and pastimes that draw millions of tourists each year to the mountain resort. Williams and five friends shared a unit at Mountain Laurel Chalets on Ski Mountain Road, while Hall and three friends stayed in the East Side Motel on Highway 73.

There is ample evidence in the incident report—including statements from numerous witnesses and friends of the drivers—to suggest that the two had something else in common beyond their plans for a weekend in Gatlinburg. Both Williams and Hall seemed to have an appetite for the illegal sport of street racing, and both appeared to share a passion for fast cars.

Included in the incident report is a copy of Hall's record of vehicle infractions, which began shortly after he was issued his driver's license. Between November 2002 and August 2004, the record lists more than 10 driving infractions, including two for "careless or negligent driving" and one accident involving personal injury.

The face-off between the two drivers began innocently enough at about 10 p.m., when Williams' red 1996 Nissan 240 SX and Hall's 1991 Honda Accord idled side by side at a stoplight at the north end of the Gatlinburg strip. In his statement about the incident, Williams' passenger describes the two occupants of Hall's white Honda "mean muggin'" him and Williams—glaring in a way that suggests a challenge to race. According to witnesses, both cars then revved their engines—"piping" in the parlance of street racers. As Williams and Hall cleared the north end of the Gatlinburg strip, both cars reportedly "kicked it in."

According to multiple witnesses, as Hall and Williams reached the straightaway leading to the Legion Field Bridge (proximate to the Gatlinburg Welcome Center), they clearly were involved in a race, jockeying for position, accelerating, and rapidly changing lanes. Eventually, Williams settled into the left (inside) lane and Hall into the right. Some witnesses estimated their speed in excess of 80 miles per hour.

At about that moment, Myra Nelson and her four passengers—all seniors from Virginia, ranging in age from 63 to 84—were returning to their condo at the Westgate Smoky Mountain Resort after a quiet day in the mountains. They were within a few hundred yards of their destination, when Nelson's green 1997 Chrysler sedan cleared Legion Field Bridge and continued east across the two northbound lanes of the Spur.

Witnesses report that as the two speeding cars approached the Chrysler crossing in front of them from the left, Williams slammed on his brakes, brought his Nissan to a near complete stop, and successfully avoided a collision. The Chrysler then entered the lane directly in the line of Hall's Honda. The GSMNP incident report uses the term "T-bone" to describe the Honda's orientation as it slammed into the Chrysler's passenger-side doors.

Williams' Nissan was so close to the point of impact that shattered glass flew in through the open passenger-side window, but Williams' vehicle was undamaged, and he sped away from the scene and returned to his friends at the chalet.

Sir Isaac Newton died in 1727, more than a century and a half before Carl Benz applied for a patent for the world's first gasoline-powered vehicle in 1886. Newton couldn't possibly have imagined the engineering marvels the coming centuries would spawn, including the sleek, powerful—and, in this case, deadly—offshoots of Benz's cumbersome and slow prototype automobile. Nevertheless, Newton's laws of motion do an apt job of describing the physics involved in the encounter between Hall's careening Honda and Nelson's Chrysler or the gruesome outcome of the collision.

Particularly applicable here is Newton's First Law: An object at rest stays at rest, and an object in motion stays in motion with the same speed and in the same direction *unless acted upon by an unbalanced force.*

In this case, Myra Nelson's Chrysler, moving at a relatively slow rate of speed across Hall's direction of travel, should have continued moving in that direction toward the condominium complex and home for the night for the car's five occupants. Likewise, Hall's Honda should have continued speeding north in the right-hand lane of the Spur. The collision, which served as the unbalanced force, abruptly altered the rate and direction of travel for both vehicles.

The impact crumpled the front end of Hall's Honda and brought the vehicle to an abrupt stop. Hall and his passenger lived but sustained serious injuries. The same force propelled Nelson's Chrysler more than 80 feet from the point of impact to a fringe of trees along the side of the road.

It's worth noting here that if Hall's Honda was traveling at, say, 70 miles per hour, his body and that of his passenger were traveling at that same rate. Had it not been for the three-point seatbelt restraints the two men were presumably wearing, they may well have exited the vehicle through the front windshield and continued moving "with the same speed and in the same direction," until gravity slammed them onto the pavement or momentum hurled them into an upright object. In effect, Hall and his passenger went from 70 miles per hour to near zero in a split second.

As for Nelson and her passengers, the acceleration process worked in reverse: When Hall's' Honda struck the passenger-side doors of the Chrysler, the car, and its occupants, accelerated rapidly from a near stop to a rate sufficient to propel an object weighing 3,400 pounds—not including the weight of the passengers—nearly 27 yards in an entirely new direction of travel.

Cars are relatively sturdy objects; human bodies, particularly those of older adults, are not. The enormous power of the impact contorted bodies, snapped bones, and slammed relatively soft brain tissue against the hard inside margins of skulls.

GSMNP Ranger Dale Culver received a call at his home at 10:05 p.m. regarding the accident and was the first park official to arrive on the scene. He immediately made his way to the green Chrysler to attend to the victims and administer first aid. It immediately was apparent that there was no need. The trauma was massive. A Gatlinburg EMT soon arrived and declared all five passengers dead on the scene.

In an instant, five people, three of them from one family and all of them with countless friends and relatives to mourn their passing, were lost in a fatal encounter with two teenagers, both borne by powerful cars, who had perhaps screened *The Fast and the Furious* one too many times.

Killed were Myra Nelson, 63, her husband, George, 80, Myra's mother, Audrey Fentress, 84, all of Norfolk, Virginia, and Anthony Deitz, 69, and his wife, Betty, 69, both of Virginia Beach, Virginia.

Sadly, the incident conforms to statistics compiled by the NHTSA: About 35 percent of 15- to 24-year-old male drivers involved in fatal crashes were speeding at the time of the crash; Williams and Hall both fell within that age range and by all witness accounts were speeding. And, like Nelson's Chrysler, about 36 percent of the vehicles involved in accidents (not necessarily fatal ones) were turning or crossing at intersections just prior to impact, according to the 2008 NHTSA report "National Motor Vehicle Crash Causation Survey."

Culver was soon joined by Rangers Ken Meyer, Rick Brown, Keith Flanery, Lorena Harris, and Kirby Styles. While some of the rangers shouldered the difficult task of identifying the dead and contacting relatives, others launched the investigation into what had caused the fatal accident and who was responsible. The latter task involved gathering evidence and inter-viewing witnesses.[1]

Hall and his passenger were transported by helicopter to the Univer-sity of Tennessee Medical Center, and National Park Service Special Agent Jeff Carlisle arrived shortly behind them to continue the interviews.

For Hall, there was no ducking responsibility. His banged up Hon-da, combined with witness statements, told enough of a story eventually to launch criminal proceedings against him. And evidence and witness ac-counts suggest that Hall may have been impaired at the time of the accident.

At the scene, Ranger Culver recovered a Styrofoam cup that witnesses alleged had been thrown from Hall's car, and Culver noted that "it smelled of an alcoholic beverage." According to the transcript of Carlisle's interview with Hall at the hospital, Hall acknowledged consuming alcohol and smok-ing marijuana prior to the incident. However, Hall's toxicology report was not included in the investigation or incident reports, so we do not know if Hall was, in fact, impaired, and, if so, the extent of his impairment.

For a time, it appeared as though Steven Williams had not only dodged the green Chrysler but may have evaded criminal prosecution as well. Though witnesses described a red Nissan 240 SX, no one had noted its plate number. On March 28, two days after the fatal accident, GSMNP dis-tributed a media briefing, seeking the public's help in identifying the driver of the Nissan.

According to friends interviewed after the fact, soon after the acci-dent, Williams' conscience had begun to work on him. In fact, shortly after the wreck, he allegedly returned to the scene (in a different vehicle driven by one of his friends) and surmised, accurately, that people had died in the crash. Eventually, beset by guilt, he turned himself in to authorities. Ranger Carlisle interviewed him on March 31, five days after the accident.

In terms of describing the legal proceedings against the two young men, Newton's Third Law—for every action, there is an equal and opposite reaction—seems particularly applicable. Hall's and Williams' actions, the deadly drag race of March 2005, resulted in a severe reaction from the judi-cial system. In January 2006, nine months following the accident, the U.S. District Court in Knoxville handed down a five-count indictment against Hall and Williams charging that "each aided and abetted and induced by the other, with malice aforethought...did unlawfully kill five human beings."

---

1   All told, rangers conducted interviews with 20 eyewitnesses and friends of the two drivers.

According to the December 10, 2006, edition of the *Mt. Juliet News*, published in Hall's hometown of Lebanon, the two agreed to plead guilty to one count each of second-degree murder. The remaining charges were dropped. Hall received a sentence of 21 years, 10 months. Williams, sentenced a month earlier, received eight and one-half years.

Though the families of Hall and Williams' five victims might argue otherwise, there is justice to be found in condemning two young men who once lusted for speed and unbridled movement to lives defined by relentless confinement.

CHAPTER 3

In an Encounter with Nature's Deadly Force, 'Under Shelter' Does Not Mean 'Out of Harm's Way'

If GSMNP's backcountry were always tranquil and predictable, the lure for trekkers would be greatly diminished. The truth is that Nature's fury doesn't strike all that often, but when it does, it can be fatal. Such was the case on a balmy summer day in 1980, when death arrived from the sky.

About 50 Americans die each year from lightning strikes, according to the National Oceanic and Atmospheric Administration (NOAA), a figure based on a 30-year average. Considering that about 100,000 thunder storms occur each year in the United States, and, by definition, lightning is present in all of them (absent lightning, there would be no thunder), an average of 50 deaths per year doesn't seem all that staggering. (More than 37,000 Americans perish each year in auto accidents, and more than 150 have died on GSMNP's roads.) Nevertheless, lightning remains one of the leading causes of weather-related deaths in the United States.

About 85 percent of the victims are male, 68 percent are between the ages of 15 and 44, and most fatal strikes occur in July, reports the Centers for Disease Control and Prevention. The victims claimed by the deadly lightning strike on the Double Spring Gap Shelter on July 10, 1980, fit neatly within all three of the CDC's parameters.

They're also reflective of the relatively high incidence of lethal lightning strikes in the Smokies region. According to NOAA's national ranking by state for lightning-strike fatalities, between 1959 and 2014, North Carolina ranked fourth (194 deaths), while Tennessee ranked seventh (140 deaths). The Double Spring Gap Shelter straddles the Tennessee–North Carolina border.

On that muggy July afternoon, as eight hikers in three groups made their way to the shelter, situated about two miles south of Clingmans Dome on the Appalachian Trail (AT), 34 years had passed since lightning had last claimed a victim in GSMNP: In August 1946, lineman George Hackman was killed when lightning struck the power line he was working on.

Early on that July afternoon in 1980, at about 2:45 p.m., Jeff Powell, 19, had arrived at the shelter with three friends, all from Michigan: brothers Ken and Jim W.[1], 20 and 17, and Todd B., 19. Inside the stone structure, Pennsylvanians James S., 28, and Frank L., 27, cooked lunch over the coals in the shelter's fireplace.

After unrolling their sleeping bags and unpacking their gear, Powell and his companions settled in the grass in front of the shelter to enjoy their lunch alfresco. A short time later, Ohioans Roger McGlone and his wife, both 32, walked past, heading south on the AT, intending to trek 1.9 miles farther to the Silers Bald Shelter. Still within sight of the Double Spring Gap Shelter, the two slid from their packs and sat on a log to eat their lunch and assess their situation.

The two-mile trek from the Clingmans Dome parking area had taken them much longer than they had expected, and the two decided to scrub their planned hike and head back to their car. As they finished eating, lightning began to flash, and it started to rain, so the two hikers ducked into the shelter to wait out the storm. They sat on the edges of two lower bunks on the right side of the shelter, as the storm intensified, and hail began to pepper the metal roof.

The weather had also driven Powell and his three friends into the shelter. (For positions of occupants in shelter at the time of the lightning strike, see diagram on page 37. Names have been added to the original diagram contained in the incident report.)

---

1   While information on fatalities that occur in national parks is public record, Exemption 6 of the Freedom of Information Act protects information contained in "personal, medical, and similar files" held by agencies of the US government that applies to living persons. Thus, survivors of the incident at Double Spring Gap Shelter are identified here by first name and last initial, to protect their privacy.

Powell stretched out on upper bunk #8, and his three friends sat on three adjacent lower bunks (Jim W. #1, Todd B. #2, Ken W. #3), with their feet on the ground. Beside them, James S. sat on the edge of #4, and, behind him, Frank L. lay on the same bunk. Roger McGlone sat on the edge of #5, and his wife sat on the edge of #6.

The occupants had been ensconced in the shelter for less than five minutes when they saw a blinding flash, followed immediately by a deafening crackle. A tree about 20 feet from the shelter had sustained a direct cloud-to-ground lightning strike. Almost instantaneously, the electrical discharge splintered the tree and vaporized its sap as it traveled to the ground. It then spread outward across the earth's surface (a phenomenon known as "side splash"). Within microseconds, the charge entered the shelter. From there, the current surged along the paths of least resistance: conductive materials, including metal, and the neurons and liquid- and electrolyte-infused tissues of the human body.

Electricity—whether carried by a charged wire or a bolt of lightning—can cause devastating, and often lethal, trauma to a human body. Consider, for instance, that electrocution served as the primary means of executing prisoners in the United States for several decades, via chairs designed for that purpose and known, often derisively, as "Old Sparky."

A direct cloud-to-ground lightning strike[2] travels at 320,000 feet per second and can carry from 10,000 to 200,000 amps and 20 million to 1 billion volts of electricity (by comparison, your home oven and clothes dryer operate on 220 volts, more than sufficient to kill). The heat of a lightning bolt can reach 50,000 degrees Fahrenheit—hotter than the surface of the sun—and fuse the molten metal of rings and watches to victims' skin.

In the moments prior to the strike, Ken W. recalls that the lag between lightning flashes and accompanying thunder had been getting shorter and shorter. The visible flash of lightning travels to the human eye at the speed of light (186,000 miles per second), while thunder reaches the ear at the much slower speed of sound (about 1,127 feet per second). Based on the near instantaneous speed of light and the relatively laggardly speed of sound, hikers have learned that a five-second delay between flash (seen instantly) and boom means that the storm is about a mile distant (5,280 feet). The lag between lightning flash and thunder diminishes as the storm draws nearer.

---

2   Cloud-to-ground lightning strikes account for about 20 percent of all lightning activity. Intracloud, cloud-to-cloud, and ground-to-cloud strikes account for the rest.

Using this rough calculation, Ken had determined that the storm was nearly on top of them, with only a second between flash and thunder.[3] Then came an "ear-piercing bang and jolt."

Ken felt an intense "tingling sensation" as the electricity surged through his body. His younger brother, Jim, leapt from the bunk, screaming and holding his hands over his ears, and he instinctively ran to exit the shelter. Ken gripped his brother in a hug to calm him down and keep him inside and under roof. Todd B. and Jim S. slowly staggered to their feet. Frank L. stirred slowly but continued to recline on his bunk.

McGlone's wife felt "a horrible force" course through her body that threw her backward on the bunk. The same jolt had, likewise, thrown McGlone backward into a reclining position. She tried to stand, but couldn't, so she crawled off the bunk and onto the floor.

She reported that her left side had gone numb. Her legs were also numb, and her right arm was completely paralyzed. She turned her attention to McGlone and soon realized that he had stopped breathing. She noticed that he smelled of smoke and that the hair on the back of his head was singed. His shirt bore burn marks on the upper chest. Meanwhile, on the top bunk, Powell also lay stone still.

Ken W., his wits slowly returning, quickly realized that, while Mother Nature had brought the lightning, human-made materials had helped carry its current to the victims. "Everyone off the bunks!" he screamed.

Today, hikers who visit the Smokies' Double Spring Gap and other AT shelters will find clean, open, and airy renovated structures, with level wood-planked sleeping platforms. By contrast, backpackers who visited the AT shelters in the 1980s will likely remember cramped, mouse-infested hovels with chain-link fences covering the shelters' open faces.

These barriers, equipped with latchable chain-link doors for hiker ingress and egress, were expressly designed to keep aggressive, marauding bears from entering the shelters and pilfering hikers' food stores.

The chain link was not the only form of metal fencing installed in the shelters. Galvanized welded-steel fencing—the type one might post around a garden—had been used to create bunks for slumbering hikers. The mesh stretched from side wall to side wall and over 10 stout logs, five on the top sleeping area, and five on the bottom, that extended at a right angle from the

---

3   Much of the information in this chapter is taken from the GSMNP incident report, which contains detailed transcripts of interviews conducted by NPS rangers with the individuals involved in the event at Double Spring Gap Shelter on July 10, 1980.

To the left is the Double Spring Gap Shelter of old with the chain link fence across the front.

The new upgraded Appalachian Trail shelter design includes more covered space for sitting and no fence.

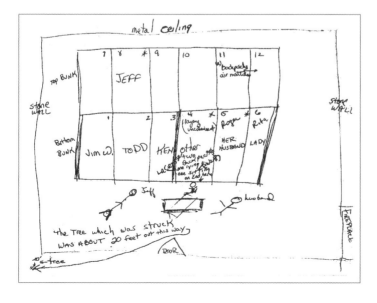

Diagram of occupants' positions from NPS incident report.

back wall of the shelter, with each rectangle defining an individual bunk.

Over the years, untold numbers of corpulent hikers had lain in the bunks and stretched the once-taut mesh metal fabric into what essentially served as body-conforming hammocks, which were comfortable and durable.

But, as the hikers discovered on the afternoon of July 10, those metal bunks were also highly conductive.

In *Pathological Features of Death from Lightning Strike*, a 2006 report published in *Forensic Pathology Reviews*, Stephan Seidl, MD, doesn't directly address electrical current carried by wire-mesh bunks in a backwoods shelter, but he does address the means by which the charge can "energize" a structure and kill those inside.

"People may rarely be struck by lightning indoors while using a telephone or an electrical appliance," Seidl writes. "In these cases, the lightning surge may energize the structure of a house, causing current to flow through the victim into the grounded telephone or appliance. Likewise, lightning may strike a cable, causing connected telephones to become electrically charged."

Ken W. moved to help his stricken friend on the top bunk. "Get up, Jeff," he called to Powell, striking the soles of his feet. Powell did not respond. Ken and his friends worked to get Powell off the bunk and onto the floor of the shelter, and as they did, they noticed that the hair on the back of his head was singed and that Powell was bleeding from a serious wound in the rear of his skull, the point at which the electrical current had entered or exited his body.

By then, Roger McGlone had also been moved to the floor. His eyes were open, but he was not breathing, and his companions could find no pulse.

According to Seidl, lightning injures and kills via three primary forces: electrical energy, thermal energy (heat), "or the enormous blast force of a thunderous lightning strike." In the case of the Double Spring Gap, the injuries likely resulted from the first, electrical energy.

And the most common cause of death associated with lightning strike is cardiac arrest, caused either by the direct electrical force of the strike (primary cardiac arrest) or resulting after the victim stops breathing (secondary cardiac arrest). The details provided by the witness testimony contained in the incident report suggest that both Powell and McGlone had suffered primary cardiac arrest.

"Despite the fact that 50 to 75 percent of those who have cardiac arrest will die," Seidl reports, "cardiopulmonary resuscitation can be successful in lightning victims far longer after the initial strike than in other types of injury."

In that regard, those attending to Powell and McGlone did exactly the right thing, though, in the end, their efforts to revive the victims proved futile.

With Roger McGlone now on the floor of the shelter, his hiking partner began mouth-to-mouth resuscitation, a process that would continue for more than three hours.

Meanwhile, Todd B. began efforts to resuscitate Powell.

Then, debunking the old adage that lightning never strikes [in the same place] twice, the hikers saw another flash and heard another resounding crackle, as lightning once again struck nearby and surged through the shelter.

Ken reports feeling "the jolt starting at my feet and traveling up to my chest." Following the strike, "everyone jumped and let out a yell."

Part of the allure of a backpacking trip to GSMNP or any other remote, wild area is the escape that such outings provide from the hustle and bustle and crush of urban living. With that escape comes isolation—blissfully rewarding under ideal circumstances, but confounding and problematic in difficult ones. The latter realm is where Ken W. and his shelter mates found themselves late in the afternoon on that stormy July day.

Two of his shelter mates were unresponsive and most likely dead. Frank L., stunned and barely coherent, was also clearly injured, though he wasn't talking, so it was difficult to assess the extent of his injuries. Rain continued to fall, lightning continued to flash, and two miles of rugged trail and 1,000 feet of elevation gain separated them from the nearest blacktop, on Clingmans Dome. And they were living in an age before the advent of cellular phones capable of conveying an instantaneous cry for help.

Just after 4 p.m., Ken W. and Jim S. laced up their boots and headed out into the storm. About an hour later, the two reached the Clingmans Dome parking area. In an unlikely turn of good fortune, two of the first three people they encountered there were medical professionals. In the parking lot, Catherine M., a registered nurse from Michigan, heard a frantic call for help as Ken and Jim emerged from the woods.

Catherine was visiting the park with her husband, Daryl, and her friend, Floridian Roni W., also a nurse. Ken and Jim struggled to catch their breath as they related the story of the lightning strike at the shelter and the two lifeless bodies. Another visitor in the parking area called out on his CB radio, trying to reach emergency responders but could not get through. He drove down the mountain to summon help. Eventually, he succeeded. Ranger Keith Nelson and Park Tech Mike Panz were at the Oconaluftee Ranger Station when the call came in at about 5 p.m.

"We loaded packs and first-aid equipment and proceeded with lights and siren to the Clingmans Dome parking area," Nelson reports.

Word soon reached the visitors in the parking area that rangers were on the way, but Catherine, Daryl, and Roni opted not to wait. They loaded a first-aid kit and some blankets into a backpack and headed south on the Appalachian Trail toward the shelter. Ken and Jim remained behind to await the arrival of Nelson and Panz.

At 6:55 p.m., the three reached the shelter and confronted a grim scene. Powell's body lay under a sleeping bag on the floor. Nearby, Mc-Glone's wife continued to expend herself in trying to resuscitate him, now more than three hours after the initial lightning strike had entered the shelter and surged through his body.

Roni and Catherine checked for a pulse on the carotid, brachial, and cardiac arteries, but found none.

They covered Roger McGlone's body and turned their attention to his wife, informing her of McGlone's status and doing their best to comfort her.

Minutes later, just after 7 p.m., Nelson and Panz arrived and began the difficult task of confirming the deaths and the strenuous process of evacuating the dead and injured. Fortunately, by that time Frank L. was ambulatory but complained of a headache and memory loss. He, along with the two fatalities, would be carried out on litters, which arrived at the Clingmans Dome parking lot at 1:30 the next morning, nearly 12 hours after the deadly lightning strike had surged through the shelter, pulsed along the metal bunks, and entered the bodies of the victims.

By all measure, the event was an unfortunate accident that could not have been predicted or prevented, except, perhaps, if all those involved had remained safely locked in their homes and away from the mountains. But, then, it's the inherent unpredictability of forays into the wilderness—the likelihood that the experiences will diverge, sometimes dramatically, from expectations and planned outcomes—that inclines hikers to shoulder risk, along with the backpacks, in pursuit of adventure. The eight hikers who converged at Double Spring Gap Shelter on July 10, 1980, no doubt shared that motivation.

At the time of this writing, Roger McGlone and Jeff Powell, who perished more than 35 years ago, remain the last fatalities claimed by lightning strike in GSMNP, but, sadly, not the last to die from electrocution.

That tragic distinction belongs to Robert Bonnetau, 30, a Canadian project supervisor of Florida-based PCL, Inc. Bonnetau was killed on August 16, 2000, while testing an electrical device on a failed piece of construction equipment used to form concrete.

CHAPTER 4
A Murdered Jane Doe in a Smokies Creek Leads to a Cross-country Hunt for Her Killer

In the days before DNA profiling and development of computerized networks that link crime fighters from different agencies and jurisdictions, connecting a missing person from one state with discovery of a battered body in another came down to good old-fashioned police work—and a bit of luck.

At 3:40 p.m. on August 14, 1976, at the end of a long hike, a University of Tennessee student was walking along the remote Parson Branch Road toward his car in Abrams Falls trailhead parking area when he made a grisly discovery. About 40 feet away from the road, the body of a woman lay sprawled across the rocks in Rabbit Creek. The woman appeared lifeless, and the student noted what seemed to be a large amount of blood spattering her clothing.

Alarmed and fearful, the student did not approach but called out to the woman, hoping to see her rouse. She remained motionless, so he set out to find help, walking two and a half miles to Forge Creek Road, where he hitched a ride to the Cades Cove Visitor Center to report the incident.

At 4:50 p.m., Ranger Lowell "Kent" Higgins received a call from Cable Mill alerting him to the discovery of what appeared to be a dead body in Rabbit Creek. Higgins swung by to pick up the UT student at the visitor center before traveling to the scene, arriving at 5:20 p.m.

Among the first things Higgins noticed were distinct scuff marks beginning at the side of the road and leading down a steep bank to where the body lay, suggesting that the woman had been dragged to the creek. Higgins then checked the body of the middle-aged Caucasian woman, which was cold to the touch, with no pulse. The woman's pupils were dilated behind half-closed eyelids smeared with heavy blue eye shadow. She wore pink fingernail polish but no lipstick. Clotted blood on the left side of the skull indicated that the woman may have been shot. She was clad in a light-blue pantsuit that was spattered with blood, and she wore hose but no shoes. There were no snags or tears in the hose covering the feet, which indicated to Higgins that the woman had not walked down to the creek.

Higgins also noted large contusions on the woman's right forearm and right side, just below the ribs, suggesting that she had been beaten. Higgins left the body as it lay and called for assistance. Roy White, the Blount County Coroner, appeared on the scene at 7:25 p.m. A murder in a national park warrants the involvement of the FBI, and there was no reason to believe that the woman had been killed elsewhere, so Higgins called FBI agent Ron Johnson, who arrived about an hour behind White.

White performed a cursory examination of the body at the scene while Higgins and Johnson gathered and documented evidence. White would conduct a more thorough examination once the body arrived by ambulance at Blount Memorial Hospital.

White's autopsy placed the time of death at about noon the day the body was discovered and confirmed Higgins' suspicions: the woman had been beaten and then shot in the left temple with a .38 caliber handgun.

Higgins and his associates may have had a body and a confirmed cause of death, but they had little else that might help them unravel the mystery and solve the crime. The woman carried no identification, and there were no missing-person reports circulating in the area.

Stumped and bereft of promising leads, law enforcement officials turned to the media for help. On August 19, the *Knoxville News Sentinel* ran a photo of the murder victim's face. Below it ran the caption: "Do you know this woman? The FBI has released the picture in an effort to identify her. The body was found, shot in the head, in Great Smoky Mountains National Park Saturday."

Nearly a week later, the *Maryville-Alcoa Daily Times* ran a similar photo. The caption noted that the deceased woman still had not been identified and offered a brief description: "approximately 40 years old, hazel eyes, bleached blond hair with dark roots, weighed 160 to 170 pounds, was 5 feet 5, fair complexion and heavy build." Further identifying marks included extensive gold dental work, an appendectomy scar, and a scar indicating the surgical removal of the thyroid gland.

The first bizarre turn in the case came by way of an anonymous call to the Blount County Sheriff's Department on August 27, the same day the woman's photo ran in the *Daily Times*. "You know that body you found in the park a couple of weeks ago?" the caller asked. "If you look close you will find another."

Two GSMNP rangers spent five hours scouring Parson Branch Road, looking for a second corpse, before officials concluded that the call was a hoax.

The first real breakthrough came on September 18, more than a month after discovery of the body, when Harold Moore, of Nashville, Indiana, traveled to Tennessee and positively identified the body as that of his sister-in-law, Emily Phyllis Moore.[1]

Emily Moore had been reported missing in Indiana on August 12, two days before her body was discovered in GSMNP. But back in 1976, at the dawn of the computer age, making the connection between a person missing from Indiana and a body discovered in Tennessee relied almost entirely on a paper-based system of record keeping managed by a jumble of jurisdictional entities that were not particularly proficient in the art of talking with one another or sharing information. At the time of Moore's murder, the advent of DNA profiling was yet a decade away. The Integrated Automated Fingerprint Identification System would not become operational until 1999, and the National Data Exchange Program would not come into being until 2008.

As it turned out, according to the *Daily Times*, mere coincidence, not police science, led to the identification of Moore's body. Following Emily Moore's disappearance, her husband, The Reverend Loren Moore, a Baptist minister, had met with his insurance agent in Indiana. During the meeting, Moore mentioned his concern over the disappearance of his wife. The insurance agent, who owned and had recently visited a home in Gatlinburg,

[1]   Neither the NPS incident report nor the newspaper accounts explain why Emily Moore's brother-in-law, and not her husband, traveled to Tennessee to identify her body.

recalled reading an article in the paper about the discovery of an unidentified
body in the park. Loren Moore called the Sevier County Sheriff's Department to follow up, and the information he shared convinced Coroner White
that his Jane Doe finally had a name and identity: Emily Phyllis Moore, 52,
of Nashville, Indiana.

Identification of Emily Moore's body marked a significant break in the
case, but two key questions lingered: who had killed her and why?

According to newspaper reports, the lives of Emily and Loren Moore
had, over previous years, been marked by controversy. The Reverend
Moore, 49, was president of Fiesta, Inc., a chain of restaurants and liquor
stores in Nashville, Columbus, and Scottsburg, Indiana. He also had served
for 18 years as the head of Baptist Home and Hospital Corporation (BHHC),
which operated a chain of retirement homes. According to newspaper
accounts, Reverend Moore was dismissed in 1974 following an audit that revealed debts in excess of $7 million for the Indiana corporation and $1 million for a subsidiary company, Samaritan Homes, Inc., in Plantation, Florida.

The fraud charges leveled against Loren and Emily Moore accused the
couple of using funds from BHHC to finance architectural work on one of
their restaurants, and Emily, who held a real-estate license, had been charged
with fraud for allegedly bilking Samaritan Homes out of $60,000 on a Flor-
ida land deal. According to published accounts, Loren Moore countered by
suing BHHC for extreme emotional distress and damage to his credit rating.

Loren Moore may have been accused of questionable business dealings, but no one suspected he had murdered his wife. It would take eight
months to locate—and arrest—the person who did.

As Emily Moore's body traveled back to Indiana for burial, law enforcement officials began to piece together details of her last two days alive,
but, at the time, they didn't have much to go on. According to Emily's
brother-in-law Harold Moore, he had last spoken on the phone with Emily
at about noon on August 12, the day she disappeared. At the time, she was
packing for a trip to Chicago. But a later search of the Moore home turned
up Emily's two packed suitcases. Her car remained parked outside, but she
was nowhere to be found. Then, two days after Emily had disappeared, the
UT student discovered her battered and bloody body in Tennessee.

When the name and identity of the GSMNP murder victim hit the
news in Indiana, it proved particularly unsettling to one resident of the
Hoosier State. Within hours, restaurant owner Leslie Diane Standifer, 44,

of Scottsburg, had taken flight. The person who would become the police's prime suspect vanished without a trace.

Two months later, on November 8, Standifer's car was found, abandoned, in Las Vegas, Nevada. Blood traces found in the vehicle matched Emily Moore's type, though Standifer had apparently ripped out the upholstery in the passenger seat—where investigators surmise Moore had been sitting when she was shot—and had it replaced.

The fatal link between Standifer and Moore involved a business deal. According to newspaper accounts, Emily, eager to sell the Fiesta Restaurant in Scottsburg, had placed an advertisement in the newspaper in spring of 1976. Standifer responded to the ad and agreed to pay $120,000 for the sale and to make a $40,000 cash down payment.

After she had inked the contract, Standifer, perhaps convinced that she had offered too much for the restaurant, suffered buyer's remorse and balked on making the down payment. According to published accounts, first she insisted that the money for the payment was in a Kentucky bank but later claimed that she had transferred the funds to a bank in Chicago. The victim and her killer planned to travel to Chicago to acquire the funds. Presumably, Emily was preparing for that trip when she had the phone conversation with her brother-in-law. According to witnesses in the neighborhood, Standifer did arrive at the Moore home, though she and Emily Moore would never embark for Chicago.

Following his wife's disappearance, Loren Moore, who was aware of the business deal, called Standifer for an explanation about the exchange of funds. He had yet to make the connection between the business deal and the disappearance of his wife.

According to newspaper accounts, Standifer offered Reverend Moore three stories: (1) she had visited the Moore home in Nashville and handed off the $40,000 to Emily in the front yard, (2) she had gone to the door and transferred the money to Emily there, and (3) she had entered the home to hand off the money. She also allegedly claimed that Emily had taken the money and fled to England, in the company of a man.

As it turned out, none of the stories was true.

According to details later pieced together by the FBI and included in the official NPS incident report, Standifer had relatives in East Tennessee and was familiar with the area. On August 13, the day before the hiker discovered Moore's body, Standifer and Moore arrived in Townsend, and, by then, Moore was likely Standifer's prisoner.

If Moore had, in fact, received a payment of $40,000 in cash from Standifer, the money would still likely be in Moore's purse or on her person. Or, perhaps more likely, Standifer never handed off the down payment, deciding instead to keep her cash and dispatch the creditor. In any case, Standifer's decision to dump Moore's body in Rabbit Creek displayed a bit of forethought. The creek is isolated with densely wooded margins, and traffic on Parson Branch Road is sparse, even through the summer. In the hot, humid days of August, the decomposition process would have progressed apace, and Moore's body would quickly succumb to the nitrogen cycle. Had it not been for the solitary hiker who happened to pass by and cast his eyes toward the creek at just the right moment, Standifer just might have pulled off the perfect crime.

On November 30, a warrant for kidnapping and murder was issued for Standifer based on mounting evidence, including the matched blood type found in the car abandoned in Las Vegas.

Sometime that same month, according to the *Knoxville News Sentinel*, an early middle-aged woman walked through the door of Ye Old Coffee Pot restaurant in Los Angeles, California, and on the application for a waitressing job, she wrote the name Stacy Jo Michaels. She was hired and went to work.

Stacy Michaels might well have sustained the alias and continued to live out her life in California, had an alleged odd twist of fate not occurred that ultimately revealed her true identity and brought her to justice.

According to an article in the *Knoxville News Sentinel*, one day a young, pregnant, and apparently unwed woman walked through the door of the restaurant, looking for a job. When the girl met Stacy Jo Michaels, she studied her closely before asking, "Aren't you my mom?"

If learning that Emily Moore's body had been identified had sent a shiver through Leslie Diane Standifer, the encounter with her daughter from a previous marriage surely must have set her on edge. The girl was hired on as a cashier.

Standifer's charade began to crumble in the spring of 1977. Though Standifer's daughter did not compromise her mother's assumed identity, another family member—or former family member—did. According to newspaper accounts, a tip from Standifer's ex-husband put FBI agents on her trail. When they confronted Leslie Diane Standifer at the restaurant, she initially held to her alias and insisted they had the wrong person. The agents weren't buying it, and on May 18, they placed her under arrest for the kidnap and first-degree murder of Emily Moore.

Nearly a year would pass before the trial began in Knox County on March 13, 1978. Though Standifer pleaded innocent, the evidence against her continued to stack up through the two-day trial: Standifer's flight on learning that Moore's body had been identified, blood in Standifer's car that matched Moore's type, the newly reupholstered front passenger seat, allegations that Standifer had asked an acquaintance to purchase an unlicensed gun for her two weeks before the murder, her familiarity with the East Tennessee region, and a collect call placed to Standifer's Fiesta restaurant in Scottsburg from Sevierville the day before the body was discovered.

It took the nine-man, three-woman jury less than four hours to reach a verdict: guilty on both counts. The judge sentenced Standifer to life in a federal prison.

Standifer's attorneys appealed the ruling in April 1979, but the conviction stood, and Standifer settled into the Federal Correctional Institute for Women in Alderson, West Virginia, for what appeared to be an extended stay. But the ever-elusive Standifer had other plans.

On October 21, the *Indianapolis Star* reported, she had cut a hole

Unanswered Questions Still Shrouding Investigation Of Emily Moore Murder

By CAROLYN PICKERING
Star Staff Reporter

Nashville, Ind.—It has been two months since Emily Phyllis Moore, the plump, matronly wife of controversial Baptist minister-promoter Loren E. Moore, left her secluded and pretentious Brown County home on an unknown mission which ended in violent death in the hills of Tennessee.

Her body, full clothed except for shoes, was identified Sept. 18, exactly 35 days after being found Aug. 14 with a bullet hole in the temple and bearing lacerations and bruises suggesting a beating had preceded the gunshot wound.

SINCE THEN, state, local and now the Federal Bureau of Investigation have pulled out all their investigative stops in a yet-futile search for the an-

swers to Phyllis Moore's murder.

The unanswered questions are many and mind-boggling.

Where, for example, is Dee Standifer, the 43-year-old Scottsburg woman to whom Mrs. Moore and her husband reportedly were selling the Fiesta Restaurant in Scottsburg?

Mrs. Standifer last was seen on Sept. 20, the day positive identification of Mrs. Moore's body was made in Tennessee.

And she may have been the last person in Indiana to have seen Phyllis Moore alive—on Aug. 12.

MRS. STANDIFER is sought on a warrant issued Friday in Brown County, charging her with the issuance of an insufficient-funds check in the amount of $1,000 on Sept. 8.

And Assistant United States Attorney Sarah E. Barker said yesterday that a

Federal warrant for Mrs. Standifer's arrest will be authorized early this week, charging the Scottsburg "mystery" woman with having fled Indiana to avoid prosecution on the bad check charge.

Issuance of that Federal UFAP warrant opens the legal door for the FBI to join in the nationwide search for Mrs. Standifer.

The $1,000 check, written on the Nashville State Bank, was made payable to Loren Moore and deposited by Mrs. Standifer in a savings account belonging to Mrs. Moore, according to Indiana State Police Detectives Darwin Scott and Don Gastineau.

How Mrs. Standifer had in her possession a deposit ticket for Mrs. Moore's account is unknown, authorities say.

THE CHECK bounced, precipitating

the issuance of an insufficient funds warrant for the woman, who has vanished, leaving behind a husband and one son still at home.

Mrs. Standifer is said to have made payments of $1,000 monthly to the Moores since May 1 and also to have made mortgage payments of $455 monthly to a Scott County bank in connection with the reported contractual purchase of the restaurant for which authorities say they can find no paperwork, no legal documents and no evidence, other than bank deposits, that the sale had been consummated.

That is just one piece of a most difficult puzzle.

Back to events leading up to the murder:

IT WAS ON Aug. 12 that Dr. Loren

Turn To Page 23, Column 1

Newspaper clipping from The Indianapolis Star, *October 10, 1976.*

through a fence and escaped with another inmate. Her freedom was short-lived, though her escape path was lengthy. Standifer was apprehended two days later in Roswell, New Mexico, and was returned to prison to serve out her sentence.

CHAPTER 5
Taken Under

GSMNP's thousands of miles of cascading rivers and streams offer cool respite from summertime heat, but they also pose risks to even the strongest swimmers, particularly when storm events swell waterways beyond their margins and turn gentle rills into raging rapids. Between 1931 and 2016, 60 individuals drowned in park streams. Prudence, awareness of subsurface hazards, and the ability to swim might have saved many of them.

On September 30, 1950, when George Michon and Alice Leonard exchanged vows and pledged to spend the rest of their lives together, neither imagined that, in their case, "'till death do us part" would involve a single week of marriage.

The couple, George, a 23-year-old maintenance engineer from Yonkers, New York, and Alice, a Pennsylvania native from Canonsburg, arrived in Gatlinburg shortly after exchanging nuptials to enjoy a honeymoon in the mountains.

On Friday, October 6, the couple departed Gatlinburg, entered the park, and drove 15 miles west on Little River Road to what was then, and remains, one of the more accessible waterfalls in GSMNP. At the destination known as The Sinks, the entire flow of the Little River narrows, passes under a bridge, and cascades more than 20 feet down a run of large boulders before emptying into a long, deep pool favored in summer by swimmers and cliff jumpers.

Today, a sign posted at The Sinks parking area cautions those who might be tempted to go for a dip: "Dangerous waters have claimed swimmers' lives here. Will you be the next victim?" The sign's placement was yet decades away when George Michon drew close to the water's edge to snap a picture, lost his footing, and plunged into the fast moving current. George may have been a competent photographer, but, according to newspaper accounts, he had never learned to swim, and he was quickly swept away. Alice, an accomplished swimmer, dove in, reached her husband, and managed to pull him toward shore but was unable to lift him out of the water.

Eventually, the swift current broke Alice's hold, and George was once again swept away. She summoned the help of a nearby road crew, but by the time George's would-be saviors arrived at the margins of the river, it was too late. The Sinks had claimed its first victim since the national park was established in 1934.

Over coming years, ten additional drowning victims would perish at the popular destination. Two others would also die there of other causes— one of a heart attack in 1984 and another of a self-inflicted gunshot wound in 1990—establishing The Sinks as the fifth deadliest location within the park.

Drowning ranks as the third leading cause of death in GSMNP (behind auto fatalities and plane crashes) and between 1931 and 2013 claimed 59 lives. Like George Michon, seven other victims lost their footing on slick rocks lining creeks or coursing along the tops of waterfalls prior to

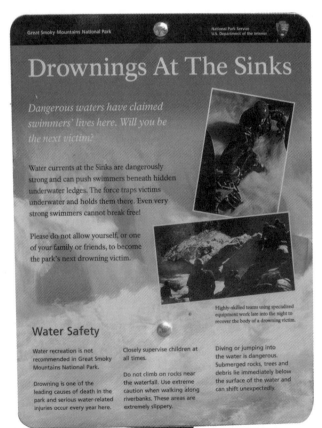

Great Smoky Mountains National Park   National Park Service
                                             U.S. Department of the Interior

Drownings At The Sinks

Dangerous waters have claimed swimmers' lives here. Will you be the next victim?

Water currents at the Sinks are dangerously strong and can push swimmers beneath hidden underwater ledges. The force traps victims underwater and holds them there. Even very strong swimmers cannot break free!

Please do not allow yourself, or one of your family or friends, to become the park's next drowning victim.

Highly-skilled teams using specialized equipment work late into the night to recover the body of a drowning victim.

Water Safety

Water recreation is not recommended in Great Smoky Mountains National Park.

Drowning is one of the leading causes of death in the park and serious water-related injuries occur every year here.

Closely supervise children at all times.

Do not climb on rocks near the waterfall. Use extreme caution when walking along riverbanks. These areas are extremely slippery.

Diving or jumping into the water is dangerous. Submerged rocks, trees and debris lie immediately below the surface of the water and can shift unexpectedly.

taking the fatal plunge. None of those seven intended to enter the water, and many were non-swimmers, raising the possibility that some might have survived had they taken time to gain that important skill. According to a 2014 report by the American Red Cross, even today, nearly half of Americans are not proficient swimmers.

A case in point is the June 6, 1956, drowning death of Donald Charles Wright, 19, of Knoxville, Tennessee. Wright slipped from a rocky ledge and fell into the Little River near the upper end of Metcalf Bottoms. According to witnesses, Wright, a nonswimmer, rose to the surface twice and called for help. Unfortunately, the other members of Wright's party were also nonswimmers and thus were unable to assist, and they watched helplessly as their struggling friend went under for the last time.

The park's waterways draw their power from two distinct features of the Smoky Mountain region: abundant rainfall and steep topography. At its higher elevations, GSMNP receives an average of 85 inches of rain per year, establishing the park as a temperate rainforest, and 2,100 miles of rivers, creeks, and tributaries carry it off. Under the relentless tug of gravity, the steep-pitched mountains shed their copious hydrologic load through a process that can hardly be described as gentle.

Anyone who has visited the park during the months of heaviest precipitation (February, March, and July) or after major storm events will note the pervasive roar of rushing water as it thrashes down the mountains on its way to the relative flats of the Tennessee Valley to the west and the rolling hills of North Carolina's Piedmont region to the east. But even during periods of light to moderate rainfall, the tumbling water traverses narrow chutes and cascades over rock ledges with sufficient force to entrap unwary victims.

George Michon may have been the first to drown at The Sinks, but at the time of his death, 12 other individuals had already lost their lives in other waterways in or proximate to the park. The first occurred on July 8, 1934, when Civilian Conservation Corps (CCC) workers discovered the body of Lewis Owl, a member of the Cherokee Nation, in a swimming hole at the confluence of the Left Fork and the Raven Fork of the Oconaluftee River. In the years since, five other persons have drowned in the Oconaluftee.

In nearly all cases, the drowning victims struggled and succumbed alone, but on August 5, 1938, a pounding deluge resulted in a mass fatality incident in which eight individuals—four of them children—shared the same fate. August 5 was an election day, and the storm struck in the evening

as dutiful citizens were returning home from the polls. Webb Creek, typically a gentle rill spanning about 10 feet, would soon be transformed into a
raging torrent as water coursed down the slopes of the Greenbrier section of
the park to the south and Webb Mountain to the north.

Just below what is now known as Cobbly Nob, about three miles east
of City Hall in Pittman Center, Alfred Ball and his wife, who had earlier cast their votes, and their four children hunkered down to wait out the
storm in their frame home situated along the creek. With them were neighbors Jesse Gillen and his wife, who lived about a mile away and had opted to
spend the night with the Balls, rather than walk home in the teeming rain.

By some reports, the Smokies region received as many as 12 inches
of rain that night over the course of about four hours. Average rainfall at
Clingmans Dome for the entire month of August is 6.8 inches. At its peak
flow, according to TVA records, Webb Creek was channeling water at 6,600
cubic feet per second (cfs). To put that into perspective, the normal flow of
the Ocoee River, near Ducktown, Tennessee, the site of the 1996 Olympic
whitewater paddling events, is 1,300 cfs.

It will never be known whether the eight occupants of the Ball home
were aware that a wall of water, described by some witnesses as looming 15
feet high, was descending on them. But this much we do know: The water
tore the structure from its foundation and swept it downstream, killing all
eight people. By some accounts, the body of one of the Ball children was
recovered seven miles from the home site.[1]

Over the years, rain-swollen streams have claimed other victims in
GSMNP. August 7, 1947, Rose Mary Mathias, 23, a school teacher from
Frostburg, Maryland, died in a flash flood of the West Prong of the Little
Pigeon River near the Chimney Tops parking area. Mathias had arrived in
Gatlinburg a week earlier with three friends from New York, according to
an article in the *Cumberland* (Maryland) *News*.

Mathias and her companions were standing within 10 feet of one
another, with Mathias closest to the stream bank, when the flood waters
struck, and all were swept away. The three companions managed to struggle
to safety; Mathias was swallowed up by the torrent.

The scattered nature of summer thunderstorms makes it possible for
heavy rains to fall at higher elevations, while visitors at the Chimneys or

---

1   The Ball home was situated just outside the boundary of GSMNP but is included in this
chapter because of its proximity to the park and because some of the water that inundated the Ball
home originated in the Greenbrier section of the park.

THE DEADLY FORCE OF RAPIDLY RISING WATERS

Flash floods rank as the leading weather-related cause of death in the United States, according to the National Weather Service (NWS), claiming an average of 127 lives per year. Nearly half of the deaths involve motor vehicles.

The week-long flooding that affected multiple Texas counties in late May and early June 2016 killed 16, including nine soldiers from the Fort Hood US Military Base in Killeen, and left others missing. Less than a month later, beginning on June 23, torrential rains triggered flash floods in West Virginia that killed 25 and damaged or destroyed more than 500 homes. According to NWS, flood waters claimed 235 victims in the United States over the 18 months extending from January 2015 through June 25, 2016.

"The two key elements [triggering flash floods] are rainfall intensity and duration," according to the NWS, while topography also plays a contributing role. Slow moving thunderstorms or those that remain stationary over small regions, which accurately describes the storm that swelled Webb Creek on August 5, 1938, are most likely to cause violent and deadly floods. The six members of the Alfred Ball family, who lived on the margins of Webb Creek just outside GSMNP, and two visiting neighbors, were killed when a wall of water tore the Ball home from its foundations and washed it downstream on the night of the storm.

Such storms overwhelm the capacity of relatively small catchments, in this case, the Webb Creek watershed, to carry off the massive load of water. As a result, water volume builds and, with insufficient drainage capacity to carry it away, begins to back up and gain depth, power, and speed. (Picture an overloaded urban storm drain during a heavy rainfall, with water backing up and flooding the street.)

When such storms strike the mountains, small headwater streams quickly overflow their banks, and the accumulating water begins to scrape away and gather up soil, rock, vegetation, and trees along the creek margins as it moves downhill. With the Webb Creek flood, massive debris slides left scars running down the sides of the mountains and in some cases retrenched stream channels. Some of those effects are still visible today.

other lower-elevation sites may be basking in sunshine. The wall of water crashing down the mountain might have been the first sign of danger, which for Mathias, left little time to scamper for higher ground.

In the *News* article, M.B. Atchley of the Tennessee Highway Patrol notes that the creek, which carries water downhill from 6,000 to 1,000 feet over a run of 15 miles, is turbulent even under normal circumstances. According to the article, the force of the flood waters was sufficient to carry Mathias' body for miles downstream from where she was last seen.

On August 10, 1984, Randall Smith, 29, of Hattiesburg, Mississippi, suffered a similar fate. Smith was swept into the Raven Fork of the Oconaluftee River near Enloe Creek Backcountry Campsite #47 while trying to cross at high water. Smith, co-leader of a Methodist Church group, was helping two young men from his group evacuate the campsite, about four miles northeast of Smokemont Campground, after having been harassed by a bear. The two young men managed to cross the rain-charged river safely. Smith was not so fortunate; he drowned in the creek.

In an October 2008 article, *Backpacker* magazine rated the trek from the Abrams Falls Trail parking area to Abrams Falls as one of the 10 most-dangerous hikes in America. The hike earned that distinction because of drowning risk, a risk borne out by GSMNP death statistics: from 1931 to 2013, seven individuals drowned in the creek, most of them at the waterfall, establishing Abrams Creek as the park's second deadliest location for drowning fatalities.

As with The Sinks, the ease of accessibility is in part to blame for the deaths in Abrams Creek. Each year, the moderate 5-mile roundtrip hike draws thousands of trekkers to the trail's culminating feature, a broad spume of water that plunges 20 feet down into a deep pool. For two of the victims, the slick, moss-covered rocks that lead to and from the falls proved to be an all-too-enticing attraction.

On July 20, 1973, Malcolm McAtee, 20, of Memphis, Tennessee, drowned when he slipped from a rock and plunged into the deep pool at the base of the falls. The same circumstances claimed the life of Christopher Drinkard, 12, a seventh-grader from Knoxville, on April 30, 2004.

The Townsend "Wye," situated at the park entrance where Laurel Creek enters the Little River, ranks as the park's third deadliest place for drowning, accounting for six fatalities. The Wye is a popular destination for waders, swimmers, kayakers, and visitors buoyed by inflated inner tubes (so-

The Sinks is a popular spot for sight seers along Little River Road. Drownings have occurred both upstream and downstream of the cascade.

called "tubers"), and members of all four groups have succumbed at or near the Wye.

On June 14, 1964, the Wye claimed its first victim. Darlene Riden, 12, of Maryville, Tennessee, a non-swimmer, was wading toward an island in the river when she slipped and fell and was carried away by the current. The Wye's next fatality involved the only drowning victim in the park who was, in fact, equipped to survive an extended stay underwater. On August 20, 1966, Richard A. Stansberry, 18, of Knoxville, reached the shores of the Little River intent on testing out his SCUBA (self-contained underwater breathing apparatus) gear.

The SCUBA equipment was working properly, but, according to the coroner's report, Stansberry had sustained a blow to the head, perhaps upon entering the river, that may have rendered him unconscious. Also contributing to the death, the river was running unusually fast and high when Stansberry entered the water.

On May 28, 1973, William Lawrence Bridge, 19, of De Sota, Missouri, became the first boater to drown at the Wye, when his canoe capsized in swift, deep water. On August 26, 2008, Isaac Ludwig, 27, of Hartford, Tennessee, became the first kayaker to die in a park stream, though not at the Wye. Ludwig was with a group of boaters who planned to paddle from the Chimney Tops Trailhead to the Chimneys Picnic Area, a distance of less than two miles. Ludwig's companions, daunted by the flood-swollen river and raging current, quickly abandoned the run and returned to shore. Ludwig pressed on. His body was recovered the next day.

Each summer, hundreds of park visitors participate in the pastime of tubing, and numerous rental outfits in park gateway communities supply the rudimentary, but effective, flotation devices.

Tubing may seem relatively safe when water levels are low and currents are gentle, but without a life preserver, children and adults alike are taking a significant risk. Two tubers fell victim to the Wye's powerful current within the same month: Gregory Michael Kirk, 15, of Seymour, Tennessee, on June 4, 1976, and Troy Titlow, 22, of Dalton, Georgia, 22 days later, on June 26. In the years since, three other tubers have drowned in park waterways.

A little-known danger facing tubers and swimmers in the park's swift streams is foot entrapment. Several drownings and near-drownings have occurred at The Sinks and elsewhere on Little River when a swimmer's foot became snagged in a slot that is part of the Smokies' river bottom geology. If the entrapped swimmer keeps calm, escape may be fairly simple, especially with the help of others. However, panic in the cold swift waters has proven fatal.

Many of the park's roadways course along rivers and streams, including Little River Road (Little River), Laurel Creek Road (Laurel Creek), and Newfound Gap Road, (Oconaluftee River in North Carolina and the West Prong of the Little Pigeon River in Tennessee), and, despite being shrouded in an armor of steel and glass, occupants of autos are not immune from drowning.

On March 11, 1967, at about 10:30 p.m., a car driven by James A. Ray, 22, of Pigeon Forge, Tennessee, careened into the West Prong of the Little Pigeon River on the Gatlinburg-Pigeon Forge Spur. According to witness accounts, Ray attempted to leave the vehicle, fell into the river, and was swept downstream. His body was recovered the next morning in more than 15 feet of water 75 feet below the abandoned car.

On January 18, 1986, James McNeel, 20, of Birmingham, Alabama, and Anthony Grisdale, 19, of Talladega, Alabama, where traveling in a Datsun 280Z when the vehicle left the road about 3.5 miles east of the Townsend Wye and plunged over a 20-foot cliff into the Little River. The car landed on its roof and quickly filled with water, killing both occupants.

Twenty-two years later, on February 25, 2008, in nearly the same location, park officials recovered the body of Matthew Johnson, 24, of Toccoa, Georgia, from a submerged vehicle. Late on the previous night, Johnson had been traveling east on Little River Road and failed to negotiate a sharp right-hand turn. His car had plummeted 25 feet into the water.

GSMNP's abundance of rushing water establishes the park as a favored destination for swimmers and anglers, particularly in warm summer months, and the vast majority of them fully savor their aquatic experiences and return home safely. But between 1931 and 2016, 60 of them did not.

Water sports, like most other outdoor activities, pose a degree of risk. Indeed, according to the Centers for Disease Control and Prevention, natural waterways, including rivers and lakes, annually account for more than half (52 percent) of all drowning deaths in America. But the risk diminishes considerably if individuals take time to calculate potential hazards and take steps to minimize or avoid them.

The fact remains that drowning deaths, except those that are caused by flash floods and other natural disasters, are largely avoidable: don't enter the water, and you won't drown. In fact, the National Park Service does not encourage swimming or boating in any park streams.

Currents in mountain streams are notoriously difficult to read, particularly those at work beneath the surface, and subsurface tangles of downed trees and jumbled rocks—so called "strainers"—can entrap a swimmer, tuber, boater, or angler and pin him or her under thousands of pounds of hydrologic force.

Diving is never a good idea in natural waterways, even if the stream bottom is clearly visible. A head-first encounter with a submerged rock can, at best, result in a nasty concussion, and at worst, cause paralysis or death.

The latter fate awaited Donald Eugene Manis, 27, of Knoxville, who, on May 20, 1977, dove into the Little River near Long Arm Bridge and struck his head on a rock, which broke his neck. Manis subsequently drowned.

Non-swimmers especially should steer clear of the park's waterways entirely or limit themselves to dangling their feet in shallow pools. Better yet, they might invest in swimming lessons before entering the park. Personal flotation devices—aka, life jackets— are requisite equipment for kayakers and canoers; tubers and swimmers who do not wish to be included in future editions of this book series should likewise adopt their use.

The official message posted at The Sinks might be applied to many of the park's waterways: "Dangerous waters have claimed swimmers' lives here. Will you be the next victim?"

With adequate caution and respect for the power of moving water, the answer will most certainly be, no. Tumbling whitewater is a key component of the GSMNP landscape and, for many visitors, a feature that's essential to their enjoyment of the park. Those who enter the water to fish, boat, float, wade, or swim should take to heart the adage that still waters run deep, but, as statistics bear out, the churning rapids and plunging falls are significantly more perilous.

CHAPTER 6
A Mother's Mission of Thanks

Each year, for more than 40 years, Wanetta Johnson arrived at the National Park Service Headquarters at Sugarlands on December 3, with an out-sized box of chocolates and a potted red poinsettia. It was a mother's way of saying thanks for the rescue of her son Eric, stranded with a friend high in the mountains, along an Appalachian Trail buried in early-season snow.

In early December, a particularly celebratory mood overtakes the National Park Service Headquarters staff at Sugarlands in Great Smoky Mountains National Park (GSMNP), as they await the arrival of a special visitor who is often dressed in red and always bears gifts.

Nope, not *that* visitor. This caller arrives in a vehicle outfitted with rubber tires, rather than sleigh runners. And the purpose of the visits relates as much to the recently passed Thanksgiving holiday as it does the approaching Yuletide.

Every December 3, for the past 41 years, Wanetta (pronounced *Wa-nee-ta*) Johnson, who turns 95 this November [2017], makes the trip from her home in Johnson City, Tennessee to park headquarters to express her gratitude for the dramatic rescue of her son Eric and his friend Randy Laws in late fall of 1974. The two boys, both experienced backpackers, had become stranded high on the Appalachian spine in waist-deep snow when a planned three-night outing morphed into a six-day struggle for survival.

Just after noon, Wanetta, a former school teacher, arrives with a potted poinsettia—"the biggest and most beautiful" she can find—and a 2.5-pound box of chocolates. Eric, 58, now a retired agent with the Drug Enforcement Administration, accompanies his mother and offers Park Service staff a tangible reminder of the value of their life-saving skills.

"Wanetta's visits are a steady reminder of how important our park rangers are to public safety and to saving the lives of the ones we love," says Nancy Gray, a former GSMNP media specialist who welcomed Wanetta to park headquarters for the past 21 years. "Having someone like Wanetta show her gratitude each year, for so many years, is a remarkable gesture. It just feels good to know that you've made a difference in someone's life." Once inside headquarters, Wanetta, clad in a sweater as red as the flowers she's bearing, greets everyone with a hug, though, for the most part, the narrative of the boys' ordeal goes untold. Indeed, the story of Randy and Eric's rescue and Wanetta's annual mission of thanks have long since passed into park lore.

The Best Laid Plans

Those who spent a traditional Thanksgiving on November 28, 1974, might recall that the Dallas Cowboys came from behind to defeat the Washington Redskins 24-23. New Yorkers lucky enough to score tickets to Elton John's concert in Madison Square Garden were treated to a guest appearance by none other than John Lennon. It would be Lennon's final concert.

Closer to home, Chattanooga logged its most frigid Thanksgiving on record, at 22 degrees. Further to the east, in Johnson City, unaware of the approaching weather system, 15-year-old Eric Johnson loaded his blue Jansport backpack into his parents' Pontiac station wagon. Likewise, Eric's friend Randy Laws, also 15, stowed his pack, a borrowed Kelty. Neither boy could know that, within a few days, the Kelty's red fabric would play a role in their very survival.

Later in the day, Wanetta and husband, Harry, deposited the boys at Davenport Gap, where the Appalachian Trail (AT) exits Great Smoky Mountains National Park and heads north. The boys had planned a three-night, 30-mile trek south on the AT from Davenport Gap to Newfound Gap. According to Eric, it was the boys' first long-range backpacking trip in the Smokies and—by any measure—an ambitious one, even under ideal weather conditions.

Wanetta recalls "the prettiest day"—chilly but clear. The couple

planned to meet the boys at Newfound
Gap at 6 p.m. on Sunday evening.

*Eric Johnson in 1974, around the time of
his rescue along the Appalachian Trail.*

NPS Official Incident Report:
Thursday, November 28, 1200 hours.
Eric Johnson and Randy Laws were taken
to Davenport Gap on 11-28 by Eric's father
[Wanetta was present as well]. They were
to begin a hike on the AT commencing at
Davenport Gap and ending at Newfound
Gap on 12-1-74. The permit was written at
Sugarlands Visitor Center by Park Technician
Cardwell who also inspected and approved their
gear. The hike the two boys were making was
too ambitious (30 miles) for the time allowed
and changeable weather patterns at this time of year.

The boys shouldered their packs, picked up the white blazes marking
the AT in the early afternoon, and began the 1-mile trek to the Davenport
Gap Shelter, where they would spend the night.

Preparation, Boy Scout Style

Eric recalls that the sky was cloudless as the two arrived at the shelter and
broke open their cache of Mountain House® freeze-dried food. Eric was
particularly excited to have with him the down sleeping bag he had received
from his parents on the previous Christmas.

In fact, the boys were well equipped, with thermal underwear, multiple clothing layers, hats and gloves, sturdy lug-soled hiking boots, and two
extra days of food. Both boys were in top physical condition. In fact, Randy
was an athlete on the high school football team. Over his years in scouting,
Eric had learned to heed to the Boy Scout motto, "Be Prepared." Under
the tutelage of his troop leader, Tom Dosser, Eric had covered many miles
on the trails of East Tennessee and Southwest Virginia and spent countless
nights out under the stars.

According to Eric, Dosser led his scouts on overnighters at least once
a month and conducted each outing like a classroom, teaching first-aid, use
of map and compass, and survival skills. Eric, who went on to earn his Eagle
Scout badge, had also earned a special patch for completing a 20-mile hike

in one day. The boys would soon have the opportunity to put their training to the test.

The following morning, the hikers began the difficult 2,500-foot, 7-mile ascent to Cosby Knob Shelter, their stopover for the night, at 4,700 feet. The following day, Saturday, the difficult climbing continued an additional 6.4 miles and 1,900 feet to the high point of the boys' trek, just below Mt. Guyot's 6,620-foot summit—the second highest peak in the park. Despite the difficult terrain, the boys reached Tricorner Knob Shelter before noon on Saturday, with 5.2 miles separating them from their planned destination for the night, Pecks Corner Shelter.

That's when the Smokies' notoriously fickle weather intervened.

"As we approached Tricorner Knob, it started snowing heavily," recalls Eric. With temperatures in the low-20s, and blinding snowfall, Eric and Randy collected firewood, settled into the shelter, crawled into their sleeping bags, and decided to hole up and wait out the storm—putting them a day behind schedule. They planned to make up the lost time on Sunday, hoofing it all the way to Newfound Gap—a distance of 15.7 miles over rugged, saw-toothed terrain—in time to meet Eric's parents at 6 p.m.

Incident Report:
Saturday, November 30, 1330 hours.

The two boys were at Tri-Corner Knob Shelter and at this point they were one day behind schedule. It began to snow heavily about 1200 hours on Saturday and the boys decided to stay at the shelter in hopes that the snow would stop. At 1330 hours, the boys were seen by a horse party at the shelter. One of the group was a Dr. Kiebler and he reported that they were gathering firewood to wait out the storm and that one of the boys complained of a stomach ache.

Though Eric struggled with a "queasy stomach," the boys were otherwise in good health and remained optimistic about hiking out the next day.

Sunday morning, the boys awoke to a world of white. Overnight, snowfall had accumulated to three to four feet, and high winds had sculpted drifts large enough to consume a man, as Randy would learn firsthand the following morning. Worse still, the snow continued to fall.

The incident report from Sunday morning notes dropping temperatures, heavy winds, snow accumulation of a foot at Newfound Gap, and "people stranded at [Clingmans] Dome, due to cars being snowed in."

Waiting and Worrying

Just after noon, Wanetta and Harry, aware of the weather conditions but hoping for the best, set out for their planned rendezvous with the boys at Newfound Gap. But when they arrived at Sugarlands, they found that the road to Newfound Gap had been closed. They appealed to park rangers, who loaded them into a four-wheel-drive vehicle and drove the 13.2 miles to the gap. There, standing up to their knees in snow, and with a stiff breeze blowing, they waited until well after dark, peering north on the AT, hoping to see a flashlight beam piercing the darkness. With no sign of the boys, the couple and their escorts returned to Sugarlands, where rangers began to organize a search and rescue.

At 10 p.m., rescue ranger Dwight McCarter received a call from Assistant Chief Ranger Jack Linahan, advising him of the missing boys and the planned rescue mission, scheduled to begin the following morning.

Wanetta and Harry settled into an upscale hotel in Gatlinburg, but their consuming worries made it impossible for either of them to enjoy the room's plush red rugs and crackling fire, which Wanetta describes as "cheerful." It would be a long night—but not the last they'd spend awaiting word on the fate of their son and his friend.

Thwarted Escape

Incident Report

Monday, December 2, 1200 hours

Decision is made to send two men into Icewater [Springs] Shelter via the AT to see if the boys made it that far. Two others will go by ATV[snowmobile] up Bradley Fork to Pecks Corner shelter.

On Monday morning, resolved to escape their predicament, Eric and Randy packed their gear and began post-holing in the snow up the short spur trail that leads from Tricorner Knob Shelter to the AT. The snow had stopped falling, but the drifts continued to mount.

"As soon as we were out of the shelter, we were in snow up to our knees," says Eric. "By the time we reached the AT, the snow was waist-deep."

The boys continued on, progressing less than a quarter of a mile in over two hours. That's when Eric heard his hiking partner yell for help. Behind him on the trail, Randy had fallen into a drift up to his chest.

"Heck with this," Eric concluded, and the two turned tail and slogged back to the shelter, where they prepared for an extended stay and began rationing their food, determining to live on one meal per day.

Rescue rangers would later credit the boys with having made the right decision. Had they pressed on, it's likely that they would have reached a point of exhaustion far from shelter and died of exposure. (See "What They Did Right" on page 73).

"The way we figured it," says Eric…at one meal per day, we could make it six days on what we had left."

Further, to conserve energy, the boys remained in their sleeping bags.

Eric soothed Randy's growing anxiety by assuring him that rescue would eventually come.

"I reminded him that we were on an established trail, that people knew we were out there, and that, somehow, they'd get to us," recalls Eric. "I wasn't concerned about them finding us—I was just concerned about how long it would take."

At one point, the two heard an aircraft pass overhead and ran outside the shelter, signaling for help, but the plane was too high to see them.

At that moment, Eric had begun to grasp that, with trail conditions as they were, rescue would likely come from the air and that Randy's bright red backpack would serve as a highly visible signaling device. The boys mounted the pack on a long walking stick planted in the snow in the clearing in front of the shelter. Determined to boost their odds, Eric also stomped the word "HELP" in large block letters in the snow.

After that, they waited…killing the hours by recounting the plot lines of old TV shows, including *Gomer Pyle*, and challenging each other with football trivia questions.

As the boys resigned themselves to meager rations and another frigid night in the shelter, the Park Service was mobilizing a rescue. At 3 p.m., Rangers Click and DeHart, en route from Newfound Gap to Icewater Springs on a snowmobile, keyed their radio and reported drifting snow, 30-40 mile-per-hour winds, and an ambient temperature of 19 degrees.

According to the National Weather Service, a 40-mile-per-hour wind turns 19 degrees into -1. Unable to proceed, the two rangers turned back halfway to the shelter.

At 5 p.m., Eugene Phillips and Bob Brantley, also on a snowmobile, reached Pecks Corner and reported that the shelter was empty. They radioed plans to continue north on the AT to False Gap, but within a half mile, they, too, turned back.

According to McCarter's account of the search in his book *Lost: A Ranger's Journal of Search and Rescue* (Graphicom Press, 1998), another team of rangers was dispatched from Cosby on a snowmobile. Within a few miles, the snowmobile foundered in the deep snow on the Snake Den Trail, and, for a time, it appeared as though the rangers themselves might be in need of rescue.

In his journal entry, McCarter writes: "I have never seen conditions as bad as these and I am very apprehensive about the young men we are trying to find. I know that they cannot survive very long under these conditions."

Back at Sugarlands, Wanetta and Harry, who had spent the day listening to the disheartening radio chatter, returned to a hotel room in Gatlinburg for another sleepless night.

Deliverance

Tuesday, December 3, dawned cold but clear. Eric and Randy were beginning the sixth day of their ordeal at Tricorner Knob Shelter. Early in the morning, on his way up to Newfound Gap in a Jeep, McCarter heard the chop of rotors and looked up to see the University of Tennessee Vertiflite chopper, manned by Robert "Doc" Lash, MD, (who would go on to found the UT LIFESTAR program in 1984) and his crew, heading northeast along the AT. Within an hour, just before 11 a.m., Lash reported seeing the red pack, Eric's HELP message, and two people waving frantically in front of the shelter.

Eric recalls seeing the chopper overhead, with an arm waving out an open window, and realized they had been spotted. Persistent high winds made it impossible for the chopper to linger long, and the boys watched it depart, thinking that their rescue was imminent.

"We immediately packed our gear, put away our sleeping bags, and were standing out in front of the shelter in our hiking clothes," says Eric. By early afternoon, the two were chilled—not to mention discouraged—and returned to their sleeping bags.

What they didn't realize was that Lash had dropped a survival kit, containing food and extra sleeping bags, along with a note informing the boys that a large Chinook helicopter, called in from Ft. Campbell, Kentucky, would return to hoist them to safety in the early afternoon.

There is nothing subtle about a Chinook. The birds stretch nearly 100

feet from fore to aft, are powered by two stalwart 3,750 horse-power engines, and can accommodate 55 troops.

Hours later, back in the recesses of the shelter, Eric heard the unmis-
takable "womp" of the helicopter's enormous rotors when he estimates the
craft was yet five miles away.

"The rotors just kept getting louder and louder," Eric recalls. "I finally
spotted the chopper when it was about a mile away, descending like an enormous praying mantis."

A coin toss earned Randy rights to the first extraction: a 300-foot,
wind-buffeted ascent on a wire that slowly winched him up into the craft.
Eric soon followed and was greeted by a medical crew—including Doc
Lash—as the chopper banked north and headed for the University of Tennessee Medical Center.

Down in Gatlinburg, Wanetta and Harry learned of the rescue and that one of the boys was sick (Eric had frostbitten toes, and both boys were dehydrated). The grateful—and greatly relieved—parents were soon reunited with their son, who lay on an emergency-room bed in Knoxville. Though Eric spent several days in the hospital and hobbled on his heels for a couple of weeks after, he returned to Science Hill High School after the Christmas break.

Wanetta Johnson and her son, Eric, on the annual visit to Great Smoky Mountains National Park headquarters.

Epilogue

As the months passed, with her boy home safe, Wanetta—eager to demonstrate her and Harry's gratitude

WHAT THEY DID RIGHT

Eric Johnson and Randy Laws, both 15, owe their survival to the Park Service Rangers and others who, in fall of 1974, rescued them after a six-day ordeal in a wind-blasted Great Smoky Mountains National Park cloaked in waist-deep snow.

But the boys' prudent and well-considered actions in the face of crisis also helped ensure their own survival. In a December 4, 1974, *Knoxville Journal* article, Park Service Ranger Jack Linahan, who supervised the search and rescue, credits the boys with doing "everything right."

In particular, Randy and Eric (who went on to become an Eagle Scout) took the following appropriate actions.

- The boys departed from home with multiple clothing layers, warm sleeping bags, sturdy boots, hats and gloves, and two extra days of food rations. When they realized that they were stranded at Tricorner Knob Shelter, Eric and Randy began to ration their remaining food supplies to stretch their stores an additional six days, if necessary.
- On Monday morning, after determining that the trail from Tricorner Knob Shelter was impassable because of deep snow, the two opted to stay put in the shelter, where they had access to ample firewood to keep warm. Had they pressed on, they would likely have succumbed to exhaustion and then hypothermia, and the story would have recounted a recovery (of bodies) instead of a rescue. Further, they conserved energy and body heat by remaining in their sleeping bags.

- The two acquired a backcountry camping permit—required of all who intend to stay overnight in the park's backcountry—which alerted Park Service personnel to their planned itinerary and helped guide search efforts. The boys had also shared detailed plans with their parents, who alerted Park Service personnel when the boys missed their planned rendezvous.

- As weather conditions continued to deteriorate, Eric realized that rescue would most probably come from above. To signal to aircraft passing overhead, he and Randy placed Randy's bright-red Kelty pack on a walking stick in front of the shelter. Eric stomped "HELP" in the snow, in block letters, in the clearing in front of the shelter. Searchers in the air saw both the SOS message and the pack and called a Chinook helicopter to carry the boys to safety.

If the boys did anything wrong, it was planning a three-night, 30-mile trek over some of the most rugged country in Great Smoky Mountains National Park—an ambitious undertaking, even under ideal weather conditions.

for the rescue—fixed on a plan.

She and Harry, bearing a large, bright-red poinsettia, arrived at park headquarters on December 3, 1975, and began a tradition that's lasted ever since (though Harry died in 2000).

His six days on the edge had a lasting effect on Eric. In years following the rescue, he became the living embodiment of Friedrich Nietzsche's dictum "What does not destroy me makes me stronger," which Eric cites in explaining the path that guided him forward from the frozen environs of Tricorner Knob Shelter.

A mere year and a half after his ordeal in the Smokies, Eric, then 16, kicked steps to the 14,410-foot summit of Washington's Mt. Rainier, the most heavily glaciated peak in the Lower 48. In 1979, he stood on the 20,320-foot summit of Mt. McKinley. And in 1987, at age 28, Eric reached the summit of Argentina's 22,841-foot Aconcagua, the highest mountain in the Western Hemisphere.

"It's empowering to go through something like that and come out the other side," he says.

While Eric found himself lured to the challenge of some of the world's least hospitable locales, his grateful mother embarked on an annual pilgrimage to a familiar site—and one she will forever associate with redemption. Fitting, it seems, for the season of red poinsettias.

CHAPTER 7
Armed, Dangerous, Ready to Kill Cops
(and Headed to the National Park)

Law enforcement rangers in GSMNP don't relish confronting armed and homicidal outlaws, but on occasion such intervention is part of the job of securing the park and protecting its visitors. Rarely have the stakes been higher than in 2004, when a ranger spotted a green Toyota 4Runner and locked eyes with the deranged man behind the wheel.

On June 7, 2004, at about 11 p.m., GSMNP Ranger Tracy J. (T.J.) Jackson, patrolling alone, pulled his cruiser into the Newfound Gap parking lot. At the time, about a dozen visitors and their vehicles occupied the parking area, but it was a dark green 2000 Toyota 4Runner parked in the lower section of the lot that caught Jackson's attention.

The vehicle's driver had turned on the interior light, so Jackson was able to identify him as a white male. Jackson noted that the subject watched him closely as Jackson shone his spotlight on the other cars in the lot, just before the subject backed the SUV out of his parking space and slowly drove toward Jackson's patrol car.

"When we were approximately 40 to 50 feet apart, the man stopped the SUV and placed his arms straight out over the steering wheel with the palms of his hands facing me," Jackson writes in his incident-report narrative of events of that night. "His fingers were spread wide apart, and he appeared to be stretching out towards the windshield with his palms on the glass, as if to show me he had nothing in his hands." As he did, the subject kept his eyes riveted on Jackson.

"His intense interest in my whereabouts, coupled with his hand gestures led me to believe that he had past dealings with law enforcement," Jackson writes. Information Jackson had received a few hours earlier served to validate that assessment.

At 4:52 p.m., dispatcher Randy Kelly had faxed a be-on-the-lookout (BOLO) notification, and a copy had arrived at the Smokemont Ranger Station. Just after 5 p.m., Jackson picked it up and shared it with colleague Ranger Joe Pond. The two had discussed the BOLO over dinner at the Ponderosa Steakhouse in Cherokee.

The description provided by the BOLO aligned perfectly with the SUV and its driver situated just ahead of Jackson's cruiser in the overlook parking lot.

With his right hand, Jackson gently eased his sidearm from its holster and concealed it under his left forearm, hidden from the subject's line of sight, as he pulled the cruiser alongside the green Toyota SUV. Jackson strategically placed his vehicle so that his driver-side door glass was positioned between the SUV's front tire and door.

"I assumed this position so he would have to lean forward and hold his head out the driver's window to talk to me," Jackson writes. "This kept him in an awkward position, and I could easily see any of his movements." Jackson's interest in the man's movement was based on more than mere prudence.

The SUV driver, John Brian Peck, was, based on the BOLO, deranged and dangerous, not to mention heavily armed. Jackson had reason to believe that somewhere in the vehicle, perhaps within easy reach, Peck had a 7.26 mm SKS assault rifle—a notoriously powerful and deadly weapon—with a loaded banana clip containing 30 or more rounds of ammunition.

Peck, 27, a dropout from the University of North Carolina-Wilmington (UNCW), had already demonstrated a homicidal bent to use the weapon. According to newspaper accounts, three days earlier, on June 4, Peck had allegedly used the weapon in murdering his ex-girlfriend, Christen Naujoks, 22, a UNCW student, in front of her Wilmington apartment.

After Naujoks had broken off the relationship, Peck had allegedly stalked and harassed her for several months, and the young woman had filed a restraining order against him. In the end, the injunction did little to stop

Peck, temper his rage, or block the nearly dozen bullets he allegedly pumped into his victim's body.

Christen Naujoks was but the first of Peck's intended targets. According to newspaper accounts, Peck's hit list, later recovered, indicated that he intended to continue his killing spree to include Naujoks' mother, his own mother, and a therapist who had treated him for severe mental illness.

The BOLO also indicated that Peck had likely stopped taking his medication and noted that, before fleeing Wilmington, Peck had informed family members that he would "shoot any law enforcement officer that approached him or tried to apprehend him."

Ranger T.J. Jackson's situation—alone, facing an armed and dangerous homicidal man not five feet away—was as delicate as they come, and he realized that the wrong move might place him, and the other visitors in the parking area, in direct danger.

Then Peck broke the silence.

"Can I camp here [in the parking area]?" Peck asked.

"No," Jackson told him.

Peck went on to explain that he had purchased new camping gear and hoped to use it. The information Jackson had received with the BOLO bore out the fact that Peck had, indeed, purchased the gear in Asheville the night before.

During the brief discussion, Jackson noticed that beads of sweat had begun to pop out on Peck's face, though the temperature hovered in the low 60s. Peck's voice also began to waver, and he "appeared very nervous," indications perhaps that a man not particularly noted for impulse control was about to act.

Here Jackson made a critical decision and one that would ultimately chart the outcome of the unfolding incident. Jackson knew that Ranger Pond, who likewise, was working the 3 p.m.-midnight shift, was on patrol south of the overlook on Newfound Gap Road, and he determined to send Peck in that direction.

"I told him [Peck] that Cherokee had good campgrounds," Jackson reports, and he advised him to turn left out of the parking lot and head down the mountain. Peck complied, and as he pulled away, Jackson noted that the tags on the SUV matched those provided by the BOLO. This was definitely their man. Without a moment to lose, Jackson keyed his radio and relayed an urgent system-wide message that specifically targeted Ranger Pond. It was now 11:16 p.m.

"Got our BOLO suspect picked up at Newfound Gap, 516 [Pond's call number], you copy? He's heading your way, Joe…Joe, watch in case he's coming down the mountain."

As Peck approached Pond's position, the 1991 veteran of Operation Desert Storm, began to think like a soldier.

"I believed that if Peck was homicidal, mentally disturbed, armed, and even somewhat prepared for entering a woodland environment, that he would gain a superior advantage [over] pursuing officers, making his capture extremely dangerous," Pond writes in his narrative on the incident. "Numerous backcountry campsites lie throughout the park, and during the summer, it can be expected that many are occupied to capacity with adults and children."

Pond's reasoning led him to the conclusion that "it would be tactically in my best interest to try and apprehend Peck in the open, on the road, preventing either escape by vehicle on the road or by foot into the woods." If Peck managed to escape into the forest, with his high-powered, highly accurate weapon and considerable cache of ammunition, "the terrain and vegetation could provide him with an instant tactical advantage at minimal risk to himself and *great* risk to law enforcement."

Pond decided to set up his roadblock and take his stand at the Collins Creek Picnic Area of the park, 10.7 miles down the mountain from Newfound Gap, and Pond knew that if Peck was punching the gas, as he was likely to do, he didn't have much time.

The Collins Creek area was likely to be unoccupied at that time of night, while, just 1.8 miles farther south, the Smokemont Campground was nearly filled to capacity, and beyond lay the community of Cherokee, teeming with summer tourists.

Pond immediately activated his in-car video recording system, which would later render valuable evidence, and at 11:17 p.m., a minute after receiving Jackson's alert, radioed the Cherokee Police Department and requested a Special Weapons and Tactics (SWAT) team and any other support it could provide.

At 11:21 p.m., Pond arrived at Collins Creek and parked his cruiser in the southbound lane, facing north, (the lane that Peck would occupy as he headed down the mountain) and switched on his emergency lights, headlights, and spotlight.

For the next eight minutes, as Pond waited for backup to arrive, he prepared for his encounter with Peck. He checked his NPS-issued rifle, an M-16, and flicked the safety switch to on. Pond was wearing a ballistic vest under his uniform but, for added protection, donned a second vest containing ceramic plates intended to stop rifle bullets. The covering vest was clearly marked "Police." Pond then advised the few visitors he encountered to leave the area.

At 11:29 p.m., Sergeant Neil Ferguson and Officer Doug Pheasant, both SWAT-trained officers from the Cherokee Police Department, arrived at Pond's roadblock. Ferguson quickly deployed spike strips (aka "tire-shredders") across the road in front of Pond's patrol car. Meanwhile, up the mountain, Jackson locked the gate and blocked the road up to Clingmans Dome, just in case Peck had veered off the Newfound Gap Road there, instead of heading south toward Pond. Once the gate was secure, Jackson, armed with his M-16, took tactical cover on the hillside overlooking the roadway.

When Pond had received Jackson's 11:16 p.m. alert from Newfound Gap, he had calculated the distance and estimated Peck's time of travel from the Newfound Gap Overlook at 15 minutes; his estimate was a mere two minutes off. At 11:33 p.m., an SUV approached his position from the north. From his vantage point less than three car-lengths from the approaching vehicle, Pond could see that it matched the description of Peck's dark green 2000 4Runner.

"That's it!" Pond advised Ferguson and Pheasant. "That looks like a Toyota!"

What happened next resolved any doubt that Peck meant to make good on his pledge not to be captured and to kill any law-enforcement officers who stood in his way.

Pond raised his M-16, flicked off the safety, and pointed it directly at the driver's side of Peck's car, and the SUV slowed to a stop. As Pond faced down the vehicle, he shouted, "Police! Show me your hands!" As he did, from the periphery, he could see Pheasant advancing toward the SUV from the other side of the road. In an equally strident voice, Pheasant echoed Pond's command to Peck.

Peck, who had no intention of yielding, dropped the SUV into reverse, and, as his tires squealed on the pavement, fired three poorly aimed rifle shots at the officers, kicking up sparks from the roadway. Ferguson and

Pheasant returned fire from their rifles.

Peck, who was not injured in the exchange, reversed course and sped back up the mountain. Pond, still in position to fire, determined that his cruiser, not his rifle, would prove a more effective tool for ending Peck's flight.

As he backed toward his patrol car, Pond keyed his portable radio and announced that shots had been fired. Jackson, up at Newfound Gap, abandoned his defensive shooting position, hopped into his car, and sped down the mountain to offer assistance. Pond's next transmission advised Jackson that Peck "was running, northbound" toward him.

Pheasant's patrol car led the pursuit up the mountain, with Pond's cruiser right behind him and Ferguson bringing up the rear.

Peck's flight was short; it was also dramatic. At 11:37 p.m., just past the Kanati Fork Trailhead, two miles north of Collins Creek Picnic Area, Peck's tail lights came into view. After Pond saw Peck pump his brakes, the car slowed before easing off the right side of the road and into the woods.

At the time, Pond, Pheasant, and Ferguson surmised that Peck had pulled into the woods, abandoned his vehicle, and was in the process of locating a hidden position from which to snipe at the law-enforcement officers. As it turned out, the short, troubled life of John Brian Peck had already come to an end. At the moment Pond had seen the Toyota brake and slow, Peck's powerful assault rifle—the very one that he had, only moments earli-

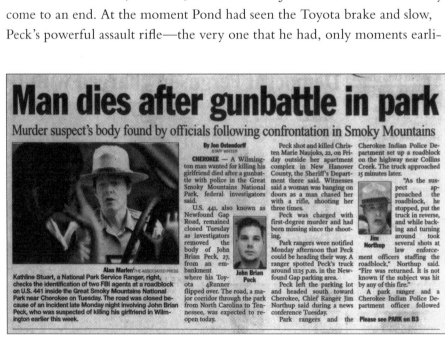

Man dies after gunbattle in park

Murder suspect's body found by officials following confrontation in Smoky Mountains

By Jon Ostendorff
STAFF WRITER

CHEROKEE — A Wilmington man wanted for killing his girlfriend died after a gunbattle with police in the Great Smoky Mountains National Park, federal investigators said.

U.S. 441, also known as Newfound Gap Road, remained closed Tuesday as investigators removed the body of John Brian Peck, 27, from an embankment where his Toyota 4Runner flipped over. The road, a major corridor through the park from North Carolina to Tennessee, was expected to reopen today.

Peck shot and killed Christen Marie Naujoks, 22, on Friday outside her apartment complex in New Hanover County, the Sheriff's Department there said. Witnesses said a woman was banging on doors as a man chased her with a rifle, shooting her three times.

Peck was charged with first-degree murder and had been missing since the shooting.

Park rangers were notified Monday afternoon that Peck could be heading their way. A ranger spotted Peck's truck around 11:15 p.m. in the Newfound Gap parking area.

Peck left the parking lot and headed south toward Cherokee, Chief Ranger Jim Northup said during a news conference Tuesday.

Park rangers and the

Cherokee Indian Police Department set up a roadblock on the highway near Collins Creek. The truck approached 15 minutes later.

"As the suspect approached the roadblock, he stopped, put the truck in reverse, and while backing and turning around took several shots at law enforcement officers staffing the roadblock," Northup said. "Fire was returned. It is not known if the subject was hit by any of this fire."

A park ranger and a Cherokee Indian Police Department officer followed **Please see PARK on B3**

John Brian Peck

Jim Northup

Kathline Stuart, a National Park Service Ranger, right, checks the identification of two FBI agents at a roadblock on U.S. 441 inside the Great Smoky Mountains National Park near Cherokee on Tuesday. The road was closed because of an incident late Monday night involving John Brian Peck, who was suspected of killing his girlfriend in Wilmington earlier this week.

Alan Marler/THE ASSOCIATED PRESS

Newspaper clipping from Asheville Citizen-Times, *June 9, 2004.*

er, fired at police—claimed its second victim.

The head wound was massive. The SUV careened more than 200 feet down a steep hillside, rolling side over side, before coming to rest in the creek. Peck's battered body was thrown from the vehicle on impact and came to rest on a rock just a few feet from the rifle that had caused so much harm.

Several days after the incident, after the adrenalin had cleared Pond's system and he had had time to rest, he began to recall the events of the chase in greater detail.

"One particular detail that I recall with some clarity...is having heard a single gunshot as Peck's Toyota was going off the road," Pond writes in his report. "I feel that I heard this with certainty on the night of the event."

Indeed, the noise Pond likely heard was the sound of Peck's murderous rampage coming to an end.

CHAPTER 8
The Smokies Prepare for Nuclear Attack

Cold War-induced fear of nuclear annihilation swept the nation through the 1950s and '60s. Rational suburbanites responded by building elaborate backyard bomb shelters. School-aged kids received instructions from a cartoon turtle named Bert on how to duck and cover under their desks. Meanwhile, Great Smoky Mountains National Park prepared to help its visitors survive a nuclear blast and outlast the deadly fallout.

All of the other chapters in this book chronicle events that directly imperiled human lives and played out in a circumscribed period of time—hours or days. This chapter, by contrast, addresses a looming threat that spanned decades and engaged not just GSMNP but the entire country. In the end, the threat came to naught and a tense nation could begin to relax.

Most visitors to Great Smoky Mountains National Park come seeking escape from the bustle and strain of life in the city in a place of peace and calm. But at the height of the Cold War, during the 1950s and '60s, park administrators came to regard "escape" in terms predicated less on recreation and more on sheer human survival.

In the realm of disaster, it's difficult, if not impossible, to imagine a more cataclysmic event than total thermonuclear war and the end to civilization as we know it. Though the widely anticipated attack never came, for the better part of two decades, most Americans lived with the palpable dread that it would.

The pervasive anxiety arose from the possibility—in the minds of many, the probability—that nuclear weapons, dispatched by former World War II ally turned adversary, the Soviet Union, would rain down on U.S. soil. The bombs would obliterate major cities, ignite all-consuming firestorms, and create a deadly cloud of windborne radioactive fallout that would sicken and kill many of those who had survived the initial blast. The same radioactive miasma would also dispatch livestock and poison farm fields and surface water for years, or even decades, to come.

The GSMNP staff, like most other federal employees and the agencies they worked for, had been assigned duties and responsibilities devised to help the nation creep back from the brink of annihilation.

Indeed, by the time Cold War tensions crested in the early 1960s, culminating in the 1962 U.S.-Soviet showdown that became known as the Cuban Missile Crisis, GSMNP administrators, prompted by a spate of regulations and requirements promulgated by the Federal Civil Defense Administration (FCDA) and its successor organizations,[1] had come to regard the park as a refuge of last resort, one capable of saving park staff and visitors from what, in Biblical terms, would amount to Armageddon.

(For more on the Cuban Missile Crisis, see "The Cuban Missile Crisis" on page 94. For more on the FCDA, see "The Federal Civil Defense Program" on page 88.)

At the time, visitors to GSMNP might have detected little in the way of overt end-time preparation. Nevertheless, behind the scenery, park staff was busy preparing for the ultimate worst-case scenario.

Beginning with the detonation of the Soviet's first atomic weapon in 1949, four years after the United States had ushered the world into the atomic age by dropping nuclear weapons on the Japanese cities of Hiroshima and Nagasaki at the end of World War II, U.S. policymakers and defense strategists realized how woefully unprepared the nation was to respond to a nuclear strike.

Adding to the sense of urgency, by the early 1950s, both the United States and the Soviet Union had successfully tested hydrogen bombs—essentially nuclear weapons on steroids. The destructive power of these ther-

---

1   The FCDA was established by an act of Congress and signed into law by President Harry Truman in January 1951. In 1958, President Eisenhower merged the FCDA with the Office of Defense Mobilization to form the Office of Civil and Defense Mobilization (OCDM). In 1961, President Kennedy changed OCDM to the Office of Emergency Planning (OEP) and assigned the Department of Defense oversight of the Office of Civil Defense. To avoid confusion created by these various organizations and administrative designations, this article will use the more generic term "federal civil defense program" throughout.

monuclear bombs far exceeded that of the weapons dropped on Japan. (For more information, see "The Hydrogen Bomb" on page 99.)

And while the incursion of a foreign fighting force on US soil seemed unlikely, thermonuclear weapons dropped from high-altitude bombers or launched from ships or submarines were another matter entirely.

By 1954, the Soviets had developed the R-7 rocket, a two-stage intercontinental ballistic missile, the world's first such weapon, capable of carrying a three-ton nuclear warhead more than 5,000 miles from its launch site. In 1957, a version of the same rocket carried Sputnik, the first human-made satellite, into Earth orbit.

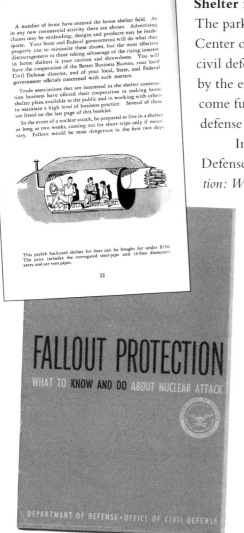

Shelter from the Nuclear Storm

The park archives stored at Sugarlands Visitor Center offer scant evidence of GSMNP's role in civil defense planning through the 1950s. But by the early 1960s, the national parks had become full-fledged partners in the national civil defense effort.

In December 1961, the Department of Defense issued the publication *Fallout Protection: What to Know and Do about Nuclear Attack*, one of dozens of instructional films and pamphlets produced through the Cold War years. *Fallout Protection* featured an introduction by then Secretary of Defense Robert McNamara, who also served as head of the federal civil defense program.

The tone of the publication is undeniably—and perhaps appropriately—grim. Here's an extended excerpt:

"There is no escaping the fact that nuclear conflict would leave a tragic world. The areas of blast and fire would be scenes

This 1961 publication warned the public they "would be prey to strange rumors and fears."

THE FEDERAL CIVIL DEFENSE PROGRAM

On January 12, 1951, President Harry Truman responded to the concern that the United States was not prepared to defend itself against nuclear attack by signing the Federal Civil Defense Act, which created the Federal Civil Defense Administration (FCDA).

Truman issued a statement explaining the law's intent: "To protect life and property in the United States in case of enemy assault. [The law] affords the basic framework for preparations to minimize the effects of an attack on our civilian population, and to deal with the immediate emergency conditions which such an attack would create."

Over the two decades that followed, the programs and public service announcements of the FCDA, and its successor organization, the Office of Civil and Defense Mobilization (OCDM), would reach into every home, every classroom, every business, and even into the national parks.

As one might imagine of an agency charged with the task of preserving a nation from annihilation, the FCDA hit the ground running. The administration's 1952 annual report, submitted by acting administrator James Wadsworth, detailed the range of programs that were being planned or had become operational.

According to the report, some 42 million Americans had taken part in civil defense exercises. Emergency sirens and whistles were in place to reach 40 percent of the population in "critical target areas." Eventually, all major cities and most towns would be equipped with blaring Thunderbolt warning sirens, which were activated on a regular schedule to keep citizens vigilant and alert.

The report also notes that plans were in place for creation of an emergency alert system that would broadcast news and information over the radio. Initially called CONELRAD (Control of Electromagnetic Radiation), it would be replaced by the Emergency Broadcast System in 1963.

In the event of an attack, CONELRAD would instruct listeners to turn their AM radio dials to either 640 or 1240 kHz, where they would receive information and instructions of what to do in the wake of the attack. Radios manufactured between 1953 and 1963 featured civil defense logos marking the two frequencies on the dial. The weekly tests of today's Emergency Alert System, often broadcast at noon on Wednesday, trace their roots to the federal civil defense alerts of the 1950s and '60s.

"Alert America" convoys, traveling exhibits sardonically dubbed "Paul Revere on Wheels," crossed the country and provided an instructional primer on surviving a nuclear attack.

Civil defense public service announcements aired on TV and radio. Not particularly renowned for their artistry—and alternately accompanied by lilting, upbeat soundtracks or those better suited to horror films—these announcements instructed homeowners on topics ranging from how to shelter in their basements to how to protect crops and livestock from nuclear contamination.

A cartoon turtle named Bert taught school children to duck and cover under their desks when they saw the flash of a nuclear detonation flood through their classroom windows. Here's a snippet from "Duck and Cover" (1951):

> There was a turtle by the name
> of Bert
> And Bert the turtle was very alert.
> When danger threatened him he
> never got hurt.
> He knew just what to do: He'd
> duck and cover.

Through the mid-1960s, the federal civil defense program released dozens of instructional films, including "Survival under Atomic Attack" (1951), "Our Cities Must Fight" (1951), "Disaster on Main Street" (1951), "Warning Red" (1956), "If the Bomb Falls" (1961), "About Fallout" (1963), and "Public Shelter Living" (1964).

The federal civil defense program also released LP records with short PSAs featuring the voices of celebrities, among them Boris Karloff, Tony Bennett, Connie Francis, Pat Boone, and Johnny Cash. "America can survive enemy attack," says Cash in his PSA, "if we support the emergency plans of our community and learn to help ourselves."

By the late-1960s, the Cold War had begun to thaw, in part through the first in a series of strategic nuclear arms agreements, in part through the détente Richard Nixon achieved when he visited then secretary-general of the Soviet Communist party, Leonid Brezhnev.

As tensions eased between the former Cold War adversaries, civil defense as a national priority began to fade. But the federal civil defense program public alert system spawned by the Cold War would retain its relevance, particularly in alerting US citizens to the approach of deadly and damaging storms.

In 1979, the successor to the original Federal Civil Defense Adminis-tration became the Federal Emergency Management Agency (FEMA). In 1963, CONELRAD became the Emergency Broadcast System, and in '97 the Emergency Broadcast System was re-placed by the Emergency Alert System.

of havoc, devastation, and death. For the part of the country outside the immediate range of the explosions, it would be a time of extraordinary hardship—both for the Nation and for the individual. The effects of fallout radiation would be present in areas not decontaminated. Transportation and communication would be disrupted. The Nation would be prey to strange rumors and fears. But if effective precautions have been taken in advance, it need not be a time of despair.

There are no total answers, no easy answers, no cheap answers to the question of protection from nuclear attack. But there are *answers."*

Among those answers, according to the publication, was the creation of a nationwide system of community fallout shelters. Those private citizens who could afford to do so were urged to construct shelters in their base-ments or backyards. And many of them did.

To accommodate park employees, their families, and any visitors who might find themselves within the park when the Soviets dropped the big one, GSMNP designated and stocked seven Civil Defense fallout shelters within the park and two on the periphery.

Six utilized stone-and-mortar structures: the basements of the park headquarters building and visitor center at Sugarlands, the basement of the Oconaluftee Ranger Station, the tunnel on the Gatlinburg-Pigeon Forge Spur, and Calderwood and Chilhowee Dams.

The seventh was, like the others, an existing structure but one not made by human hands. To protect vulnerable populations in the western-most zone of the park, GSMNP explored use of Gregory Cave as a suitable shelter.

Gregory Cave, situated about a half mile north of the Cades Cove Loop Road, is perhaps the only limestone grotto in Great Smoky Mountains National Park to have played a role in two wars, one hot and deadly, the other, well, notoriously cold.

In the years before, during, and after the Civil War, Gregory Cave likely served as a source of potassium nitrate, or saltpeter, an important component of gunpowder. Some of the saltpeter was produced by bacteria, which oxidized the nitrogen present in the cave soils into nitrate. This chemical process was also supported by rich deposits of bat guano, another source of nitrate.

Scientists reasoned that, owing to the half-life of the nuclear fallout—or rate at which its deadly radioactivity would degrade—shelters should be stocked with at least two-weeks' worth of supplies. After two weeks, radioactivity in the environment would have declined to a relatively safe—or, at least survivable—level.

Thus, shelter stores included a 14-day supply of food (along with special provisions for babies and the sick) and water, budgeted at a rate of seven gallons per person per day. The shelters also stocked covered pails for toilet purposes and a 10-gallon can to store human waste, along with flashlights and radios, extra batteries, bedding (including rubber sheets for the sick), first aid kits, cooking equipment, and a number of medical publications, including *What to Do until the Doctor Comes* and *Ship's Medicine Chest and First Aid at Sea*.

While the headquarters building, visitor center, and Oconaluftee ranger station were deemed capable of sheltering a hundred or so individuals, the more capacious Gregory Cave was stocked with sufficient supplies to sustain a population of 1,000 refugees.

On January 17, 1963, a scant three months following the Cuban Missile Crisis, GSMNP Superintendent Fred Overly sent a letter to Colonel W. Merle DeLaney of Maryville, the Blount County Civil Defense Director, expressing his support for DeLaney's proposal to use Gregory Cave as a fallout shelter "for those persons who happen to be in the Cove and Park who can safely reach it in the event they must seek shelter." Overly further offered suggestions to DeLaney on where the civil defense director should place signs directing visitors to the cave.

As for the signage, the National Park Service's managing agency, the Department of the Interior (DOI) was, and remains, ever mindful of the provisions of the so-called Organic Act of 1916, which established the Park Service. In part, the act obliges the NPS to "conserve the scenery and the natural and historic objects and the wild life therein and to provide for the enjoyment of the same in such manner and by such means as will leave them unimpaired for the enjoyment of future generations."

Reflecting the spirit of the act, a February 1963 memo from DOI headquarters to park superintendents made it clear that garish or outsized signs were not going to be tolerated, regardless of the urgency of the civil defense mission.

"Adequate safeguards should be taken to control the size, design and location of the signs so that they will not adversely affect the appearance or use of the facility by visitors…" the memo reads. A memo issued by DOI headquarters three months later further stipulates the requirement that the signs be "conservative and unobtrusive" so as to "avoid damage or interference with [the park's] natural features."

In his letter to DeLaney, Superintendent Overly articulated plans to improve the access road to the cave and clean out the rotting wooden walkways, remnants of pre-park days when the cave served as a privately operated tourist attraction.

"Although the cave is damp and the floor uneven," Overly writes, "we intend to make no move to rectify these conditions because any use would be on a survival basis…."

In January 1963, Overly, on behalf of DOI, signed the federal fallout shelter license form and invited DeLaney to begin stocking the cave with supplies. "These supplies I have been told are to be placed in the cavern and are of such a nature that they can be safely stored there for a period of at least five years and will occupy a space equivalent to a 10-foot cube," Overly writes in the letter.

At the time, Gregory Cave was off limits to park visitors, unless they had received special permission to enter. In fact, a slatted iron barrier still blocks the entrance. If and when the alert went out, Overly explained, rangers would promptly unlock the entrance to the cave to afford access.

The other park civil defense shelters were likewise stocked with supplies, and all awaited the arrival of the first of the temporary residents.

Post-attack Registration

Other civil defense duties and responsibilities also fell to GSMNP staff. The

Civil Service Commission regularly prompted administrators of federal agencies, including DOI, to remind their employees annually of their obligations as required by Nationwide Post-attack Registration procedure.

"A strong, united America is one of our greatest assurances of maintaining peace and deterring aggressive forces," reads a memo dated May 31, 1961, from DOI Regional Director Elbert Cox to Interior employees. "Each of us, as citizens and as Federal employees, has a responsibility to contribute to the strength of our nation."

In particular, "in the event of an emergency, brought about by an attack," the procedure required federal employees, including those with and without specific emergency assignments, to report promptly to their regular places of employment. If, however, the enemy attack prevented the employees from reporting to work, the procedure instructed them to go to the nearest U.S. Post Office and fill out a federal employee registration card "as soon after enemy attack as possible." This directive clearly is predicated on the belief that the post offices would still be standing. The postmaster would have been instructed to send the card to the Civil Service Commission, so the commission could keep track of its employees.

The federal government even went so far as to draft plans to ensure that employees, including GSMNP staff, would continue to draw their pay following the attack, wherever they happened to wind up.

On September 3, 1963, the US Comptroller General issued a memo to heads of federal departments and agencies, including DOI, under the subject heading "Guidelines for Developing Fiscal Procedures Re: Emergency Evacuations."

It reads, in part: "To the extent possible and practical, pay, leave, and travel data should be sent from the evacuated installation to the safe haven post as soon as possible after the evacuation order has been issued so they will be available to support future payments."

Such provisions were generous and thoughtful but perhaps a tad over-optimistic in projecting the state of business and commerce after the nuclear fallout had cleared. Were federal employees to be paid in cash? If so, who would safeguard the sizable payroll? If by check, would banks be open to cash it? And, further, would printed money or coinage have any value at all amid the post-attack Darwinian struggle for survival?

Civil defense preparedness also called on the national parks to devise plans to protect historic objects and buildings, in the event of enemy attack.

THE CUBAN MISSILE CRISIS

In the fall of 1962, the deterrent effect of so-called "mutually assured destruction"—a tenuous balance established by the ever-increasing US and Soviet stockpiles of thermonuclear weapons, riding atop ballistic missiles capable of crossing continents—began to totter. Proof emerged that Soviet nuclear-tipped missiles had arrived within 100 miles of US shores.

On October 14, 1962, the high-resolution cameras aboard a Lockheed U2, a spy plane capable of flying at 70,000 feet and reaching speeds of 500 miles per hour, captured images that analysts at the National Photographic Interpretation Center later determined to depict three launch sites for Soviet-made medium-range ballistic missiles, located near San Cristobal, in Fidel Castro's Cuba.

Unbeknownst to US military experts, beginning in September, Soviet Premier Nikita Khrushchev had clandestinely shipped the nuclear missiles, along with intermediate-range IL-28 bombers, to the island—and more were on the way. Once operational, those rockets, pointed north, would be capable of traveling 1,000 miles to reach strategic targets within the United States. The seat of government, in Washington, DC, was within range, as were missile silos in the Midwest. Some 50,000 battle-ready Soviet troops had arrived with the missiles, and Soviet submarines, armed with nuclear-tipped torpedoes, trolled the ocean.

The Cuban Missile Crisis, as it became known, spanned 13 days and seemed to usher the world to the very brink of nuclear war. Some of the more hawkish Pentagon officials had resigned themselves to the loss of millions of American lives in an end-times throwdown that would annihilate the Soviet Union while leaving the United States with sufficient survivors to begin the centuries-long process of repopulation.

Reflecting that sentiment, General Tommy Powers, commander in chief of the Strategic Air Command (SAC) from 1957 to 1964, famously quipped: "At the end of the war, if there are two Americans and one Russian, we win!"

On October 22, 1962, President John Kennedy appeared on TV to address the nation. In his address, Kennedy noted the arrival of Soviet missiles in Cuba and announced his intentions to create a naval blockade around the island. Within the week, tensions only escalated. On October

27, Cuban defenses shot down a US U2 spy plane flying over the island, killing pilot Major Rudolph Anderson, the only confirmed US casualty of the crisis. Meanwhile, US armed forces massed in Florida and readied for an attack of the island nation.

In the end, the conflict wasn't resolved through belligerence and brinkmanship, as many believed at the time. As the crisis escalated, the president's attorney general, his brother Robert Kennedy, began working behind the scenes, meeting secretly with Soviet Ambassador Anatoly Dobrynin. The two managed to shape a solution acceptable to both nations, and on October 28, the crisis drew to a close.

Ultimately, the Soviet Union agreed to remove its missiles if the United States pledged not to invade Cuba. The United States further agreed, though tacitly, to remove its Jupiter nuclear missiles from Turkey.

A memo dated November 2, 1962, from E.M. Lisle, DOI acting director of the Southeast region, used as an example the National Historic Park at Yorktown, site of the 1781 British surrender to General Washington that ended the Revolutionary War.

"Someone should be fully prepared to dismantle safely the Washington tents, fold them without creases and wrap them…," the memo reads. "He should decide just which of the salvaged artifacts are to be taken to safety and have everything in readiness for packing them." The ultimate destination for the Yorktown relics was to be Mammoth Cave. One can only imagine where, on the list of priorities amid the post-attack panic, meticulous tent folding might fall.

On November 7, 1962, Superintendent Overly replied that GSMNP had not identified any artifacts or buildings of national significance worth saving in the event of a nuclear strike, though he pledged that he and his staff would do what they could to protect the restored historic cabins in Cades Cove.

Monitoring the Wind
The blast of a nuclear weapon merely represents phase one of a cascade of potentially lethal effects. Subsequent to the blast, a cloud of highly radioactive particles (nuclear fallout) spreads outward from ground zero and is borne

by prevailing winds. In March 1954, the United States tested a 15-megaton (the equivalent to 15 million tons of TNT) hydrogen bomb on Bikini Atoll in the Marshall Islands. By contrast the bomb dropped on Hiroshima had a yield of about 15 kilotons (or the equivalent of 15,000 tons of TNT). By some estimates, the resulting cloud of nuclear fallout after the Bikini Atoll blast blanketed 7,000 square miles of the Pacific Ocean.

While radioactive particles in the air, particularly if they are large enough, may be visible to the human eye, radiation itself is an invisible but potentially deadly energy force, and the effects often do not appear until minutes to hours following exposure. Assessing the risk of this invisible menace requires tools that can read what the human eye cannot see or the human nose smell, and one of those tools is the Geiger–Müller counter.

A nation comprising nearly 4 million square miles would require an extensive network of monitoring sites, since, as we know, the Soviets were a bit tight-lipped about the intended targets for their bombs.

As of January 1961, the National Plan for Civil Defense and Defense Mobilization responded to the threat by calling for the establishment of a national network of 150,000 fixed stations for monitoring radioactive fallout, and DOI was charged with creating 400 of them within in the national parks.

These fixed monitoring sites were to be equipped with radiological monitoring devices provided by the federal civil defense program. These included the CD V-700, a Geiger–Müller counter capable of measuring alpha, beta, and gamma radiation, and CD V-750 dosimeters, each about the size of a cigar tube and equipped with pocket clip, used to measure the cumulative radiation exposure of the person wearing it. The fixed monitoring sites also were equipped with reliable communications equipment—telephones and two-way radios—for relaying readings to the county Emergency Operations Center, which, in turn, would relay the information up the chain.

GSMNP headquarters met these criteria, so it was established as the park's fixed monitoring station.

All fallout shelters—including Gregory Cave—were also equipped with monitoring equipment, which arrived prepackaged in cardboard boxes bearing the Civil Defense logo: a triangle bearing the initials CD contained within a blue circle. Meanwhile, aircraft equipped with the CD V-781 Geiger–Müller device would perform aerial monitoring.

Select park employees were trained to operate the monitoring equipment and to plot the direction and range of radioactive particles carried in the lower and upper atmosphere, based on weather conditions and wind speed.

Thomas F. Ela, chief park ranger, received training to serve as a radiological monitor instructor, while six other park staffers were trained to operate the monitors and interpret the readings.

On May 26, 1961, Superintendent Overly sent a missive to his regional director, asking where to send an inoperative CD V-700 and a dosimeter recharger for repair. Fred Arnold, region one chief of ranger activities, suggested that Overly send the units back to the manufacturer, Universal Atomics, based in New York City. He further added: "We have no funds provided for civil defense or radiological monitoring requirements, hence it will be necessary to pay the costs from Park funds."

The Office of Civil Defense Staff College in Battle Creek, Michigan, offered courses in, among other topics, Civil Defense Planning, Shelter Management, and Radiological Defense. Instruction was available closer to home as well and provided by the Tennessee Office of Civil Defense in cooperation with the University of Tennessee.

"Emergency Preparedness for Public Officials and Community Leaders" convened at 7 p.m. on September 26, 1966, at Alcoa High School. Harry Price, of the UT Extension Civil Defense Program, welcomed those in attendance.

GSMNP Superintendent George Fry received an invitation, but Robert Perkins Jr., acting chief ranger at the time, attended in his stead. In a follow-up letter, Perkins mentioned that he had made a number of new contacts at the program that he believed "beneficial" and noted that the instructors would be willing to teach courses of "special value to the park," including "riot control."

A Plan for Emergency Operations

On August 5, 1963, the National Park Service issued the *Emergency Operations Handbook*, which prescribed a service-wide set of instructions designed to guide the Park Service response to a nuclear attack. Each park, including GSMNP, was required to draft a supplement to the handbook that focused on the park's individual response plan.

In January 1964, GSMNP submitted its six-page supplement, which, according to the document's introduction, intended "to establish a basic staff for emergency administration...and designate the functions of that staff" and "to outline measures for survival of employees of GSMNP and their families."

As for the latter, the document's section "Survival and Post-Attack Procedures" notes that, following a nuclear attack, "personnel and their families will be alerted by telephone and radio" and directed to assemble at the park's established civil defense shelter nearest them. Further, before they fled their homes, they were advised to collect "uncontaminated food and blankets."

Meanwhile, the park's maintenance staff would shut off water supplies flowing into the buildings (presumably contaminated by fallout), and residents would henceforth rely on purified water preemptively stored in the shelters. Staff trained as radiological monitors would check the radiation levels of individuals and goods entering the shelter, though the document does not specify the fate awaiting anyone who set off the Geiger–Müller counter.

Among the action items listed in the supplement is maintaining "minimum records necessary for operations, controlling expenditures, protecting property, and managing personnel." The document acknowledges, though, that carrying out these duties in time of "extreme emergency" might require "considerable adjustments to normal fiscal procedures."

The document also outlines a succession plan. Should the superintendent be incapacitated, the assistant superintendent would take over. If he fell, the chief ranger was next in line, followed by the park engineer, the administrative office, and, finally, the chief park naturalist.

A Whimper, Not a Bang

With its emergency response plan drafted and filed in 1964, GSMNP had fulfilled one of its last major obligations as required by the federal civil defense program. Though the park staff, like all Americans, remained vigilant through coming years, and GSMNP representatives continued to attend meetings and undergo training in preparation for a nuclear strike, fears of the anticipated attack had slowly begun to abate following the peaceful resolution of the Cuban Missile Crisis in October of 1962.

President Kennedy remained a strident proponent of the federal civil defense program and saw that it received generous funding. In fact, he was largely responsible for the call to create a national system of fallout shelters, but following his assassination, funding for the civil defense effort began to

THE HYDROGEN BOMB

Atomic weapons like the ones dropped on Hiroshima and Nagasaki at the end of World War II rely on a process of nuclear fission—splitting atoms apart—for their destructive power.

Hydrogen bombs, also known as thermonuclear weapons, rely on the process of fusion—forcing hydrogen atoms together to form helium, which produces enormous amounts of energy and heat.

Hydrogen bombs, which exploit the same energy source as our sun, are many times more destructive than atomic weapons. In fact, most hydrogen bombs utilize an internal atomic bomb as a trigger. When the spherical atomic bomb detonates, it implodes, forcing sufficient heat and pressure into the hydrogen contained within to initiate a fusion reaction.

The United States tested its first hydrogen bomb on November 1, 1952, on Eniwetok Atoll in the Pacific. The Soviet Union responded in kind less than a year later, detonating its first thermonuclear weapon in Siberia on August 12, 1953.

---

wane. It's a bit ironic that a program based on the presumption of a big bang would, instead, die with a whimper.

With budgets for federal civil defense programs slashed, several individuals attempted to fill the void by creating the not-for-profit American Civil Defense Association in 1962. The organization is still in operation, and President Ronald Reagan was one of its staunchest supporters.

By the time the Soviet Union dissolved in December 1991, the U.S. federal civil defense program had undergone many of the changes in mission and focus that would shape its current incarnation.

In 1979, President Jimmy Carter signed Executive Order 12127, merging the successor to the Federal Civil Defense Administrations, the Defense Civil Preparedness Agency (DCPA), into today's Federal Emergency Management Agency (FEMA). In 2003, FEMA was merged into the US Department of Homeland Security.

Other remnants of the federal civil defense program survive and continue to provide for the protection of the nation's citizens. CONELRAD (Control of Electromagnetic Radiation), created in the early 1950s to broadcast warnings of attack over AM radios, became the Emergency Broadcast System in 1963, which, in turn, evolved into the Emergency Alert System in 1997. Today, Emergency Alert System advisories, broadcast over radio and TV, carry, among other messages, warnings of approaching severe weather.

It's easy enough to imagine how the employees of GSMNP came to regard the complex and often cumbersome overlay of additional tasks and responsibilities the civil defense program imposed on them through the early 1960s. They knew that the national parks would have been of little strategic importance to an enemy intent on destroying our nation's economic, social, military, and political nodes and nerve centers. But, being the good patriots that they were, they engaged earnestly in the process of preparing for a menace that never materialized. But perhaps the exercises paid a dividend. Compared to anticipating—and planning for—Armageddon, managing the ever-increasing throng of arriving visitors must have seemed like a walk in the park.

CHAPTER 9
Star-crossed Lovers Part Ways on a Remote Mountain Ridge

A hysterical young woman wearing a dress spattered with blood, an orange Volkswagen Beetle abandoned at the Abrams Falls Trail parking area, and a frantic call from a worried parent whose child had gone missing served as the converging clues that lead rangers to a tragic discovery deep in the park's backcountry.

At 7:15 p.m., on Sunday, March 29, 1981, Park Technician Bill Webb answered a knock on the door of the Abrams Creek Ranger Station and confronted a troubling scene. Just beyond the threshold stood a young woman, barefoot and wearing a lavender dress covered in blood.

Webb also noticed that the woman had a slashed wrist with a quantity of dried blood on her arm. Despite the bloody dress and clotting wound, the girl otherwise looked as if she were groomed to attend a party. Her long hair was clean, neatly combed, and parted in the middle, and she wore makeup.

The wild gaze in her eyes told a different story, as did her demeanor, which Webb termed "hysterical."

Webb invited the woman inside, where she began to relate a rambling and bizarre story. At the outset, Webb had one important question for her: "Are you alone?"

"I am now," the girl cryptically replied.

About a half hour after Webb had welcomed the confused and bloody visitor into the ranger station and her perplexing story began to unfold,

Ranger Lowell "Kent" Higgins, at park headquarters, received a call from
a man named John Rudd. Rudd was calling from Coral Gables, Florida, to
ask whether Higgins had any information about his son, also named John
Rudd, who was believed to be somewhere in the park.

Just then, an emergency call came in, and Higgins put Rudd on hold
to answer it. It was Webb at the Abrams Creek Ranger Station, calling about
the wounded, hysterical woman who had shown up at his door.

The proximity in time and connection in theme between the two
calls was more than a mere coincidence, Higgins surmised, and he began to
connect the dots.

A week earlier, on Sunday, March 22, at about 7 p.m., Higgins had,
per park routine, closed and locked the gate at the entrance to the Cades
Cove Loop Road and in his patrol car began making a final sweep of the 11-
mile road before locking the gate at exit. When he reached the Abrams Falls
Trail parking area, about half-way around the loop, he encountered a young
couple standing near an orange 1971 Volkswagen Beetle bearing Florida
plates. As Higgins pulled up, the couple were about to shoulder green alumi-
num-frame backpacks and start hiking.

Higgins was pleased to see that the couple had complied with the rules
for camping in the park's backcountry and had acquired a permit to camp at
sites in the Abrams Creek area over the next four nights. But he also noted
that their first scheduled site lay five miles from where the couple now stood,
and the sun had already dipped behind the mountains to the west. Concerned for their safety, Higgins urged them to stay the night in the Cades
Cove Campground and begin their hike the next day, and the two complied.

According to Higgins, the couple did not break camp and head out
until 2 p.m. the next day. Though there's no way Higgins could have known
it at the time, the couple may have acquired the requisite permit to camp in
the backcountry, but they had no intention of adhering to their scheduled
itinerary. Instead, they had schemed a far more tragic set of plans.

Unbeknownst to their parents, John Rudd, 19, and Janet Rudd, 18,
had married in secret on March 5 in Bradenton, Florida, and they arrived in
GSMNP intent on carrying out a suicide pact that they had been planning
for several months.

But on Monday, March 23, when Higgins confirmed that the couple
had left the Cades Cove Campground, he had no reason to suspect that they
were any different from the thousands of other hikers who explore the park's

backcountry each year.

That changed the following day, when Higgins received a call from headquarters dispatch, with instruction to be on the lookout (BOLO) for a young couple driving an orange VW Beetle with Florida plates.

Janet's mother had contacted the park after receiving a letter from her daughter postmarked Knoxville, March 22, explaining that she had abandoned her VW in GSMNP and was leaving the country with her new husband. According to newspaper accounts, Janet indicated that their destination was Canada and requested that her father come retrieve the abandoned vehicle. Rudd also allegedly sent his family a letter, indicating that the couple was heading to Peru.

But according to their plans, the two had already arrived at their final destination; they intended to remain in the park—forever—in a place where no one would ever find their bodies.

Then, on Sunday, March 29, Janet had emerged from the woods, unaccompanied by her husband. At the Abrams Creek Ranger Station, Webb struggled to make sense of Janet's bizarre story about the events of the previous seven days.

Yes, she was now alone, she explained, but she had arrived in the park with her husband, John Rudd, who was now dead.

"Did he fall?" Webb asked her.

"No, he didn't fall," Janet said, smiling dimly.

After repeated questions and vague, confused answers, Janet came out with it: "He took his own life," she said. "It's what he wanted to do."

Okay, if Janet was telling the truth, John was out there somewhere, likely dead, but perhaps not. Maybe he was alive but gravely wounded.

Webb probed for information that would help him and his colleagues locate, and perhaps, save, John. All Janet could recall was that the couple had wandered around in the woods for a week, and they had stayed off trails so the rangers would not find them.

"Did you camp near a stream?" Webb asked.

"No, streams are cold."

As park officials would later learn, Janet's testimony was riddled with inaccuracies. Perhaps these were mere lapses of a troubled mind; perhaps they were intentional, to allow John, as per his wishes, to repose in a place where he would never be found.

In reality, the couple *did* adhere to established trails for part of their odyssey, including the Rabbit Creek Trail, and searchers would later locate their final campsite proximate to a stream.

Janet noted, accurately, as it turned out, that on their march through the woods, they had discarded items they no longer needed. Their decisions on which items were essential and which were dispensable likely reflected their frame of mind in the context of their planned actions. Discarded were a canteen, a backpack, a sleeping bag, and an orange tent.

Janet shared with Webb that the couple had burned their passports, marriage license, and any other documents that might lead to their identification.

According to Janet's testimony, as recorded in the official incident report, on the fateful morning of March 29, John had announced to Janet that he was going for a walk and ambled away from their camp. He did not return. She searched for him and soon found him, bleeding from several razor-blade slits to his wrist. Whether John was still alive at that time remains uncertain. Janet initially claimed that he was motionless, his skin cold to the touch. She would later indicate that when she reached him he was still alive, but the quantity of blood from his wound revolted her. She had left John there and walked to a stream and began her own work with the razor blade, but she found the pain unbearable. The small wound on her wrist eventually stopped bleeding, and she determined to join John later, "on the other side," via a less painful method of suicide.

Then she began to wander, directionless, through the forest, "looking for people," according to Webb's interview. Eventually, she showed up at the Abrams Creek Ranger Station.

Following his conversation with John's father, Higgins made his way to the ranger station, and by 9 p.m. that evening, he believed he had enough information to allow a search party to retrace Janet's steps, which, he hoped, would lead them to John. Rain was forecast, and Higgins realized that if the storm broke, it would make following Janet's trail all that much more difficult, so he quickly dispatched the tracking team, which included noted GSMNP tracker Dwight McCarter.[1] The trackers found barefoot prints on both sides of Abrams Creek along the Rabbit Creek Trail before the cloudburst began at 10 p.m. Through the night, 1.22 inches of rain fell, and Janet's footprints vanished into the muck.

---

1   McCarter is author of several books based on his years as a NPS tracker, including *Lost*, about searches for missing persons, and *Mayday!* about plane crashes in the park.

Back at the ranger station, Higgins examined Janet's wrist and determined that the wound was relatively minor and could await medical treatment, while he probed for whatever additional information he could extract from her. At 2 a.m., park personnel transported Janet to University of Tennessee Medical Center in Knoxville. The wound, a vertical incision on the palm side of the wrist, required six stitches. The attending physician made the observation that if John had employed the same technique and sustained a similar wound, he might well still be alive.

The rangers returned with Janet to the Abrams Creek Ranger Station, fed her a meal, and afforded her a few hours of sleep.

The Search: Day One

The next morning, Monday, March 30, an FBI team with tracking dogs joined the GSMNP search crew, which set out an hour or so after dawn. Near noon, an Army National Guard helicopter, a Bell UH-1D Iroquois "Huey" from the base near Knoxville's McGhee-Tyson Airport, began searching from the air, hoping to spot the couple's campsite.

At 3:30 p.m., the Huey crew spotted the tent, sleeping bag, and pack on Polecat Ridge, about two miles south of the ranger station, and hovered in place until the ground searchers arrived at the site. According to information Higgins had received from Janet, the tent and sleeping bag marked the couple's next to last campsite. Janet told them that they would find John near a white and brown blanket that marked the couples' last campsite—and their last night together.

Later in the evening, as darkness fell, Higgins knew that his searchers

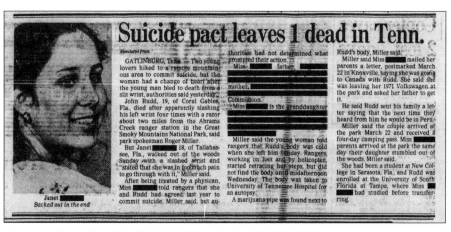

Suicide pact leaves 1 dead in Tenn.

Associated Press

GATLINBURG, Tenn. — Two young lovers hiked to a remote mountainous area to commit suicide, but the woman had a change of heart after the young man bled to death from a slit wrist, authorities said yesterday.

John Rudd, 19, of Coral Gables, Fla., died after apparently slashing his left wrist four times with a razor about two miles from the Abrams Creek ranger station in the Great Smoky Mountains National Park, said park spokesman Roger Miller.

But Janet ███████, 18, of Tallahassee, Fla., walked out of the woods Sunday with a slashed wrist and "stated that she was in too much pain to go through with it," Miller said.

After being treated by a physician, Miss ███████ told rangers that she and Rudd had agreed last year to commit suicide, Miller said, but authorities had not determined what prompted their action.

Miss ███████ father ███████ mother ███████ Commission.

"Miss ███████ is the granddaughter

Miller said the young woman told rangers that Rudd's body was cold when she left him Sunday. Rangers, working her steps, but did not find the body until midafternoon Wednesday. The body was taken to University of Tennessee Hospital for an autopsy.

A marijuana pipe was found next to

Rudd's body, Miller said.

Miller said Miss ███████ mailed her parents a letter, postmarked March 22 in Knoxville, saying she was going to Canada with Rudd. She said she was leaving her 1971 Volkswagen at the park and asked her father to get it.

He said Rudd sent his family a letter saying that the next time they heard from him he would be in Peru.

Miller said the couple arrived at the park March 22 and received a four-day camping pass. Miss ███████ parents arrived at the park the same day their daughter stumbled out of the woods, Miller said.

She had been a student at New College in Sarasota, Fla., and Rudd was enrolled at the University of South Florida at Tampa, where Miss ███ had studied before transferring.

Janet ███████
Backed out in the end

Newspaper clipping from The Philadelphia Inquirer *on April 3, 1981.*

were close, but John Rudd—alive or dead—could have been a mile or more away in any direction.

By then, Janet's father, mother, and stepmother had arrived at the ranger station, after traveling from Florida, and Higgins, having no legal grounds for holding the teenager further, released her to the custody of her blended family for the evening. She would return the next morning to assist with the search.

Earlier in the day, GSMNP officials had contacted John Rudd's parents in Florida and informed them of the unfolding drama, and they arrived at the Abrams Creek Ranger Station the next morning.

The Search: Day Two

On Tuesday, March 31, the search team departed the ranger station at 6:45 a.m. and traveled by jeep nearly three miles to Scott Gap, the center of the search zone, via the Rabbit Creek Trail. At about 8:30 a.m., a search crew, now on foot, located the white and brown blanket, along with soap, shampoo, and several single-edged razor blades removed from their paper wrappers. This site lay about two-tenths of a mile south-southeast of the abandoned tent and sleeping bag and, according to information from Janet, marked the couples' last campsite.

Higgins immediately launched a grid search, which, as evening drew on, had turned up nothing. By then, Janet had offered details that contradicted her earlier statements, and Higgins realized that either "something was wrong with Janet's story," he recalls, "or that John had moved." If, in fact, John had moved, he clearly had still been alive when Janet had left him.

The Search: Day Three

The following morning, April 1, Janet accompanied the search team to the couple's alleged last campsite, the location of the white and brown blanket, and Higgins noticed that the woman had become progressively more composed, perhaps because she was in the care of her family.

"If he was here, you would have found him," she told the search team. "He was very near here."

Then a curious smile crossed Janet's face, as she conspicuously fixed her gaze to the north.

"Is John in that direction?" someone asked.

"No, he's back the other way," Janet answered. The odd smile roused the suspicion that she might have been intentionally deceiving the search effort to throw them off John's path. As it turned out, the gaze north was a feint.

By that time, Higgins' and Webb's questioning had allowed them to piece together Janet and John's back story. The couple had met the year before, in September, at the University of South Florida, Tampa, and, nearly from the beginning of their relationship, had discussed the suicide pact. They hoped to disappear, so that no one would worry or grieve over them. John loved the woods and mountains and wanted to die in a setting of natural beauty. They were not in love but had determined that it would be nice to be married when they died. They had begun their hike on Monday, March 23, and over seven days had traveled just over five miles to Scott Gap, using the map in the *Hiker's Guide to the Smokies* to help them navigate. By the time they reached their final campsite, marked by the white and brown blanket, they were out of food.

At 2:30 p.m., the mystery was resolved when a search team led by Bob Wightman discovered the body of John Rudd about a half mile from the white and brown blanket where Janet had plunged her arm into the stream's icy water before making the small cut on her wrist.

John was reposed on his back, with legs crossed, as if he had toppled backward from a sitting position. His left wrist bore four deep lacerations. Evidence at the scene suggested that after John had made the incisions in his wrist he had moved under a large downed tree spanning the stream to shelter from the rain—the same rain that had obliterated Janet's bare footprints on the margins of Abrams Creek near the ranger station. After the rain ended, he apparently had moved about 10 feet to his final resting place in the gravel and mud on the edge of the streambed. Higgins believes that John may have been alive for several hours after he had made the first cut.

The search crew hauled John's body three-quarters of a mile to Scott Gap on a Stokes litter and laid the body in a Jeep for the ride down the mountain. John's father identified his son at the Abrams Creek Ranger Station before the body was transported by ambulance to UT Medical Center for an autopsy, though evidence at the scene left little doubt about the cause of John's death. Janet returned to Tampa, Florida, with her family.

In March 1981, a pair of troubled star-crossed friends—young, on the cusp of adulthood—entered GSMNP intent on spending an anonymous eternity there on a remote mountain ridge. The fates had other plans. In the end, the anonymity eluded them. The incident received widespread media coverage—as did their hoped-for final resting place. John's family presumably took him back to Florida for burial.

As for Janet, the small slash on her wrist was superficial and would soon heal, but the psychological wounds resulting from her husband's death, no doubt, cut much deeper.

CHAPTER 10
Storm of the Century

In March 1993, gale-force winds, frigid temperatures, and several feet of snow slammed Great Smoky Mountains National Park (GSMNP), stranding more than 150 people in the park's half-million acres. For many of the victims—including 80 students and staff from a Michigan prep school—the storm's crucible severely tested winter survival skills. Those sent out to rescue them turned one of the worst disasters of the past century into GSMNP's finest hour.

Section One: The Gathering Storm
March 1993 arrived in the Southeast with much more of a bleat than a roar. A gradual warming trend that began on March 7 reached a daytime high of 71 degrees in Gatlinburg on Thursday, March 11. Even 6,593-foot Mount Le Conte registered a relatively mild 48 degrees that day. Throughout the region, greening grass and budding flowers ushered in what appeared to be an early spring.

In Great Smoky Mountains National Park (GSMNP), rangers welcomed the arrival of the first of the early-season campers and backpackers, including dozens of high school and college spring breakers. Eighty students and staff from Cranbrook Kingswood Upper School in Bloomfield Hills, Michigan, were distributed among campsites deep in the park's backcountry. The students, organized into 10 eight-person teams, were participating in a 10-day wilderness experience that had begun on March 6. Several other Cranbrook teams explored the backcountry of the Joyce Kilmer-Slickrock

Cranbrook's wilderness outings usually lasted 10 days and involved some of the most remote areas of the Smokies.

Wilderness in Cherokee National Forest.

Meanwhile, forty sixth- and seventh-graders from Mount Washington Middle School, located near Louisville, Kentucky, set out for an overnight educational field trip at the Great Smoky Mountains Institute at Tremont on Friday, March 12.

Seven long-distance hikers—two of them from New Zealand—made their way north from Georgia along the 2,180-mile Appalachian Trail (AT) and approached the park's boundary at Fontana Dam. By departing the trail's southern terminus, Springer Mountain, Georgia, in February, all had hoped to avoid the AT's notoriously crowded conditions through the South. The early start, they realized, also exposed them to the risk of encountering a wintry blast, though the prevailing mild conditions seemed to indicate that their gamble just might have paid off.

More than a dozen other hikers had locked their cars at trailhead parking lots and were making their way into the backcountry.

None of them anticipated anything more than a pleasant visit to the mountains.

From Improbable to Inevitable

Meteorologists at the National Centers for Environmental Prediction, a division of the National Weather Service located in Washington, DC, had a hard time reconciling the warm temperatures and calm conditions they glimpsed through their office windows with the troubling images that appeared on their computer screens.

Several days earlier, their weather prediction models had begun to indicate that a major winter storm might slam the East Coast if forces converged as the models suggested they might. An arctic high plunged down through the Central West toward the warm, humid air over the Gulf of

Mexico, while the sagging U-shaped trough of the jet stream dipped south all the way to Texas—requisite ingredients for a fierce extratropical cyclone.

By Thursday, March 11, the possible—as unlikely as it seemed—started to look more probable, and by March 12, TV meteorologists from Florida to Maine began urging their viewers to dismiss past erroneous predictions and heed their warning: a deadly storm—packing gale-force winds, tornadoes, tidal surges, and, for GSMNP, frigid temperatures and feet, not inches, of snow—was unquestionably heading their way.

The events of the next few days would validate those predictions and go on to rank as one of the worst disasters of the past century. The blizzard, which became known as the Storm of the Century, manifested itself on a weather map as an enormous inflamed comma, its tail hooked below Mexico's Yucatan Peninsula and its broad, angled head spanning from Arkansas to Maine and plowing northwest into Canada.

Before the storm blew itself out on Sunday, March 14, nearly 300 people in 13 states would be dead, 15 tornadoes would rage across Florida, Flattop Mountain in nearby Pisgah National Forest would clock winds in excess of 100 miles per hour, all major East Coast airports would be closed, and 159 people would be marooned in GSMNP.

Friday, March 12

In Gatlinburg, the daytime high reached only 50 degrees, 21 degrees cooler than the previous day's high, before it began its plunge to a low of 26, and misting clouds began to mass over GSMNP. Nothing unusual there—wafting clouds had given the park its name.

By late afternoon, the clouds produced a light snow—certainly more welcome than cold rain to the backcountry travelers distributed throughout the park.

Six friends—four men and two women—from a suburb of Atlanta watched the first snow fall at the Spence Field Shelter. They had hiked up from Cades Cove.

Two days earlier, on March 10, Patricia Hammann, from Indiana, and sister Kathy Davidson, from Missouri, also had left their car at Cades Cove and set out for Russell Field Shelter. According to Hammann, it was warm enough for the two to hike in T-shirts. They stayed at Mollies Ridge Shelter on March 11 before returning to Russell Field the next day. University of Tennessee students Jeff Burns and Todd Graves arrived at the shelter just behind them.

Before departing their homes, Hammann and Davidson had loaded their packs with several pounds of extra cold-weather clothing and gear, just in case. Twenty years of backpacking had taught Hammann always to prepare for rough mountain weather, regardless of prevailing conditions. Many others in the park had not been so thoughtful in selecting their gear, and they would suffer the consequences.

Also on March 10, George Griffin of Maryville had dropped off his 40-year-old son, David, at Newfound Gap, according to an article in the Maryville *Daily Times*. David was resuming his northbound thru-hike of the AT, which he had begun on February 14, after spending a few days off the trail. David, an experienced hiker with plenty of food, planned to take two days to cover the 23.3 miles from Newfound Gap to Cosby Knob Shelter. He arrived at the shelter on March 12; it would remain his home for the following five days.

Four other AT hikers, including New Zealanders Gary Boyland and Sonya Baldwin, along with Susannah Chaplin, from Maine, and Courtney McCollum, from Maryland, entered the park at Fontana Dam on March 12, destined for the Birch Spring Gap Shelter, 5.3 miles north on the AT. (The Birch Spring Gap Shelter has since been removed.) Ranger Glenn Martin inspected the group's gear, informed the hikers of storm predictions, and advised them not to proceed into the backcountry. The hikers opted not to heed Martin's advice.

AT thru-hikers the Reverend Richard Maloney, from Maryland, and New Yorkers Walter Pawlowski and Tom Schembri also entered the park at Fontana on March 12. They, too, were bound for Birch Spring Gap Shelter. They, likewise, received but dismissed the warning from a ranger about the approaching weather system; they were carrying sufficient food to last nearly two weeks.

As evening fell, the Cranbrook students, now on the sixth day of their planned 10-day outing, occupied backcountry campsites, most of them in the remote southwestern section of the park, along the north shore of Fontana Lake or in the rugged mountains above.

For more than 20 years, faculty advisors from Cranbrook, a private college-prep boarding school in a Detroit suburb that counts Mitt Romney among its alumni, had been guiding groups of their students through the southern Appalachians as part of the school's annual Wilderness Expedition

Program. Each eight-person team included six sophomores, one faculty leader, and one student leader, usually a junior or senior who had participated in the program in the past.

Cranbrook English teacher Tom Murdock's team had been on the west side of Hazel Creek, hiking northeast, when the snow began to fall about 3 p.m. Earlier in the day, the group had been forced to wade across two branches of the creek, and, Murdock says, keeping his students warm and dry was becoming increasingly difficult.

According to sophomore Jay Nicols, one of Murdock's student campers, "Friday night was one of our worst scenarios come true." Nicols reports that one of his schoolmates had earlier fallen into a creek and was on the verge of hypothermia when the group hastily established camp. Murdock's students, like their Cranbrook schoolmates, would shelter under tarps, not in tents.

Hypothermia is a potentially deadly drop in core temperature caused by exposure to cold, wind, water, or a combination of those factors. The condition occurs when the body loses heat faster than it can produce it. The storm of 1993 packed more than ample amounts of all three contributing conditions.

Near dark, as the snow began to accumulate, Murdock's team erected a tarp large enough to cover all eight of them. The packs formed a wall at the back of the sheltered area, and Murdock placed his sleeping bag and pack at the tarp's open front, hoping to block the intrusion of blowing snow.

"The kids were great," recalls Murdock. "They worked together and put on dry clothes from different packs, helping each other stay warm."

Murdock's team and the other Cranbrook students expected to awaken to a light dusting of snow, more of a novelty than a nuisance to individuals schooled in contending with backcountry challenges.

The "light dusting" never let up. In fact, snowfall would continue and intensify, borne by high winds, over the next two days. On Saturday, March 13, more than 30 inches of snow fell on Mount Le Conte. The next day, the storm added another 30 inches to the mountain's snow load, marking the largest accumulation anywhere along the storm's path. Even the Florida panhandle received half a foot.

"Friday was the only really dramatic night for me," says Murdock. "I was watching the snow pile up along the edges of the tarp until it eclipsed the light. I got pretty wet, too, so I had some frightening dreams about what might happen to us."

Nicols awoke Saturday morning to find his sleeping bag buried under more than a foot of snow.

Section Two: Paralysis
Saturday, March 13

Floridians living on the Gulf Coast, who had suffered through tornadoes, violent thunderstorms, and hurricane-force winds on Friday, now braced for a tidal surge. The 12-foot wall of water hit Florida's west coast just before dawn on Saturday. The combination of wind and water claimed 44 lives in the state, according to a report by the National Climatic Data Center. Residents of Georgia experienced a blinding whiteout accompanied by flashes of lightning and rolling thunder.

In GSMNP, paralysis swept in with the storm. Hikers, by definition, are a mobile lot, moving from point to point through the mountains, often with their homes tethered to their backs. But the storm moored them in place. Most who tried to venture out were soon exhausted by chest-deep drifts and battered by howling winds, and they straggled back to their previous encampments.

The nation's most visited national park, itself, was likewise paralyzed. Staff could not escape their own homes, owing to hundreds of toppled trees and snow so deep it was impassable in places even by rugged four-wheel-drive vehicles.

On Saturday, while the blizzard gained intensity and snow began to pile up, a skeletal staff reported for work. A maintenance crew began cutting downed trees and plowing the road (U.S. 441) from park headquarters (HQ) at Sugarlands to Gatlinburg. Ida May Hobbs, who had stayed overnight in anticipation of the storm, assumed dispatch duties.

Other crew members began barricading roads to prevent additional visitors from attempting to enter the park. The effort to clear and plow the two miles of road to Gatlinburg proved hopeless and was abandoned.

A report came in of eight hikers stranded on Meigs Mountain, southwest of the Elkmont Campground. A search and rescue (SAR) was planned and then postponed; interviews with families of the stranded hikers indicated that the group was prepared for winter conditions.

Two Cranbrook teams led by Expedition Program coordinator Frank Norton, a physics instructor, and Kristen Smith, occupied campsites 73 and

Scenes from the National Park Service headquarters area at Sugarlands. The blizzard knocked out power to the site for over a week.

74, about a mile apart on the Lakeshore Trail near Forney Creek. Norton and his students had passed a difficult night.

"My first indication that we were dealing with really heavy snow was when my tarp collapsed at about 3 a.m.," Norton recalls. After helping his students dig out, Norton returned to his sleeping bag. A couple hours later, near dawn, his tarp collapsed a second time. By then, about two feet of snow lay on the ground, and the storm raged on.

Norton wrestled with the critical decision to stay put or try to hike out, realizing that the wrong decision could trigger what he terms a "domino effect."

The decision to break camp and move or remain in place is never an easy one for backcountry travelers to make, particularly in the face of potentially deadly conditions. Staying put allows hikers to conserve vital energy stores, pool food supplies and gear, and establish a functional and protective base camp.

Provided the hikers have conformed to their planned itinerary and are camped where they were scheduled to camp—which was true in Norton's case—SAR teams likely have a general idea of where they are. Further, in unfavorable weather conditions, hikers on the move can stray from the trail, particularly one buried under feet of snow, and wind up not only stranded, but lost as well. And there's always the risk that a mobile group will become fragmented, forcing rescue teams to search for isolated individuals rather than a group situated in one place.

But staying put also exposes hikers to the continuing ravages of harsh weather and requires them to rely on an ever-dwindling reserve of food and fuel. Uncertainty about whether a rescue operation is even underway and, if so, when it might arrive can prompt fear and even panic. A prudent decision to depart camp can instill in a group of hikers a sense of purpose and, ultimately, lead them to safety. Such so-called self-rescues also allow SAR teams to focus their limited resources on locating and extracting other groups.

After carefully evaluating his group's options, Norton instructed his students to pack up their gear; they were heading out. One of his students, unable to locate her backpack buried under the snow, made do with a duffel bag.

Norton's team reached Smith's camp later in the morning. From there, the two groups set out for the tunnel marking the end of the Northshore Road (also known as the Road to Nowhere because it was never completed). It took them all day; they finally reached the tunnel near dark. Beyond the tunnel, Norton realized, the road—provided it was passable—would lead them to Bryson City.

Cranbrook team leader Peter Fayroian and his students had already made their way to safety. On Friday, Fayroian, one of whose students was ill, had led his entire team one mile from Campsite 50, on the Chasteen Creek Trail, into the Smokemont Campground, which served as a base camp for the Cranbrook teams dispersed in the backcountry. Fayroian's group was safe, but Nicole Schack's team was not only stranded at Campsite 61 on the Noland Creek Trail; it was also leaderless.

According to Norton, Schack and her student leader had hiked ahead of the rest of their group, giving the students instructions to continue straight on the Pole Road Creek Trail and turn left at the junction with the Deep Creek Trail to Campsite 54. Instead, the students turned left 3.3 miles too soon, when they reached the junction with the Noland Divide Trail, and headed northwest toward the Clingmans Dome Road. After realizing their mistake, they backtracked to the junction. It was late in the day and beginning to snow, so the students decided to return to Campsite 61, where they had stayed the previous night.

Meanwhile, Schack and her student leader were encamped at Campsite 54 on the Deep Creek Trail when the storm struck. The next morning,

Saturday, Schack and the student leader were unable to reach their stranded students, so they hiked out to the Deep Creek Campground to summon help.

"Nicole's kids did exactly the right thing," says Norton. "They stayed put. They had plenty of food and fuel."

For team leaders Charlie Shaw, Jim Meehan, and Tom Murdock, self-rescue wasn't an option. The three groups were camped in the mountains along the upper reaches of Hazel Creek, where the snow was waist deep in places.

Murdock realized that there would be no ground rescue for his team, so after he and his students emerged from their "hole" under the tarp, they ate a quick breakfast and started hiking northeast along Hazel Creek. "We didn't plan to go far, but we did want to get to a clearing," says Murdock. "If someone flew over us, we wanted to be visible."

Though he had slept under a mound of snow, camper Jay Nicols had remained warm and comfortable in his sleeping bag through the night and awoke rested and ready to move. As the group prepared to break camp, Nicols noticed that one of his friends was struggling.

"As we packed up our camp, he kept lying down in the snow; he was exhausted," says Nicols. "He just wanted to continue sleeping, but it was not an option, we had to move on."

As they departed camp, the students contended with snow that had drifted to five feet deep in places, Murdock recalls. "We were sinking about two feet down with each step."

Traveling through deep snow without benefit of skis or show shoes—a process known as post-holing—is an exhausting ordeal, particularly for the lead hiker breaking trail. With each step, the hiker must extract his foot from the "post hole" and lift his leg high enough to clear the snow. Heavy snow and ice clinging to boots only adds to the challenge.

Murdock estimates that the group progressed only about 150 yards when he spotted a suitable clearing on the other side of Hazel Creek. The group's river-fording shoes (sneakers) had been lost under the snow the previous night, so Murdock devised a plan to keep the hikers' boots dry during the crossing.

"We found garbage bags and wrapped them around our boots, holding the bags up with our hands," he says. "I walked to the creek and slid down the steep wall of snow into water that was about thigh deep."

It quickly became apparent that the plastic bags were "a terrible idea," says Murdock. The creek water collected in the bags and infused his boots. He managed to get to the other side and drop his pack, but as he turned around, he saw that several of his students had already followed his lead. "I watched their faces fall as their dry boots filled with water," he says.

Murdock slipped off his boots and, one-by-one, carried several of his students across the creek, wearing only thick wool socks on his feet.

Now on the other side of the creek, the team hastily began to stomp down a camp area. A cleared area for packs allowed the hikers to store and organize gear. A living area included bench seats crafted from snow. A kitchen provided space for cooking and heating water for hot drinks. Cocoa with butter was a favorite among the students, says Murdock.

According to Murdock, during the warm early days of the trip, Jay Nicols had taken some good-natured ribbing for having brought a bright-yellow ski jacket. With their camp nestled among the trees, Nicols surmised that it would be difficult for a chopper pilot to spot them from the air, so he suggested that they use the jacket as a signaling device.

After the evening meal, Murdock found another creative application for the stoves and frying pans, using them to "melt the ice balls that were our socks." The group also pan-warmed scarves, hats, and boots, but when Murdock tried to thaw his now-frozen down sleeping bag, the nylon burst into flames.

Back at park HQ, four-wheel-drive vehicles proved no match for the snow, so National Park Service (NPS) staffer Ron Parrish made his way to Gatlinburg, rode the tram to Ober Gatlinburg, and borrowed the resort's tracked snow vehicle. He arrived with it at park HQ at 4 p.m.

Just after 5 p.m., park HQ lost power. The power would remain out for more than a week. Shortly after, the phone system, with the exception of a single line, crashed. Snow and downed trees had also taken out power to the Fry Mountain repeater, a device that picks up and amplifies two-way radio signals. With roads impassable and electronic communication with the outside world all but cut off, the park staff might as well have been operating in the 19th century.

At the Birch Spring Gap Shelter, AT hikers Maloney, Pawlowski, Shembri, Baldwin, Boyland, Chaplin, and McCollum spent the day gathering firewood, hanging tarps over the shelter's open face, and filling cracks in shelter walls. They later draped collapsed tents over their sleeping bags for additional warmth. The snow finally stopped falling at about midnight, but then temperatures began to plunge.

Sunday, March 14

The cargo ship Gold Bond Conveyor, carrying 24,000 tons of gypsum ore, had departed Halifax, Nova Scotia, in clear weather bound for Tampa, Florida. Saturday afternoon the storm struck, battering the ship with 90-mile-per-hour winds and 100-foot waves, according to a report posted on the National Gypsum website. The ship began to take on water and list to port; water had seeped into the port-side cargo holds and mixed with the gypsum, creating a heavy cement-like paste.

The willingness of U.S. Army pilots to make dangerous maneuvers in heavily-forested mountain terrain ultimately rescued over 100 people in the aftermath of the March 1993 blizzard.

Late in the evening, as the ship continued to lean farther and farther to port, Canadian Coast Guard pilots circled the ship in a fixed-wing aircraft and watched, helpless, as a large sea swell struck and sank the crippled ship just after midnight on Sunday. All 33 crew members perished in the icy waters of the North Atlantic.

Back on land, 3 million American households and businesses were without power and, in many cases, heat, including some of the luxury chalets and vacation homes that perched on mountainsides above Gatlinburg. Many of the cabins' occupants, like the hikers in the park's backcountry, were stranded and, thus, forced to rely on whatever supplies occupied their pantry shelves. Over coming days, hovering Black Hawks would drop boxes of meals ready to eat (MRE) to the marooned vacationers.

Early Sunday morning, a Pigeon Forge Police Department 4X4 picked up NPS staffers Keny Slay and Don Utterback and escorted them to HQ.

Twenty inches of snow and toppled trees had rendered most roads impassable. Road crews cleared the parking lot at Sugarlands to serve as a landing
zone for the first of 12 Black Hawk helicopters that would soon begin arriving from the 101ˢᵗ U.S. Army Airborne Division in Fort Campbell, Kentucky, and North Carolina and Tennessee Army National Guard units.

Other specialized equipment was en route as well, including two Bell
UH-1 Iroquois (Huey) helicopters from the Tennessee Air National Guard,
four tracked vehicles and five High Mobility Multipurpose Wheeled Vehicles (HMMWV) from the Tennessee Army National Guard, and three
fixed-wing aircraft from the Civil Air Patrol. All told, 167 NPS staff members, 32 National Guard troops, and 75 U.S. Army and 23 Civil Air Patrol
flight personnel would play a role in the six-day SAR operation.

The reports of stranded hikers continued to trickle in: Three adults
and five children were stranded in the horse barn near Elkmont. Thirty people—most of them 6ᵗʰ and 7ᵗʰ graders—were stranded at Tremont. Campers
were also stranded at the Cataloochee, Elkmont, and Cades Cove Campgrounds.

Ranger Jack Piepenbring, who lived in Maryville, picked up a few
maintenance workers in his four-wheel drive truck and drove them to the
park boundary at Townsend. Blount County plows had already cleared US
321. Piepenbring knew the Kentucky middle-schoolers were trapped at
Tremont and at least 22 campers were stranded at Cades Cove.

"There were a lot of trees blocking the roadway in the park, and since
all the snow-removal equipment was kept at Cades Cove, the only thing we
could do was to attempt to chain saw our way in to the students at Tremont," says Piepenbring. "We were able to clear only about a mile, to the
Tremont Road intersection with Laurel Creek Road."

Ron Parrish, en route to Newfound Gap in Ober Gatlinburg's tracked
snow vehicle, found and rescued two hikers at the Alum Cave Bluffs trailhead mid-afternoon. Holed up in the Cosby Knob Shelter, stranded solo
AT hiker David Griffin, turned on his portable radio and was encouraged
to hear that rescue operations had begun in the park, the *Daily Times* article
reported.

For many hikers stranded in GSMNP's backcountry, small battery-powered radios provided a vital link to the outside world and the only
source of information on the burgeoning rescue operation. For those who
heard their names referenced in broadcast reports, the radios provided com-

fort—they knew help was on the way. For those not mentioned, the radios only compounded their worries, suggesting that they and their whereabouts remained unknown to search crews.

Frank Norton's and Kristen Smith's Cranbrook teams emerged from their camp in the Northshore Road tunnel and set off down the road toward Bryson City. The clouds cleared and the sun began to shine. According to Norton, the road was choked with downed trees, but he and his students were able to get through, affirming the judgment of his decision to break camp and move.

Norton advised the students to "think like a caterpillar." The 16-person group formed a single line, with the person in front kicking steps in the snow. "Each person kicked 25 steps, or 50 if they were feeling strong, before stepping aside and letting the next person take the lead," says Norton. "No one was a passive participant; everyone contributed to the good of the group."

By late afternoon, the human caterpillar approached the park boundary, where the group encountered a maintenance crew out clearing debris from the road, and the group was soon in Bryson City. Later, they would check into the Holiday Inn in Cherokee and await word on the fate of their schoolmates.

Cranbrook advisor Cara Martin and seven students managed to self-rescue by hiking out nearly three miles from Campsite 17 to Abrams Creek Ranger Station. They would be evacuated by an NPS truck the next day and taken to Maryville.

In the Russell Field Shelter, Patricia Hammann, Kathy Davidson, Todd Graves, and Jeff Burns occupied their time by playing word games ("we thought of foods that started with each letter of the alphabet") and discussing religion and politics. According to Hammann, temperatures dropped through the day, but the wind abated. Graves and Burns, hoping to reach the spring for water, tried to fashion snow shoes from wire mesh they had found at the shelter. The plan failed, and they were forced to burn precious fuel to melt snow.

At 5:20 p.m., the first three Black Hawks arrived at Sugarlands. One was dispatched to the Oconaluftee Visitor Center, and a second set out to cover the AT from Mt. Collins to Charlies Bunion and the road to Clingmans Dome.

The Sikorsky UH-60 Black Hawk helicopter was first put into service in the late 1970s, replacing the Bell UH-1 Iroquois (Huey), which had seen extensive use during the Vietnam War, as the U.S. Army's main tactical transport chopper. The aircraft can accommodate two pilots and 12 passengers, and when equipped with an external motorized hoist, can lift soldiers—or, in this case, stranded hikers—to safety. The aircraft would assume the lead role in the ensuing rescue operation, assisting both in locating stranded hikers and extracting them from the snow-draped backcountry.

As darkness fell, the AT hikers at Birch Spring Gap Shelter discussed plans to push on toward Mollies Ridge Shelter the next day. Though they wrestled with the same decision Cranbrook team leader Frank Norton had faced the day before, their ultimate decision would prove far less auspicious.

Section Three: GSMNP Intensifies the Search
Monday, March 15

On Monday morning, the NPS staff continued to trickle in. Some were forced to cut their way out of their neighborhoods with the same chainsaws they would later apply in clearing roads in the park. By then, bitterly cold temperatures had compounded existing problems. Sunday night had reached a low of -10° on Mount Le Conte, a record for March. The low would bottom out there again Monday night, while the low in Gatlinburg would plummet to 1°. The widespread power outage meant most area residents were enduring the frigid temperatures without the benefit of heat in their homes.

The hikers stranded in the backcountry, depending on the elevations of their bivouacs, were forced to contend with temperatures somewhere in between. The luckier ones huddled in tents. The Cranbrook students lay under sagging tarps.

In the backcountry, hikers may have been cut off and stranded, but the NPS had a pretty good idea where most of them were. The park rigidly enforces its backcountry registration system, which requires all backcountry travelers to acquire permits listing all planned campsites for the duration of their visits. In the end, the system created a vital paper trail that led SAR crews to many of the stranded hikers.

At 7:30 a.m., NPS Ranger George Minnigh departed in a Black Hawk en route to the Luftee Overlook near Newfound Gap and evacuated three hikers from Syracuse, New York, two of them suffering from frostbite and exposure. They were flown to Sevierville Medical Center.

At about 9 a.m., AT hikers Maloney, Pawlowski, and Shembri depart-

ed Birch Spring Gap Shelter en route to Mollies Ridge Shelter, five miles to
the north. McCollum, Chaplin, Baldwin, and Boyland left shortly after. All
encountered chest-deep snow. Seven hours later, they had covered less than
half the distance to the shelter.

Piepenbring had arranged for snow-removal equipment operators to
meet in Townsend in the morning, where a Black Hawk landed on US 321
and flew them to Cades Cove.

"Once the equipment operators got the plows moving, they were able
to push the downed trees out of the roadway and plow a one-lane road from
Cades Cove to Townsend," Pipenbring says. "After that I had a ranger lead
the 22 stranded campers down Laurel Creek Road to Townsend."

Public Information Officers Bob Miller and Nancy Gray arrived at
a "dark and cold" HQ and set up a temporary public affairs office in two
rooms at the Conner Motor Lodge in Gatlinburg. The motel, Miller reports,
had power, phone, and FAX. Miller and Gray, along with many of their
NPS colleagues, would remain on the job and not return home until Thursday evening.

"On Saturday and Sunday, March 13-14, few contacts with the park
were possible, as only one emergency phone line was in service," Miller
wrote in a post-incident report. "This inability to communicate directly
with the park meant that, by the time we [Miller and Gray] came on line on
Monday, much speculative, and often erroneous, information had already
been put out by the media."

Among the misinformation was the assertion that the NPS was searching *only* for the Cranbrook students, leaving the impression that the rest of
the park's backcountry travelers would have to fend for themselves. Some of
the marooned hikers received the disheartening, though false, news via their
battery-powered radios.

Miller pressed administrative worker Lisa Rolen into service to begin
logging calls from the dozens of worried relatives of hikers stranded in the
park. Meanwhile, Miller and Gray responded to the first media queries.
Over the next five days, the two would field nearly 500 calls and interview
requests from media representatives, many of them based in the hometowns
of the stranded hikers.

National media also recognized the newsworthy nature of the situation, and Miller and Gray talked with reporters from *Life Magazine*, *The
New York Times*, *USA Today*, *Good Morning America*, National Public Radio,

CNN, NBC, CBS, and ABC, among many others.

The parents of the stranded Cranbrook students used their clout to generate pressure from their senators and Congressional representatives and Department of the Interior administrators—all of whom contacted the park to check on progress.

Miller and his colleagues realized that they were racing against time; the longer the hikers remained trapped in the backcountry, under conditions now made worse by frigid temperatures, the more likely that the SAR operation might, at some point, evolve into an mission to recover bodies.

"We knew from previous experience that the equipment and judgment of those individuals stranded in the backcountry varied greatly," says Miller. "We expected that some of the more skilled and better equipped and supplied hikers would just hunker down and be okay. But we feared that others would be woefully underprepared for those extreme conditions and make bad decisions and get into life-threatening situations to which we would be unable to respond."

At 10:40 a.m., the NPS officially closed the park's backcountry. Park staffers already had their hands full, and if there's one thing they didn't need, it was a few overconfident daredevils straying into the park and themselves becoming stranded and further stressing limited SAR resources.

A few minutes later, a Black Hawk spotted a lone hiker on the Clingmans Dome road and dropped a sleeping bag. At 11:35 a.m., another Black Hawk hovered over the tight clearing near the Spence Field Shelter. Jack Piepenbring, who was on-board the chopper, said that the pilot executed a "dust-off," revving his engines to blast away any loose debris and snow before he landed the aircraft. The clearing proved to be too small; as the pilot lowered the chopper, his rotor tips cut a landing zone in the rhododendrons on either side of the clearing, "slicing through the branches like a chainsaw."

Once on the ground, the pilot sent part of the crew out with a "crash kit" to cut away the branches that entrapped the now-motionless and sagging rotors while he inspected the damage. Piepenbring noticed that all four rotors were damaged, with pieces of rhododendron hanging from the cracked rotor tips. Nevertheless, the pilot, a Viet Nam War veteran, deemed the craft airworthy and invited the six stranded hikers to climb on-board. Though no doubt a bit unnerved by the rough landing, the battered backpackers were more than ready to leave.

The day before, they had aborted an attempt to hike out when they were unable to find the trail, buried under feet of snow. That night, the group contended with sub-zero temperatures and snow blowing into the open-faced shelter past the plastic tarps they had hastily erected to seal off the interior space.

Early in the afternoon, Ranger Keith Nelson, aboard a Black Hawk, located Nicole Schack's group of six students near Noland Creek, winched them out, and flew them to McGhee-Tyson Airport. At that point, Schack, who had hiked out to Deep Creek the day before with her student leader, was safe at the Holiday Inn in Cherokee.

A Black Hawk spotted and rescued Cranbrook advisor Fred Higgins and seven students from Campsite 41, in Cataloochee. Tom Murdock's Cranbrook team, supplied with ample food, decided to head north along the Hazel Creek Trail toward the AT.

"We left all our gear at camp and began breaking a trail," says Murdock. "After working for a while, we'd walk back to the camp to rest." The group did not progress far before they began hearing and seeing aircraft and realized that rescue was imminent.

At Cosby Knob Shelter, David Griffin spotted a Black Hawk hovering overhead. The chopper dropped a sleeping bag, food, and a note instructing him to stay put; help would arrive within 24 hours. The chopper's rotors shook loose some dead limbs and provided Griffin with his only source of firewood, according to the *Daily Times* article. To keep his mind sharp, the article reports, Griffin checked and rechecked his gear.

At 2 p.m., Chief Ranger Jason Houck assumed the role of Incident Command and directed his small available staff to establish a command center in the training room at park HQ in Sugarlands. The Tennessee Emergency Management Agency (TEMA) provided a generator large enough to power the entire command center. A telephone repairman installed four direct phone lines.

At 2:40 p.m., an NPS vehicle with Cherokee Tribal Emergency Medical Technicians on board rescued several teenage hikers who had made it out to the Oconaluftee Visitor Center. Three of them were suffering from frostbitten feet.

Shortly after, a chopper hovered over the Russell Field Shelter and dropped a package instructing Patricia Hammann and her sheltermates to wave their hands if they were okay, to wave a blue flag if they needed food, or to wave an orange flag if anyone was injured. Hammann says they deployed the blue flag; they were running low on rations. The chopper dropped a case of MREs before departing. The four hoped the helicopter crew would convey news to their families that they were cold and hungry but safe. Hammann's husband, Tim, who had traveled from Indiana, awaited word in a Gatlinburg motel.

At about 4:30, a Black Hawk spotted the AT hikers—now splintered into two groups—struggling to make their way from Birch Spring Gap Shelter to Mollies Ridge and lowered a medic. According to post-incident interviews, Shembri, the only one who interacted with the medic, insisted that all were okay but needed food. The chopper dropped food rations before departing.

The helicopter returned a short time later. A corpsman descended on a winch cable and asked McCollum, Chaplin, Baldwin, and Boyland if they wanted to be extracted. Thinking the shelter was only 15 minutes away, and assured that the chopper would drop food rations, the group decided to remain on the trail.

As the chopper departed, its cable temporarily snagged on Chaplin's pack, and its rotors showered the hikers with snow. They watched as the chopper dropped a load of food near the shelter, more than a mile away, and realized just how far they yet had to travel.

By now, the AT hikers had difficulty locating the trail. At 7:30 p.m., they dug out an emergency campsite in a cluster of trees. They kept their stoves burning to provide additional warmth in their tents. Boyland's boots had frozen to his feet, and he was forced to cut the laces to remove them.

Tuesday, March 16

The Tennessee Interagency Mobilization Center dispatched 15 personnel with winter survival skills to assist NPS rangers in searching the backcountry on foot. As crews began to clear park roads, rangers catalogued cars parked at trailheads and matched license plates with the names of missing persons.

Public Information Officer Miller, now operating from the emergency HQ at Sugarlands, discovered that a number of media representatives were calling and massing at the Oconaluftee Visitor Center and dispatched Nancy Gray, via helicopter, to handle press relations on the other side of the mountain. There, Ranger Tom Robbins assisted Gray, while Ranger Karen Ballentine joined Lisa Rolen in helping Miller.

At about 10:30 a.m., about two miles south of the Mollies Ridge Shelter on the AT, Chaplin, McCollum, Baldwin, and Boyland broke camp. According to a post-incident interview with the hikers, at that point, their boots were frozen, and they had no dry socks or gloves. They reached Mollies Ridge Shelter at noon and found the shelter filled with snow. Shembri, Maloney, and Pawlowski had arrived before them and had begun gathering firewood. The hikers set up their tents inside the shelter to conserve body heat and protect them from blowing snow.

Just after 11 a.m. Ranger Dave Panebaker appealed to the Federal Aviation Administration to close airspace over the park to avoid congestion and reduce interference with rescue operations. The FAA complied.

On the upper reaches of Hazel Creek, a chopper hovered over Murdock's Cranbrook team and dropped a small package, instructing the group to form their arms into a Y if they needed help or to the sides if they were uninjured. According to Murdock, the group signaled that they were okay.

"We wondered if other people in the woods might need help more than we did," he says. Soon after, the helicopter departed but returned and dropped a box of MREs. With the supplemental food, Murdock says, "we had enough calories to last us weeks."

Murdock interpreted the food drop as a sign the campers would not be rescued for a couple more days, and he instructed his students to empty their packs to inventory gear. "Just when the students had taken apart their packs, the helicopter returned," says Murdock. The chopper's rotors scattered the loose gear.

A corpsman descended on a cable and informed Murdock that bad weather was blowing in; the students would have to be evacuated immediately, and their belongings would have to remain behind. The Black Hawks operating in the park were equipped with extraction devices known as Jungle Penetrators (they were first used in Vietnam to hoist ground troops into hovering Hueys), which were lowered on a steel cable. The weighted device's three arms are folded up as it's lowered through the jungle, or in this case, forest canopy. Once lowered, the arms open to create small seats.

The chopper hovered about 100 feet above Murdock's students on the forest floor, and for each extraction, a student, belted to the extraction device, hugged a chopper crewman seated opposite him or her, and the two rose together to the chopper. According to Piepenbring, each extraction took about five minutes. Jay Nicols, who describes the ascent to the chopper as "beautiful, with great views," confesses that he was "a little scared but more pumped to be going home."

Once Nichols was on-board, the pilot confirmed that Nicols' signaling device—the bright yellow ski jacket—had helped him and his crew locate the stranded hikers.

As the students were lifted one-by-one into the chopper, Murdock rifled through the students' packs and the piles of belongings, grabbing cameras, journals, and other valuable items before he, too, was lifted to safety.

When the chopper landed at Oconaluftee Visitor Center, Murdock's team was confronted by what he describes as "a crazy crowd of reporters. We were completely amazed by the level of interest."

At about 2:30 p.m., Ranger George Minnigh, traveling on snowshoes, reached thru-hiker David Griffin at the Cosby Knob Shelter, and the two soon began their hike out. By that time, above-freezing daytime temperatures had begun to melt and consolidate the snow, making foot travel possible, though still enervating and slow.

Late in the afternoon, Murdock was able to provide the rescue team with the approximate location of Jim Meehan's Cranbrook team. Two pilots powered up their chopper and took off with Ranger Pat Patten on-board. Patten spotted Meehan's group near the junction of the Hazel Creek and Lakeshore Trails. By then, according to Norton, Meehan and his students had managed to hike nearly eight miles down the mountain from Campsite 82, hoping to reach a ranger cabin they knew would provide shelter. They never got there. The chopper crew extracted Meehan and his seven students and flew them to the Oconaluftee Visitor Center. Shaw's Cranbrook team was likewise rescued.

At 5:22 p.m., Incident Commander Houck advised his crew that the last of the Cranbrook students were safely on the ground. That left only 11 hikers marooned in the backcountry: the seven AT hikers at Mollies Ridge Shelter and Hamman, Davidson, Graves, and Burns at Russell Field.

By that time, Graves had managed to reach the spring near the shelter, and Hammann says they could hear helicopters in the distance. Graves learned from his radio that several people were yet unaccounted for in the park, and Hammann wondered if the four of them were part of that group.

That evening, weather conditions declined, with rain and clouds, and at 8 p.m., Houck shifted the SAR from air to ground.

Wednesday, March 17

A warming trend brought rain and dense fog, preempting any attempt at air-borne rescue. At Mollies Ridge, the seven AT hikers spent the day scouring the ridge for wood and idling in their sleeping bags.

In the Russell Field Shelter, Graves' radio broadcast a discouraging report suggesting that the search might be called off because of its skyrocketing costs, according to a post-incident NPS interview with the hikers. (An NPS assessment would later put the cost of the operation at $118,000.) Though he heard news reports about other hikers missing in the park, he and his three shelter-mates were not mentioned.

Later in the day, Graves picked up another broadcast, which featured his and Burns' fathers. According to Hammann, the young men's fathers cited their "faith in their sons' ability to survive the storm." In another interview, Hammann's husband, Tim, mentioned his wife's 20 years of experience as a backpacker.

The four were heartened—even moved—by the news. "We all had an emotional period after we heard the interviews," recalls Hammann. "We all cried knowing that our families were worried about us."

At Mollies Ridge, Baldwin, Boyland, Chaplin, and McCollum packed their gear, hoping that a helicopter would arrive the next day to rescue them. Meanwhile, Shembri and Pawlowski desired a different outcome, wishing instead that the NPS would leave them alone and not disrupt their journey north on the AT.

Thursday, March 18

At the Russell Field Shelter, Hammann, Davidson, Graves, and Burns prepared to hike out to Cades Cove. The group was down to the last of its food rations, so they forewent breakfast. Before departing, they filled their water bottles at the spring.

As they reached the grassy clearing just beyond the shelter, Hammann says she could hear a plane fly overhead. The fog that had persisted through the previous day began to lift. Hammann tied a strip of orange plastic to the top of her pack so they could be spotted from the air.

Though now seven days into a difficult ordeal, Hammann still managed to find beauty in the snowy landscape that spread around her. She noted in particular the ample hoar frost that adorned the trunks and branches of the trees and shimmered in the sun.

As they hiked down through snow that, in some places, was hip deep, the two young college students pulled ahead, and about a mile from the shelter, Hammann could hear Graves and Burns talking with someone. She soon discovered that they were talking with NPS rangers. One of them got on his radio to call in a transport for the hikers to the University of Tennessee (UT) Medical Center, but Hammann, a registered nurse, assured him that they were okay—just eager to get out.

The rangers led the four hikers back up the mountain to a clearing near the shelter, where, at 8:12 a.m., a chopper set down, loaded them up, and flew them to HQ. From there, a van took them to a motel in Gatlinburg, where Hammann was reunited with her husband.

In the morning, Shembri and Pawlowski departed the Mollies Ridge Shelter on handcrafted snowshoes but made little progress before the devices broke. Maloney, Baldwin, Boyland, Chaplin, and McCollum followed. According to the NPS post-incident interview, the group spotted a plane at 9 a.m., and 45 minutes later, a 101st U.S. Army Airborne helicopter arrived to extract them and carry them to Sugarlands Visitor Center.

Piepenbring, who was on-board the Black Hawk, says that Shembri turned out to be a reluctant, even resentful, evacuee. According to a post-incident interview with the two hikers, "It was evident that Shembri and Pawlowski probably would have stayed on the trail if they had been given that option. Shembri was quite vocal in expressing his desire to have continued." Piepenbring did not afford Shembri any options. The hiker was ordered onto the chopper, and Piepenbring was forced to confiscate the lock-blade knife that Shembri clutched in this fist.

Once on the ground at Sugarlands, according to an article in the *Bar Harbor Times*, Chaplin was greeted by an old friend wearing an NPS uniform. Chaplin, from Maine, had babysat Ranger Carroll Schell's kids when he was stationed at Acadia National Park. According to the report, Schell had been in contact with Chaplin's father over the previous three days.

Section Four: Epilogue

Early afternoon on March 18, with all missing hikers accounted for and safe, the NPS began to shut down what had become known as Operation Blizzard.

At 3:30, the last of the helicopters transported Public Information Officer Nancy Gray from Oconaluftee back to HQ, before departing. Three hours later, the Tennessee Army National Guard caravan of tracked vehicles and HMMWVs set out for its home base in Knoxville.

NPS crews continued to remove snow and fallen timber from park roads. By Saturday, March 20, eight days after the storm hit, Sugarlands Visitor Center was still without power, but GSMNP had reopened US 441 and the Laurel Creek Road from Townsend to Cades Cove. As of March 31, some of the park's more remote roadways remained closed.

A few days after Shembri and Pawlowski had been plucked from the mountains, they resumed their hike on the AT. By summer's end, they and David Griffin would achieve their quest; their names are included on the Appalachian Trail Conservancy's "2000-miler List" for 1993.

The NPS, with invaluable assistance from the Army National Guard, U.S. Army Airborne Division, and TEMA, directly rescued 135 people from the park's 800-square-mile backcountry. Twenty-four other hikers effected self-rescues, bringing the total to 159. In recognition of its efforts, GSMNP staff would later be awarded a Unit Award for Excellence of Service from the U.S. Department of the Interior.

The Cranbrook students boarded buses the morning of Wednesday, March 17, and arrived home late that afternoon. The students—and their parents—had endured a dramatic ordeal, and all who had ventured into GSMNP left the park with plenty of stories to share with friends and eager media representatives.

Murdock says that two years after the incident, when the sophomore participants were by then seniors, he read "a huge number of college entrance essays focused on the storm experience."

With their students reunited with the families back in Michigan, Expedition Program coordinator Frank Norton gathered his staff in a hotel conference room and did what he could to help them process the difficult situation they had all endured. Murdock recalls Norton saying, "Your work as a leader is done. The kids are home safe."

Then he asked them to reflect on their own thoughts and memories of the experience. "At that point," recalls Murdock, "we were all crying and laughing in the exhausted way of people who had spent several sleepless nights worrying about everything and living on adrenaline."

The skills they had nurtured in their students through the Wilderness Expedition Program had been severely tested and proven. According to Norton, many of the students returned home brimming with newfound self-confidence, and no regrets.

"When you're 16, life hasn't really tested you very much. Your tools to handle difficult situations are limited," says Norton. "The Wilderness Expedition Program was designed to provide students with a more extensive set of tools. This event was extreme, and the kids were tested in a potentially life-threatening situation. I can't help but think that this experience played a key role in their ability to handle difficult challenges down the line."

After the faculty leaders had returned to Michigan, Norton says, the Wilderness Expedition Program went through "an extensive internal and external review process." Among other changes, guided by "best practices" at the time, Cranbrook shifted from a one- to a two-adult leader model for each team, while retaining a role for the student leaders.

Not all Cranbrook expedition participants emerged from the 1993 experience unscathed. Cranbrook sophomore Danielle Swank and faculty leader James Woodruff, a math teacher, who had been among groups stranded in Joyce Kilmer-Slickrock Wilderness, suffered severe frostbite and remained hospitalized at UT Medical Center. But that was the worst of it.

"I wouldn't have given you a nickel on Sunday night that we wouldn't lose somebody in this storm," said Bob Miller, as quoted in the *Chattanooga Times*.

Miller's post-incident report references "much finger-pointing." According to the report, some parents of the Cranbrook students castigated the NPS for failure to adequately warn the students and their leaders or to close the park's backcountry. Other parents lay part of the blame on the leaders of the school's Wilderness Expedition Program.

According to Miller's report, four NPS rangers, three in North Carolina and one in Cades Cove, had, in fact, cautioned some Cranbrook leaders about the impending storm. Frank Norton acknowledges that a ranger had visited him on Thursday and advised that a storm was headed his way.

"We knew a storm was coming in," says Norton, "but we did not anticipate three to four feet of snow." Indeed, until the storm actually hit, its arrival and intensity were still only part of a forecast—and one that pushed the limits of credibility.

Weather—or, more accurately, predicted weather—creates an inconvenient conundrum. Meteorologists are well aware of the effect of Chicken Little syndrome, where repeated warnings of weather crises that fail to develop incline their audiences to discount their predictions. If you get it wrong too many times, when you get it right, no one pays much attention.

The conundrum for consumers of the local news, particularly for those who have their backpacks loaded for a long-anticipated trip to the mountains, is to weigh the risk of adverse weather—no matter how seemingly remote—against the disappointment and frustration that would result from scrubbing the trip only to discover that your target destination is basking in warm sunshine.

In the storm's aftermath, interest in assigning blame, for the most part, eventually gave way to gratitude. Indeed, no one can question the Cranbrook leaders' commitment to protect their kids and lead them to safety or the NPS response to the crisis, which was aggressive, organized, and remarkably effective.

In the end, the story of GSMNP and the Storm of the Century is more about deliverance than disaster. The blizzard, one of the deadliest storms on record, claimed nearly 300 lives, 19 in North Carolina and 14 in Tennessee, according to the report by the National Climatic Data Center. Not one of those deaths occurred in GSMNP.

CHAPTER 11
A Suspected Mass Murderer Arrives in the National Park, but Does He Leave?

Few alleged crimes have been more vicious or flights from justice more protracted than those of the mid-level U.S. State Department employee who, in 1976, left the last definitive clue to his whereabouts in GSMNP before becoming one of the longest sought-after fugitives in U.S. history.

On March 2, 1976, a ranger of the North Carolina Division of Forest Resources, perched 120 feet up in a fire tower, detected a plume of dense smoke rising from a low-lying pine forest just outside of Columbia, a community near the famed Outer Banks.

When he went to investigate, he discovered the source of the smoke: five bodies, drenched in gasoline, smoldered in a hastily dug ditch the size of a bathtub. Nearby lay a shovel. The youngest of the victims, three boys, were dressed in pajamas. The other two bodies appeared to be those of adult women.

Soon after, the Tyrrell County authorities arrived. The five partially burned bodies in the make-shift grave were clearly victims of homicide—autopsy reports would later conclude that all had been bludgeoned to death—but who were they, who had killed them, and why were they there?

The police would have a week to mull those questions before a resident of an upscale Bethesda, Maryland, neighborhood called the local sheriff's department with a report on the house next door. For nearly a week, the home of a successful U.S. State Department employee—a man who had served at foreign embassies around the world—and his family had been eerily quiet. Meanwhile, unretrieved newspapers continued to pile up in the driveway.

William Bradford "Brad" Bishop Jr., 39; his wife, Annette, 37; sons William Bradford III, 14, Brenton, 10, and Geoffrey, 5; and Brad Bishop's mother, Lobelia, 68, who lived with the family—all were apparently away. But it wasn't like the well-liked family to head out of town on an extended trip without alerting their neighbors and canceling delivery of their newspaper.

When police entered the home to investigate, they found the house empty, but masses of coagulated blood in multiple rooms told a story of violent struggle. Notably, the family's 1974 Chevrolet station wagon was missing, along with the family dog, Leo, a golden retriever. It didn't take long for law enforcement officials to connect the dots. The recent discovery of five partially burned bodies in coastal North Carolina and the vacant, blood-stained Maryland home might have been separated by 300 miles, but they were clearly linked.

Before long, a third dot would emerge, this one 500 miles to the west and located smack dab in the middle of Great Smoky Mountains National Park.

Within a few days, the FBI conclusively identified the remains of Annette Bishop, her mother-in-law, and her three sons. The grave contained all the Bishop family members except one. Brad Bishop, a once-promising member of the U.S. diplomatic corps, had become the prime suspect.[1]

Bishop was hardly your stereotypic homicidal maniac. He had graduated from Yale University with a degree in American studies and later earned a master's degree in Italian from Vermont's Middlebury College. He had served four years in the U.S. Army in counterintelligence. He had an aptitude for learning languages and spoke French, Serbo-Croat, Italian, and Spanish fluently.

His foreign service postings had taken him to Italy, Addis Ababa, Ethiopia, and Botswana before he returned stateside, where he served as assistant chief of the U.S. State Department's Division of Special Trade Activities and Commercial Treaties, and he had represented the U.S. government in

---

1   William Bradford Bishop has not been tried and convicted of the crimes, so, technically, he should be presumed innocent. However, the preponderance of evidence points to him as the perpetrator.

high-stakes international trade negotiations. His salary afforded him and his family an upper-middle-class lifestyle and a comfortable, 2,500-square-foot home on Lilly Stone Drive in Bethesda's Carderock Springs subdivision.[2] His smarts, good looks, and affable nature had endeared him to neighbors and coworkers.

But beneath the surface of the seemingly well adjusted All-American family, some cracks had begun to form. According to the FBI, Bishop was prone to violent outbursts and had long suffered from insomnia. He was under a psychiatrist's care and was taking heavy doses of the drug Serax.

In the days before the advent of modern psychotropic medications, Serax, a potentially habit-forming tranquilizer, was used to treat anxiety, depression, and alcoholism, though it's unknown precisely which of those symptoms, or constellation of symptoms, the drug had been prescribed to treat in Bishop's case.

The trigger point had come on March 1, when Bishop learned that he had been passed over for an anticipated promotion. Complaining of flu-like symptoms, he left the office early. On his way home, he withdrew several hundred dollars from his bank and stopped at a hardware store to buy a hammer and a gasoline can. He filled the can at a service station near his neighborhood.

Whether the gasoline he purchased in Maryland was used to immolate his slain family members in North Carolina can't be known for certain, but it's likely. The FBI managed to trace a partial price tag on the shovel found near the grave to a hardware store in Potomac, Maryland. There's little doubt about how Bishop allegedly used his newly acquired hammer.

Though the precise details of how his killing rampage unfolded are unknown, evidence suggests that Bishop first bludgeoned his wife and then waited for his mother to return home after walking the dog. She was likely his next victim. Then he crept to the bedrooms where his three young sons slept and used the now-bloodied hammer to dispatch each of them in turn. He allegedly struck his sons with such force that he left indentations in the ceiling. He loaded the bodies into the station wagon, covered them with blankets, called to his dog, and headed south, beginning what would become a decades-long flight from justice.

The last confirmed sighting of Bishop occurred one day after the

---

2   In 2015, average home listings in the Beltway community of Bethesda approach $1 million, according to realtor.com.

murders, on March 2, when Bishop used a credit card to purchase a $15 pair of sneakers from a sporting goods store in Jacksonville, North Carolina. According to witnesses, Bishop was accompanied by a woman about his age who walked the dog as he shopped. The woman's identity has never been determined.

On March 18, a more incriminating piece of evidence turned up in Great Smoky Mountains National Park. According to the GSMNP incident report, Roy Owenby, a resident of Elkmont[3], reported that a rust-colored station wagon, a Chevrolet, had been parked near the Jakes Creek trailhead for nearly two weeks. Early that afternoon, Ranger C.E. Hinrichs arrived to investigate. Hinrichs inspected the interior of the locked vehicle through the windows and noted nothing out of the ordinary.

Then he checked the Maryland license plate and called the numbers into dispatch. Within a few seconds, he received an urgent response: the car belonged to murder suspect William Bradford Bishop Jr. The dispatcher then called the Knoxville office of the FBI, and just over two hours later, 10 federal agents arrived on the scene.

The agents gained entry to the car and, inside, found, among other items, men's clothing, a shotgun and shells, an opened box of dog biscuits, and blankets covered in blood. Dog biscuit crumbs littered the front seat.

Ranger Hinrichs turned the investigation over to the federal agents but pledged to make Park Service personnel available to assist with whatever was needed.

The FBI agents surmised that Bishop might still be somewhere within the park, and what they needed most was trained trackers familiar with the park's rugged terrain and complex network of hiking trails, and nobody knows the park's half-million acres better than GSMNP's backcountry rangers. For the next two days, as many as 25 FBI agents, guided by a team of GSMNP trackers, performed an ever-widening grid search that radiated outward from the area surrounding Elkmont. Among the GSMNP trackers were park technicians Dwight McCarter, Jack Collier, Lennie Garver, J.R. Buchanan, and park ranger Bill Burke. Numerous tracking dogs accompanied the searchers, including two German shepherds who had been involved in the hunts for Patty Hearst and Jimmy Hoffa. Helicopters combed the area from the sky.

---

3   At that time, a collection of cottages occupied by lease-holders comprised parts of Elkmont, even though the land fell inside the national park. In 1992, the National Park Service declined to renew the leases, and ownership eventually transferred to the federal government.

Park Ranger Bill Burke, center, was part of a tracking team sent out from the Elkmont area in search of Bishop.

One of the dogs seemed to pick up Bishop's trail and led to the front porch of one of the Elkmont cottages. The dutiful dog could not be pulled from the scene until his handlers had gotten inside and searched the dwelling. The search turned up nothing, and torrential rains soon set in, obscuring whatever clues might have remained from Bishop's movement through the park.

On March 20, the park closed the backcountry and began interviewing hikers as they emerged from the woods. Several promising leads began to surface from the hikers and other park visitors, and for a time it appeared that the illusive Bishop was everywhere at once.

Someone reported seeing a man matching Bishop's description walking along the road toward Gatlinburg. Another reported seeing the suspect wearing a backpack and walking along Little River Road a half-mile west of Sugarlands Visitor Center. A group of Boy Scouts from Texas reported that they had encountered a couple from Ohio, identified only as Mike and Betty, who claimed that they had been joined in camp by a man dressed in city clothes and shoes and carrying a duffel bag and tent.

Searchers found tracks in the mud, made by soles with no tread (street shoes), near Double Spring Gap Shelter. Another reported sighting came in from near Pittman Center and yet another from Cades Cove, near the Primitive Baptist Church. The man in the cove, who allegedly exhibited strange behavior, wore a dirty checked flannel shirt and blue jeans, and had dyed black hair. A man fitting Bishop's description and driving a small foreign car entered the Qualla Grocery in Cherokee.

Another man who looked like Bishop allegedly tried to swap a loaded .38 caliber Colt pistol for a .357 Magnum—a much more powerful weapon—at a gun shop in the small, sleepy town of Spindale, North Carolina. According to the shop owner, the man had identified himself as a U.S. State Department employee and presented his official ID card.

Law enforcement officials diligently pursued every lead, but, in the end, none of them led to their fugitive. Just after 5 p.m. on Saturday, March 20, park officials called off the search and reopened the backcountry. Bishop most likely was out there somewhere, but he apparently wasn't in the park. At least he wasn't *alive* and in the park. A few members of the law-enforcement community believed that Bishop, who had left home with a loaded handgun, had wandered into the backcountry and shot himself.

By then, his supply of tranquilizers had probably run out. The withdrawal symptoms—among them heightened anxiety and deepening depression—combined with whatever degree of remorse and shame Bishop experienced over what he allegedly had done to his family, just might have pushed him over the edge. If he had committed the final desperate act off trail and in a remote section of the half-million acre park, rangers and park visitors might never discover his body. Over the years, numerous individuals have vanished in the park, never to be found, including Dennis Martin (1969), Trenny Gibson (1976), and Derek Lueking (2012).

But FBI profilers had cast Bishop as a different type of fellow, one who would run until he was caught. Bishop, with his fluency in several languages and knowledge of cultures around the world, clearly was an international flight risk. Airport security, as comparatively lax as it was back in 1976, had likely been alerted and would have nailed him at the gate, had he proffered his official diplomatic passport. But Bishop was also resourceful enough to have altered his appearance and crafted bogus identification documents. All he had to do was make his way to an airport, purchase a ticket, and climb on board.

In the months and years following the murders, Bishop's alleged crime and flight from justice prompted extensive media coverage across the United States and around the world. Indeed, hundreds—perhaps thousands—of articles have been published on the murders, but one of the more recent, extensive, and thoughtful appears in the May-June 2013 edition of *Bethesda Magazine*.

The article, "The Man Who Got Away," by Eugene L. Meyer, presents several fresh details and a bit of reasoned speculation that suggests a potential conspiracy. According to Meyer, Maryland law enforcement officials examined the State Department's file on Bishop and found it to contain a certified letter from Albert Kenneth Bankston, a now-deceased prisoner once housed in a federal penitentiary in Illinois. The letter, addressed to Mr. Bradford Bishop Jr. at his State Department address, was dated 16 days following the murders and hinted at a murder-for-hire plot involving several other people. Among them was David Paul Allen, "who was familiar with the area where the bodies ended up," Meyer reports.

According to Meyer, in an interview with law enforcement, Allen acknowledged that he and his associates had received money to kill the family members while Bishop was away on business, though he insists that they never went through with the crime. As Meyer's reports, when law enforcement officials later returned to the State Department to reexamine the letter, it was missing, allegedly removed by an unnamed FBI agent. The letter's disappearance, along with the alleged conspiracy, creates an enticing mystery, no doubt, but ultimately it proved to be yet another dead end.

Then, Meyer reports, in 2000, 24 years after the murders, a woman in North Carolina paid $38 for a diary at a flea market purportedly belonging to Bishop and recording the events of his life between 1965 and 1971. The diary allegedly reflects an ambitious ladder climber eager to scale the State Department rungs but also beset by "accursed insomnia."

Meyer terms the diary's provenance "murky." By that time, Bishop had become something of a macabre cult figure, and the document might well have been a forgery.

More compelling, perhaps, are the numerous individuals—many of whom knew Brad Bishop personally—who have claimed to have seen him, in the flesh, in the years following the murders. Most of the sightings have occurred in Europe, a reasonable place for Bishop to wind up in his efforts to elude authorities.

In 1978, a former State Department employee who knew Bishop well reported that a bearded man who bore a striking resemblance to the fugitive was following her in Stockholm, Sweden. A year later, in Sorrento, Italy, another former coworker stepped up to a public urinal, turned to look at the man standing beside him, and recognized a bearded Brad Bishop.

According to Meyer and other sources, the man said, "You're Brad Bishop, aren't you?" Bishop, or his *doppelganger*, reportedly began trembling and fled, muttering "Oh, my God, no."

Shortly after the murders, as the hunt for Bishop continued, the State Department followed official procedure for eliminating Bishop from its roster of employees. Within a month of Bishop's disappearance, the department had filled his job and stopped issuing paychecks. By the end of July, the department sent a registered letter to Bishop, presumably at his Bethesda address, ordering him to return to work or be dismissed.

According to the *Washington Post*, in February 1977, 11 months after the murders, the Bishop house went on the market and sold to a family hoping to dispel the dwelling's grim history and make a comfortable home for themselves. In July, the Bishop family possessions—including household goods, playthings, and clothes—went on the auction block. In October, GSMNP ranger Jack Collier paid $1,750 for the station wagon in which Brad Bishop had allegedly hauled his dead family members' bodies to the fiery grave in North Carolina.

Flash forward nearly 40 years. Law enforcement agencies have, as the expression goes, "long arms," but they also have even longer memories. Few who were involved in investigating the horrific 1976 Maryland crime scene or who have been part of the four-decade-long hunt to apprehend the ruthless perpetrator will ever forget the crime or Bishop's flight from justice.

In April 2014, the FBI reopened the Bishop case and added the fugitive to its 10-Most Wanted List, hoping that social media, nonexistent in 1976, might reach a global audience with information on Bishop and his alleged crime. The FBI's wanted poster features a picture of the handsome, square-jawed Bishop as he appeared in the 1970s. Forensic artist Karen T. Taylor also created an "age-progressed" bust showing what Bishop might look like today. As further inducement for people to keep their eyes peeled for the alleged mass murderer, the agency is offering up to $100,000 to anyone providing information leading to Bishop's arrest.

Bishop's countenance—in both the youthful and age-progressed forms—also appeared on John Walsh's *America's Most Wanted*, which prompt-ed a call from Scottsboro, Alabama, in 2014. An apparently homeless man who was struck and killed by a car while walking along the road in 1981 had never been identified. The Scottsboro Police Department had reopened the case and noticed that the morgue photo of the dead John Doe bore a striking resemblance to Brad Bishop. In October, the body was exhumed. The FBI compared DNA from the unidentified dead man with DNA taken from a cigarette found at the murder scene. The deceased drifter's identity remains a mystery, but the results of the DNA test were conclusive: it was not Bishop.

So the hunt continues. Law enforcement officials still believe the now-aged Bishop is alive, probably somewhere in Europe. But maybe, just maybe, they're wrong. Perhaps he never strayed more than a few miles from the station wagon he abandoned at Elkmont in March 1976.

GSMNP's vast expanse of mountainous terrain, with its countless tucks and folds, dense copses and impenetrable thickets, holds many secrets. Perhaps someday, a hiker blundering off trail through the backcountry will happen upon what's left of William Bradford Bishop, decades after the mi-crobes and scavenging animals had consumed flesh and scattered his bones, and one of the great mysteries of the 20th century will, at last, be solved.

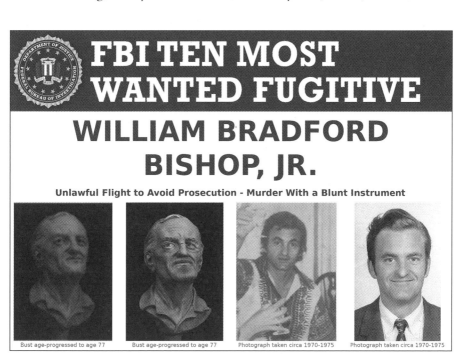

FBI's poster with age-progressed bust.

CHAPTER 12
When Bears Attack

Alpha predators still roam the forests of Great Smoky Mountains National Park. In spring 2000 a lone hiker encountered two of them in the park's backcountry near Elkmont. The outcome would mark a tragic turn in GSMNP—and National Park Service—history.

In the late morning of Sunday, May 21, 2000, as Glenda Bradley started up Little River Trail in the Elkmont section of GSMNP, nearly 84 years of National Park Service (NPS) history indicated that she had already avoided the leading cause of death in most NPS units, including GSMNP—auto accidents—when she safely exited her vehicle at the trailhead.

As for the other potentially fatal hazards lurking in the backcountry, drowning, falls, lightning strikes, and toppling trees had, over previous years, all claimed their share of victims in the parks. But, in terms of historical precedent, Bradley had little to fear from GSMNP's resident population of black bears (*Ursus americanus*).

Yes, in the years since 1916, when the NPS was established, and since GSMNP's official dedication in 1934, black bears had crashed countless picnics, shredded numerous tents, and unnerved scores of backpackers bearing loads of food, but the worst outcomes of those encounters had involved damaged equipment and the occasional painful, but nonlethal, scratch or bite.

Such injuries were all too common in the 1950s, when bear management policies were yet a bit lax and feeding the animals—or watching them feed (often on garbage)—was regarded as a key element of the Smoky Mountain experience.[1]

In 1976 GSMNP began implementing a comprehensive, science-based strategy for managing the park's bear population, and the policy has been enhanced and strengthened over the years since. Ironically, the rigidly enforced policy is aimed chiefly at managing the behavior of humans.

In many, if not most, cases of personal injury, the victims had only themselves to blame for the attacks, which often resulted after they had crowded too closely around bears to take pictures or had proffered cookies, candy bars, and other unhealthful treats to panhandling animals that occasionally grew testy when the handouts stopped.[2,3]

In some cases, the offenders themselves escaped without incident, while other park visitors were later molested by bears that had received offerings of sugary, store-bought foods and, as a result, had lost their natural fear of humans. Such behavior may have contributed to the outcome that awaited Bradley.

The notoriously territorial and unpredictable grizzly bear (*Ursus arctos horribilis*), which can weigh 800 pounds or more and stand over seven feet tall when erect, had claimed numerous victims in the Western parks, beginning in 1916 with the mauling death of Frank Welch, 61, a government employee, in Yellowstone.

But not one person had been killed in a U.S. national park by the grizzly's smaller and, by nature, more mild-mannered cousin, the black bear. Not one. (For more information on black bears, see "GSMNP's Most Iconic Species," on page 151.)

That was about to take a dramatic turn as Bradley made her way 3.5 miles along the Little River Trail toward its junction with the Goshen Prong Trail.

---

1   GSMNP documents stored at the National Archives in College Park, Maryland, include "Report[s]of Personal Injury" drafted during the 1950s. Between June and October 1956, the park filed reports on 14 injuries caused by bears. Eleven such injuries occurred the previous year between May and October. On the line "Cause of Accident," most reports note that the victim was "scratched" or "bitten" by a bear. In many cases, the injured parties had been feeding bears through open car windows prior to the incidents.

2   A typical black bear's diet in nature is 85 percent plant material, while animal and insect protein makes up most of the rest.

3   It is a violation of park policy to willfully approach within 50 yards of a bear, or any distance that disturbs or displaces the animal. It is also illegal to intentionally feed a bear or any other wildlife species in the park. Violations of these regulations can result in fines and arrests.

GSMNP'S MOST ICONIC SPECIES

The black bear, *Ursus americanus*, has come to symbolize the Great Smoky Mountain region, and an image of a bear paw is incorporated into the logo of Great Smoky Mountains Association, publisher of this book.

Black bears are the smallest and most widely distributed bears in North America. Average weight for males is about 250 pounds, while females average just under half that weight.

The sow that attacked and killed Glenda Bradley in the Elkmont section of the park in May 2000 weighed 111 pounds but was determined to be undernourished by the University of Tennessee College of Veterinary Medicine, which performed the necropsy on the animal after it had been killed by park rangers.

As of this writing, there are about 1,600 black bears in GSMNP, about two bears per square mile, the largest population on record.

Black bears are true omnivores, meaning they will eat just about anything that provides nutrients, including fruits, berries, grasses, buds, grubs, insects, fish, and meat, but plant material comprises 85 percent of the bears' natural diet.

Given the opportunity, black bears will also avidly consume calorie-dense and often sugar-laden human foods, but access to such food products is harmful to bears' health and may also condition them to associate humans with food. As a result, bears can lose their natural fear of people and become aggressive or engage in panhandling behavior.

Bears can live beyond 15 years, but the life-expectancy of bears fed on human food is about half that length.

Contrary to popular belief, black bears in GSMNP do not hibernate through the winter. They do spend longer periods of time in their dens during cold weather but may stir and emerge for a look around quite frequently.

Black bears mate in mid-summer, and females deliver their young in January or February, during the denning season. Cubs are typically born in pairs and weigh only ounces at birth. The cubs remain with their mothers for about 18 months.

With some 1,600 black bears sharing Great Smoky Mountains National Park with 11 million annual human visitors, it's something of a miracle that direct conflicts are so rare.

Bradley, 50, an avid hiker and respected teacher at Jones Cove Elementary School in Cosby, Tennessee, had entered the park at about 11:30 a.m. with her ex-husband Ralph Hill, 52, also of Cosby. The two had divorced in the fall of 1999, after less than a year of marriage, but, according to Park Service interviews with Hill and Bradley's family members, the two had remained on good terms and continued their relationship, though they maintained separate households.

At about 1 p.m., near the junction of the Huskey Gap and Little River trails, about 2.5 miles from where they had left their vehicle, the couple had parted. While Hill fished the river, Bradley continued along the foot path toward the metal bridge that spans the Little River near the junction of the Goshen Prong and Little River trails. Bradley and Hill had planned to meet back on the Little River Trail, where they had split up, between 2:30 and 3 p.m.

Evidence in the official incident report indicates that bears had been unusually active in the area over the previous days, in particular an adult female and a yearling female. Between Thursday, May 18, and Sunday, May 21, several groups of backcountry visitors reported encountering the bears, and all encounters occurred within a mile of the metal bridge.

On May 18, about 3 p.m., a group of soil scientists taking samples encountered the two bears on Little River Trail between Huskey Gap and Goshen Prong. When the adult bear became aware of the group's presence, according to witnesses, she charged the lead hiker. The group responded by backing away, but the sow continued to advance toward them, maintaining a distance of about 20 feet.

At that point, witnesses noted the presence of a yearling off the trail to the group's right. Once cub and sow were reunited, witnesses report the sow's intimidating behavior began to ease. To drive away the bears, the group threw rocks and banged shovels, which seemed to have little effect. The bears left the area on their own accord about five minutes later.

Wildlife biologists will tell you that a sow separated from her cub by a group of humans would naturally resort to intimidating behavior; what may have seemed a bit unnatural was the bears' indifference to the hurtling rocks and banging shovels.

On the following day, Friday, May 19, several members of the Middle Tennessee Fly Fishers Association occupied Backcountry Campsite 24, less than a half a mile southeast of the bridge.

Late in the afternoon, one group member encountered the sow and yearling about a quarter mile from the campsite. The animals were about 10 feet away, and the man slowly backtracked, creating a distance of about 100 feet between himself and the bears. The sow stepped onto the trail and, for a time, began to follow him. Eventually, the fisherman gave the bears a wide berth and bushwhacked around them back toward Campsite 24.

According to another member of the group, an adult bear arrived at the campsite a short time later, just before dinner, and moved through the collection of tents. Someone noted the presence of a cub. One group member reports being awakened the following morning, Saturday, May 20, at 7:30 a.m. by the sounds of cook pots banging together (a common tactic for driving away bears), but the bear then present in the camp—and whose behavior the witness describes as "bold"—seemed little phased by the racket and remained in the camp for another three hours, eventually entering a tent and gaining access to some of the group's food supplies.

It's uncertain whether this was the same sow spotted earlier or a different adult bear, but the presence of a yearling suggests the former. The group appointed look-outs to watch for the bears' return while the others packed up their gear, and they soon abandoned the campsite.

Representatives of the group later reported the bear activity to the ranger station at Elkmont Campground. A communications specialist received the report and routed it to the park's wildlife division. Other, more disturbing, reports would follow the next afternoon, but, sadly, not in time to change the fate that awaited Bradley.

On the morning of Sunday, May 21, a scouting troop from Hattiesburg, Mississippi, packed up and departed Backcountry Campsite 23, on Goshen Prong Trail about 1.5 miles southwest of the junction with Little River Trail, en route to Campsite 24, their destination for the night. The group had lunch on the metal bridge spanning Little River before continuing on, arriving at the campsite at about 1 p.m. According to a witness with the group, shortly after they arrived, the adult female entered and explored the camp, while the yearling remained on the periphery. The bears soon moved on, and the scouts began setting up their tents. At the time, according to witnesses, the bears seemed more curious—or perhaps hungry—than menacing.

Through the afternoon, several members of the Knoxville chapter of Trout Unlimited conducted water-quality sampling near the metal bridge. The group did not encounter any bears, but they did meet and talk briefly with a lone middle-aged female hiker sometime about 3 p.m. One in the group described her as tanned, with short hair, and carrying a daypack. He noted that she was smiling and "did not appear to be upset or frightened." The group and the hiker, Glenda Bradley, exchanged pleasantries before Bradley continued along the trail, and the Trout Unlimited group resumed collecting water samples. They would be the last people to see Glenda Bradley alive.

Not long after, one of the group members, positioned in the creek about 250 feet downstream (north) of the metal bridge, heard what he described as a "screeching sound"—like the sound "of a muffled whip-poor-will." Another in the group likewise reported hearing a series of four shrill screams, spaced about 10-15 seconds apart. He described them as the sounds of kids playing in a creek and splashing cold water on each other. A light rainfall gained intensity, and henceforth all the men could hear was the sound of the pounding rain and the roar of the creek. While there's no way to accurately trace the source of the sounds, their timing may be relevant, particularly in view of the events that followed.

Sometime after 3 p.m., the group encountered Bradley's partner, Ralph Hill. Hill had waited for Bradley at their appointed rendezvous point, near the junction of the Huskey Gap and Little River trails, until 2:45 p.m. When Bradley failed to arrive, he had begun hiking toward her, heading southeast along Little River Trail. He encountered the Trout Unlimited team just north of the bridge.

According to members of the group, they briefly discussed fishing with Hill before Hill asked if anyone had seen a woman on the trail. Yes, they told him, they had recently encountered a lone female hiker a short distance up the trail. Hill left the group and continued on toward the trail junction and bridge. Though Hill could not have known it at the time, as he moved south along the trail, Bradley was likely locked in a desperate struggle for survival only a few hundred yards away. Or, perhaps, the struggle had already ended.

Hill continued southeast along Little River Trail, past the junction with the Goshen Prong Trail, toward Campsite 24. While en route, he encountered two hikers who informed him that they had not seen a lone female hiker on the trail. With this information, Hill decided to reverse course and head back toward the trail junction and bridge.

Just before Hill reached the bridge, at about 4 p.m., an angler from Newport, Tennessee, arrived at the site and slid down the bank to a gravel bar to retrieve the hiking shoes he had deposited there earlier in the day after donning his waders. As he did, he noticed a black daypack lying on the rocks, a few feet from the southeast corner of the bridge. The pack appeared to be in good condition, and its position suggested that someone may have tossed it from the top of the metal structure.

A few minutes later, as the fisherman changed into his boots, Ralph Hill approached and asked if the fisherman had seen a woman hiking alone. No, he said, but he directed Hill's attention to the abandoned pack. Hill raced to the pack, opened it, inspected the contents, and quickly realized that the pack was Bradley's.[4]

According to the fisherman, on examining the pack and its contents, Hill suddenly seemed stunned, alarmed. Hill mentioned that he and the woman were supposed to have met over an hour earlier and asked the fisherman to keep his eye out for the woman as he hiked out toward the trailhead.

---

4   According to GSMNP investigators, Bradley's pack contained 2 candy bars and 5 packages of peanut butter crackers. The food items were unopened and had not been disturbed by the bears.

If the fisherman did not encounter her, Hill urged him to alert park rangers. The fisherman would comply, after he had hiked the 3.5 miles to Elkmont Campground.

A short time later, a day hiker from Wisconsin arrived at the bridge to snap some photographs. At some point, he peered northeast, and saw a man, Hill, standing at the junction of the Little River and Goshen Prong trails. The hiker approached and spoke with Hill, whom he described as clearly "worried." The hiker left Hill and continued along the Little River Trail heading southeast past Campsite 24, where the scouts occupying the site reported an earlier encounter with the sow and cub.

Hill continued to search the area around the bridge, following the right riverbank downstream and, on his return, the left bank. As he re-approached the bridge, he peered across the river to his left and confronted a scene of unimaginable horror and one that resolved the mystery of his missing companion.

There, less than 200 feet away, Hill saw two bears, an adult sow and yearling, hovering over and apparently feeding on what appeared to be a lifeless human body. As he approached, he realized that the body was that of his ex-wife, Glenda Bradley.

Hill approached the bears, brandishing a large stick, hoping to drive them off, but the sow charged at him, clearly intent on protecting her prey. Unable to expel the bears on his own, Hill ran toward Campsite 24 to summon help. On the way to the site, Hill again encountered the Wisconsin hiker, who was then returning to the trailhead in Elkmont. The hiker advised Hill to return to the scene of the attack while he ran to Campsite 24, where he enlisted the help of one of the campers. The two quickly returned to assist Hill. The three pelted the bears with rocks and shouted at them, but each time they approached Bradley's body, the sow reared and charged, refusing to leave or to afford them access. Eventually, the Wisconsin hiker sped down the trail to alert park rangers.

Just before 5:30 p.m., at Elkmont Campground, Ranger Robert Harris received a report of a missing female hiker from the fisherman who had located Bradley's pack near the bridge. While en route to the location where she had last been seen, Harris encountered the Wisconsin hiker, who reported that the missing woman had been found and that she had been attacked, and likely killed, by bears. Harris arrived on the scene just before 6 p.m. and noted two bears guarding what appeared to be a lifeless body. By then, several other individuals had joined Hill in his unsuccessful attempts to drive the bears away. One of them, an emergency medical technician visiting the park, noted the extensive wounds to the body, the pallor of the skin, and the apparent absence of respiration and concluded that the woman was likely dead.

Like Hill, Ranger Harris attempted to repel the bears, but on each approach the sow reared and displayed aggression. Harris called for backup and requested that responding rangers bring a "long gun" (a rifle) to dispatch the bears.

The park employs a series of measures to contend with troublesome bears, including capture and release in a distant and more-remote section of the park. Park personnel kill bears only in extreme situations, when they're bereft of other options; the current situation, with two bears poised over the body of an apparently deceased hiker, certainly fit the requisite criteria.[5]

Harris carried his sidearm but was concerned that he would be unable to kill both bears without endangering the others present or himself. Harris also realized that, had he opted to shoot, his field of fire would have swept the Little River Trail, placing in jeopardy any hikers passing through the area.

At 6:15, Rangers Jerry Grubb and Chip Nelson arrived on the scene. Though neither carried a rifle, Grubb, who believed he saw the bears feeding on Bradley's body, advanced toward the animals and fired three rounds from his .40 caliber pistol into the sow and then sighted on the yearling and fired two more into her. The bullets from Grubb's weapon immobilized the bears, but both were still alive. Nelson then moved in and fired a total of 14 rounds into the two animals, killing both.

Whatever grim cycle of life and death that had played out in Bradley's final moments had been brought to an end by the 19 rounds fired from Grubb's and Nelson's pistols. Park Service staff then did their best to comfort a clearly distraught Hill as they escorted him from the scene. They would do likewise with Bradley's grieving family members. A team of rangers soon arrived to carry out Bradley's body, and a second team removed the bears.

As the immediate tragedy ended, a probe into what had happened—and why—was about to begin. Any death that occurs in GSMNP or in any

5   According to a 1977 report, "Black Bear Management in Great Smoky Mountains National Park," by park scientists Francis Singer and Susan Power Bratton, between 1964 and 1976, the park had captured and relocated 332 bears, an average of 28 per year, and killed 18. By contrast, according to Bill Stiver, GSMNP supervisory wildlife biologist, the park currently captures and relocates only 5-10 bears per year, as a result of improved bear-management efforts and visitor education.

NPS unit, for that matter, sets in motion an intensive and thorough investigative process that, in the case of Bradley's death, spanned nearly a year.

The park's bear management policy had evolved considerably since the 1940s and '50s, when panhandling bears were a major attraction at roadside pullouts and picnic areas and when visitors commonly rewarded the bears with handouts of cookies and candy. The park's policy would be further bolstered as a result of Bradley's death, with a primary emphasis on efforts to educate visitors. (For information on the park's ongoing efforts to improve bear management and enhance visitor education in the years since Bradley's death, see "The Park's Evolving, Proactive Approach to Bear Management," on page 170.)

Bradley's body was transported to East Tennessee State University's (ETSU) James H. Quillen College of Medicine, where forensic pathologists would perform an autopsy to determine exact cause of death. The slain bears were sent to the University of Tennessee's College of Veterinary Medicine for post-mortem examinations known as necropsies.

Ranger Steve Kloster was appointed to head the investigation. Over the course of the following days, Kloster and his colleagues would interview more than 16 individuals, including on-the-scene witnesses as well as members of Bradley's immediate family.

In August, GSMNP convened a board of inquiry to investigate the incident. On March 19, 2001, the board issued its final report, ruling Bradley's death an accident and determining that the actions of the responding rangers were appropriate, including Harris' decision not to shoot the bears while he awaited backup. The board further recommended that the park take eight specific actions to enhance visitor education and prevent the future human-bear accidents. (See "The Recommendations," on page 168.)

In her initial findings on Bradley's cause of death, Ellen Wallen, MD, an ETSU forensic pathologist, notes "major trauma" to the neck, left femur and buttocks. Of particular significance, Wallen reports that Bradley's right carotid artery and left femoral artery—two major vessels that carry large volumes of blood away from the heart—were both severed in the attack. Either wound, by itself, would have proven fatal through blood loss—or exsanguination—but combined, they would have ensured that, once Bradley had sustained the injuries, her death would have been mercifully rapid. She probably lost consciousness within seconds and expired within minutes.

The NPS investigation of the scene of Bradley's death suggests that

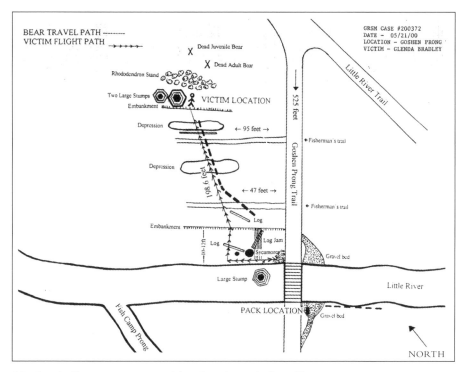

Map from incident report reconstructed from footprints and other evidence.

the victim likely was on or near the Goshen Prong bridge when the two bears approached. Based on descriptions provided by other park visitors who had earlier encountered the bears, the animals, particularly the sow, seemed to have little fear of humans and had, on occasion, displayed intimidating behavior.

When Bradley, alone at the time, saw the approach of the two animals, she did what many park visitors would have done in a similar circumstance and pulled her camera from her pack to snap pictures of the animals. According to Bill Stiver, GSMNP supervisory wildlife biologist, film taken from Bradley's camera and later developed rendered images of the two bears positioned on the trail near the bridge, only a few yards from where Bradley snapped the photos. In the images, the bears are not displaying intimidating behavior.

At some point after Bradley took the photos, the bears likely began to display more aggressive behavior, if not overt signs of predation. Bradley may initially have frozen in place, in hopes that the bears would lose interest in a seemingly inert human and move on. (For more on the involuntary

A HARDWIRED—AND ANCIENT—RESPONSE TO DANGER

What preceded Glenda Bradley's lapse into unconsciousness during the fatal bear attack of May 2000 likely involved a series of involuntary reactions and behaviors hardwired into the brains of most mammals, including humans. Those responses arise from an almond-shaped structure, known as the amygdala, part of the limbic system and positioned in the medial temporal lobe near where the spinal cord enters the brain.

Also known as the "fear hub," the amygdala activates our instinctive, autonomic physiological reactions to acute, life-threatening stress, and those reactions take several forms, all designed to enhance our chances for survival. If, for instance, an animal visually perceives a threat at a distance—say it spots a predator—the animal's first instinctive response may be to freeze to avoid drawing the predator's notice.

The autonomic nervous system facilitates the cessation of motion by slowing heart rate and respiration and causing a drop in blood pressure. If this tactic fails, and the predator spots the potential prey and begins to approach, the amygdala initiates another set of self-protective behaviors.

In 1915, Harvard physiologist Walter Bradford first described the "fight-or-flight" response, which, in times of direct threat, short-circuits the more-evolved prefrontal cortex and allows the more primitive structures in our brains to take control.

In low-stress settings, the prefrontal cortex remains in charge, allowing us to consider thoughtfully a range of responses to challenging, but not directly life-threatening, situations, say a careless driver cutting us off in traffic.

But in cases of extreme threat, including an attack by an alpha predator, our ancient brains, under the influence of the amygdala, pump the stress hormones cortisol and adrenalin into our systems and prime us to take one of two actions. One is to run away, to flee the threat to a place of safety. The second, when the first action has been precluded by circumstances—say, the predator has caught us and dragged us to the ground—is to fight to neutralize the threat.

Evidence indicates that Bradley resorted to both actions during her final moments of life and struggled heroically to survive.

animal reaction to a perceived threat to survival, see "A Hardwired—and Ancient—Response to Danger," on page 160.)

If that didn't work, Bradley may have held her ground and attempted to keep the animals at bay or drive them off by shouting or hurling rocks or sticks—appropriate responses for anyone confronted by a bear that's exhibiting aggressive behavior. It's worth noting that Bradley was an experienced hiker who had spent countless days exploring the park's trails and probably had some sense of how to react in an encounter with a bear.

But as demonstrated in other encounters with the two bears implicated in Bradley's death, the animals were not easily deterred. At this point, Bradley may have begun to experience unease, even fear. Perhaps the bears continued to approach. As they did, the initial fear may have escalated to panic, and Bradley's body responded by initiating the acute-stress, or flight-or-fight, response. It's possible, too, that Bradley began to run after she had taken the photographs, when the bears were still a distance away. We will never know.

However, clear evidence at the scene indicates that Bradley began her flight near the northwest corner of the bridge, below the embankment on the north side of the river. Distinct human footprints pressed into an area of open, moist soil clearly chart her path, and the distance between the footprints suggests the long strides consistent with someone running at a full sprint. Bradley ran parallel to the Little River for a few feet before making a sharp right-hand turn and heading north, away from the bridge and moving nearly parallel to the Goshen Prong Trail. The tracks of the bears, also pressed into the soft soil, reveal a path that converged with and then moved in parallel with that of the victim. After running approximately 200 feet, as Bradley struggled to clear a shallow rise, the bears made their attack.

Just as Bradley's instinctive brain had commanded her actions, the bears' lethal attack was likewise guided by instinctive behavior honed over many thousands of years of evolution. While Bradley's instincts prompted a response aimed at ensuring her survival, the bears, following their own predatory urges, were doing the same, allowing them to overpower and ultimately kill a source of food.

The autopsy suggests that when Bradley's flight failed to secure her safety, she shifted tactics and fought fiercely against the attacking bears. The autopsy notes that "defensive type wounds were observed on the hands." But in the end, Bradley's efforts to fight off her attackers failed, and she soon

DEATH BY ALPHA PREDATOR IS STILL A REALITY IN TODAY'S WORLD

When Ralph Hill first saw the two bears, an adult sow and female yearling, poised over the lifeless body of his ex-wife, Glenda Bradley, he was witnessing a macabre relationship between predator and prey that traces to the days of our most ancient ancestors.

Millennia ago, before humans developed the defensive weapons, social behaviors, and evasive tactics necessary to avoid, or fend off, attacks by menacing predators, our species occupied a slot midway down the food chain.

As our ancestors devised ever more sophisticated tools that provided for self-defense as well as the harvest of wild meat—advancing from stones and sticks to clubs to spears to bows and arrows and finally to firearms—our species ascended toward the pinnacle of the food chain, a position occupied by alpha, or apex, predators. There, for the most part, our species remains, though in the world's wild, untamed regions, the hierarchy can tip in favor of the beasts that inhabit the forests, jungles, rivers, and oceans, and humans continue to become their prey.

Though death by alpha predators—including, but not limited to, bears, crocodiles and related species, large cats, and sharks—is still relatively rare in richer and more advanced nations, it remains a reality of life for humans living in more primitive cultures that occupy regions that remain largely undeveloped. According to the worldwide database CrocBITE, crocodilian attacks cause about 1,000 human deaths per year, mainly in Africa (home to the Nile croc, *Crocodylus niloticus*) and the Indo-Pacific (home to the saltwater croc, *Crocodylus porosus*).

But as Bradley's death proves, alpha predators do, on occasion, continue to kill humans in North America. According to "Fatal Attacks by American Black Bear on People: 1900–2009," an article that appeared in the *Journal of Wildlife Management* in May 2011, 63 people were killed by noncaptive black bears between 1900–2009, but 78 percent of them occurred in Canada and Alaska.

Bradley's death conforms to several key findings presented in the report: May, when Bradley was killed, is the second most deadly month for bear attacks, behind August. The majority of victims (69 percent) were alone at the time of the attack, as was Bradley. And 70 percent of the attacks took place during the daytime. Bradley was killed mid-afternoon.

And, as the report makes clear, nearly 90 percent of fatal black bear attacks were predatory, vs. defensive, which describes the circumstances of Bradley's death. The report indicates further that fatal black bear attacks have been increasing over time, with 86 percent of the fatalities occurring between 1960 and 2009. Stephen Herrero and his coauthors speculate that the rise in fatal bear attacks has resulted from the increase in both human and bear populations and an increase in the numbers of individuals pursuing recreation in established black bear habitat, including GSMNP.

GSMNP's black bear population now stands at between 1,500 and 1,600 animals, two bears per square mile, the largest ever recorded, and the number of annual park visits has approached or exceeded 10 million for more than a decade, making GSMNP the most visited U.S. national park.

According to Herrero's report, in about 30 percent of fatal attacks, health problems may have contributed to the bears' predatory behavior. Indeed, food-stressed bears may be particularly willing to take the risks associated with "attempted predation." The necropsy reports on the two bears that attacked and killed Bradley noted that both animals were undernourished.

sustained the wounds that would quickly have killed her.

Bradley's untimely death was, based on the park's extensive investigation and that of the board of inquiry, a tragic event that occurred at the convergence of a number of contributing factors, some alterable, some not.

First, as the necropsy reports concluded, the bears were both malnourished, which likely contributed to their aggression in seeking and securing a source of food. The park's resource managers can, and do, monitor the wild food reserves available to bears and other wildlife species, but beyond providing a protected environment for the animals to inhabit and doing all they can to ensure visitor safety, managers rarely play a direct hand in the life-and-death struggles that occur among animals in the wild. A notable exception is the eradication of invasive—and often destructive—nonnative species.[6]

While the Appalachian Bear Rescue, located in Townsend, Tennessee, nurses orphaned, injured, and malnourished bears back to health, the Park Service does not directly undertake that role.

Second, though as many as a dozen people were within a mile of the attack site at the time of Bradley's death, she was hiking alone and was alone at the time of her death. Had she been accompanied by even one other person, the bears may have decided that an attack—daring and atypical under normal circumstances—was not worth the risk.

The aggression displayed by the sow and yearling that killed Bradley reflected the behavior of animals that had lost their natural fear of humans and/or that had learned to associate humans with the reward of food.

According to the necropsy reports, the two bears implicated in Bradley's death had both previously been captured to serve as research animals for the University of Tennessee's Department of Forestry, Wildlife, and Fisheries. The adult was ear-tagged and tattooed under the upper lip with the number 1514. The yearling was tattooed on the upper lip with the number 350.[7]

But bears captured and tagged as part of research projects—disruptive and even traumatic events for the captured animals—nearly always emerge from those encounters with a heightened—not diminished—fear of humans. Intimidating and panhandling behavior on the part of the parks' bears nearly always traces to transgressions or missteps on the part of park visitors.

"Most of the unfortunate incidents with black bears in the park are the result of human error in terms of food issues and in human reactions in the presence of the animals," says Mike Pelton, professor emeritus of the University of Tennessee's Department of Forestry, Wildlife, and Fisheries. In 1968, under Pelton's leadership, UT launched the longest continuous bear research project in the world, and most of that research was conducted on GSMNP bears.

While some of those transgressions are overt—directly feeding bears or allowing them to pilfer the contents of coolers, grocery bags, or trash

---

6   Among them is the Russian wild boar, a prolific and highly destructive species that entered and began spreading through the park in the early 20th century, after escaping from a hunting preserve on Hooper Bald in North Carolina. Rangers continue to cull the hogs from park lands.

7   University of Tennessee's Department of Forestry, Wildlife, and Fisheries began its research on bears in GSMNP in 1968. Over its history, the project has amassed records on more than 2,500 captures of approximately 1,500 individual bears in the park and has produced countless valuable research findings.

cans—others are less intentional, but, in the end, no less harmful. Indeed, bears that confine themselves to the backcountry—which includes the two bears implicated in Bradley's death—can also become habituated to humans if backcountry visitors fail to manage their food supplies properly. We know, for

When bears become habituated to human-related food, they may lose their natural fears of humans and become more dangerous.

instance, that the sow and yearling were able to access food in at least one of the backcountry campsites prior to the attack.

According to the 1977 report "Black Bear Management in Great Smoky Mountains National Park," by GSMNP scientists Francis Singer and Susan Power Bratton, from 1973 to 1976, park resource managers noted a shift from bear-related incidents occurring primarily in the frontcountry (i.e., in campgrounds, picnic areas, and along roads) to increased incidents occurring in the park's backcountry, as backpacking gained popularity and overnight backcountry use increased.

GSMNP has equipped all backcountry campsites—including shelters along the Appalachian Trail—with cable systems for hanging packs and food supplies beyond the reach of marauding bears. But, if campers fail to use these devices, and bears gain access to the relatively calorie-dense offerings carried by most backpackers, the reward of easily gained sustenance can quickly transform a bear from natural forager to camp raider.

Campers should realize that food items on the evening menu or stored in packs can entice bears from more than a mile away. The black bear has one of the keenest senses of smell in the terrestrial animal kingdom, much greater than that of the bloodhounds that track missing persons. Bears with their natural aversion to humans intact will likely remain at a distance; those that have become habituated may well intrude on a camp expecting to acquire food.

Third, there may have been an evolutionary flaw in Bradley's response to the perceived threat posed by the bears. Her flight, at a full sprint, may in fact have triggered in the animals a natural reaction to give chase. And Bradley's decision to photograph the bears may also have prompted an aggressive response, particularly if her camera's flash unit had fired when she took the pictures.

In "Black Bear Aggression in the Backcountry of Yosemite National Park," a paper from the Sixth International Conference on Bear Research and Management, 1983, authors Bruce C. Hastings *et al.* suggest that "photographing bears and running away from bears were more likely to precede bear aggression than other specific human behaviors."

In a footrace with a predatory bear, humans are assured of losing. Consider that black bears can travel as fast as 35 miles per hour over short distances. Granted, humans *can* achieve speeds of 40 miles per hour over a very short distance, but we're talking elite, Olympic-class sprinters moving along groomed tracks, not middle-aged women running off-trail through rugged terrain.

The paper further reports that "being unaggressive toward bears may increase the likelihood of precipitating bear aggression."

Again, we will never know for certain the specific set of events and actions that precipitated the deadly attack on Bradley, but, based on the paper's finding, a more aggressive and forceful response to the approaching animals might have increased Bradley's chances of survival.

"People often forget that bears are the park's largest predators," says Stiver. "When we see them along the side of the road eating acorns, they may seem docile, but they're wild animals whose behavior is often unpredictable."

According to Stiver, once a black bear becomes predatory toward a human, the animal can be relentless in pursuing its prey. "A predatory black bear can be very persistent," he says. "They'll repeatedly approach and try to test you, and you need to be equally aggressive in your response to them." (For information on proper ways to respond in the presence of a bear, see "Rules of Engagement," on page 167.)

Glenda Bradley's death—specifically, the means of her death—ranks among the more profoundly tragic events in the history of GSMNP, and it deprived Jones Cove Elementary School of an accomplished teacher and the Bradley family of a beloved sister, daughter, aunt, and mother. But rather than suggest that death by alpha predator in the park is in any way probable or likely, Bradley's death should indicate that it is merely possible. And in that sense, context and perspective are warranted.

Sixty-three people were killed by non-captive black bears in North America between 1900 and 2009, but only 18 of them occurred in the contiguous 48 states. The rest occurred in Canada and Alaska.[8] Some 16,121 persons were murdered in the United States in 2013 alone, and more than 90 people die annually from allergic reactions to insect stings, according to the Centers for Disease Control and Prevention.

Between 1931 and 2013, 470 persons perished in GSMNP, more than half of them (287) from motor vehicle accidents, plane crashes, and drownings. Meanwhile, down toward the very bottom of the list of death by cause, are the fatal events least likely to occur: non-lightning electrocution, sudden infant death syndrome, insect stings, aspiration (choking to death), and predator attack. The number of deaths resulting from each is the same: one.

And that perspective should be part of the mindset of every park visitor who probes the backcountry. Many, if not most, hikers who observe bears while exploring the park's trails, cherish the encounter. And while there's no reason to fear *Ursus americanus*, there is ample reason to educate ourselves about the animals' behavior and to respect them and afford them the space they need to remain creatures of the wild.

....

Rules of Engagement: What to Do If You Encounter a Black Bear[9]
Bears in GSMNP are wild, and their behavior can be unpredictable. Although extremely rare, attacks on humans have occurred, inflicting serious injuries and, in the case of Glenda Bradley, death. Treat bear encounters with extreme caution.
If you see a bear:
> Remain watchful.
> Do not approach it.
> Do not allow the bear to approach you.

If your presence causes the bear to change its behavior (for example, it stops feeding, changes its travel direction, watches you, etc.) you are too close.

---

8   According to "Fatal Attacks by American Black Bear on People: 1900–2009," by Stephen Herrero *et al.* The article appeared in the *Journal of Wildlife Management* in May 2011.

9   From GSMNP's website: https://www.nps.gov/grsm/learn/nature/black-bears.htm

Being too close may promote aggressive behavior from the bear such as running toward you, making loud noises, or swatting the ground. The bear is demanding more space. Don't run, but slowly back away, watching the bear. Increase the distance between you and the bear. The bear will probably do the same.

If a bear persistently follows or approaches you, without vocalizing, or paw swatting:

Change your direction.

If the bear continues to follow you, stand your ground.

If the bear gets closer, talk loudly or shout at it.

Act aggressively to intimidate the bear.

Act together as a group if you have companions. Make yourselves look as large as possible.

Throw nonfood objects such as rocks at the bear.

Use a deterrent such as a stout stick.

Don't run and don't turn away from the bear.

Don't leave food for the bear; this encourages further problems.

If the bear's behavior indicates that it is after your food and you are physically attacked:

Separate yourself from the food.

Slowly back away.

If the bear shows no interest in your food and you are physically attacked, the bear may consider you as prey:

Fight back aggressively with any available object.

Do not play dead.

Help protect others by reporting all bear incidents to a park ranger immediately. Above all, keep your distance from bears.

....

The Recommendations

In August 2000, GSMNP convened a board of inquiry to investigate the fatal bear mauling of Glenda Bradley in the Elkmont section of the park in May of that year. The board released its final report in March 2001, and it includes the following recommendations to the GSMNP management staff. In the years since, the park has taken steps to implement the board's recommendations.

The recommendations:

1. The GSMNP Black Bear Management Guideline, February 1993, should be revised and updated. While no major changes are required, the guideline has become dated. Information and insight gained from the Bradley fatality, the first in the history of the National Park Service, would be a useful addition to the handbook.

2. The GSMNP Trail Map should be revised. The "Bears and You" section should include advice and recommendations of what to do if encountered by a bear. More attention should be given to evaluation of a bear's behavior during an encounter, with guidance for the proper response.

3. Backcountry signs should be revised to include the potential for bear encounters. These signs advise visitors of the potential danger of bears. The bear warning sign has been revised to include language that bear attacks on humans have occurred.

4. The ranger division should devote a segment of its annual law enforcement training to problem bear management. Wildlife staff should review the protocols for identifying and managing recurring problem bear behavior.

5. The GSMNP Bear Management Report has been revised and reaffirmed. The procedure for reporting after-hour/weekend observations has been reaffirmed to ensure that bear reports are received by the appropriate resource management staff in a timely manner.

6. The Resources Management and Science Division should identify one person who will be assigned as the point of contact for problem bear reports. This employee will coordinate his or her response with the wildlife biologist and the ranger staff.

7. Other Park information distributed in visitor centers, the communications center, and by Resource Education personnel should be modified to include the lessons learned from this tragedy [the fatal attack on Glenda Bradley]. Written materials should describe the appropriate measures to take when encountered by a bear. Research by Professor Steve Herrero and others clearly shows that, during an encounter, people should respond according to specific types of bear behavior. More attention should be given to evaluation of a bear's behavior during an encounter, with guidance for the proper visitor response.

8. The Resource Management and Science Division should resume sponsorship of an annual bear management workshop in the spring of the

year. Employees from all operating divisions would benefit from open discussion of bear management issues as bears emerge from their dens concurrent with the arrival of spring break campers and backpackers.

The members of the Board of Inquiry:
Jason Houck (chair), GSMNP Chief Ranger
Lance Lewis, GSMNP Occupational Health and Safety Manager
Reed Detring, Superintendent, Big South Fork National Recreation Area
Dr. Mike Pelton, Professor Emeritus, University of Tennessee

....

The Park's Evolving, Proactive Approach to Bear Management
In the years since the fatal attack on Glenda Bradley in 2000, GSMNP has engaged in a continuing effort to enhance management of its increasing population of black bears, educate visitors, and reduce the likelihood of future attacks. Many of those efforts are grounded in the growing body of scientific research on the American black bear and its behavior.

The following provides information on key elements of the park's ongoing bear management program.

Earlier closing times for park picnic areas during summer. In the past, picnic areas remained open until dark, the time when bears become most active. Now, during summertime, picnic areas close at 8 pm, while it's still light, and the park has assigned maintenance personnel to the evening shift to ensure that these areas are cleaned and free of food waste.

Visitor education. Annually GSMNP logs about 10 million visits, the most of any national park, and these visitors often arrive with little knowledge about bear behavior or how to respond in the event of an encounter.

"We've made significant strides in educating visitors about bears, but one of our biggest challenges results from the sheer number of people who come to the park," says Bill Stiver, GSMNP supervisory wildlife biologist. As Stiver points out, the park does not have entrance stations, which, in other parks, allow staff to interact one-on-one with visitors and provide important information on appropriate wildlife viewing and interaction.

Instead, Stiver and his staff are taking the message directly to visitors through educational signage posted throughout the park (even in bathroom stalls) and social media. GSMNP's homepage (www.nps.gov/grsm/index.htm) provides links to the park's Facebook page (www.facebook.com/GreatSmokyMountainsNPS) and Twitter feeds (twitter.com/GreatSmokyNPS).

The short video "Day Hiking and Wildlife" (posted on YouTube) features now-retired supervisory wildlife biologist Kim Delozier explaining appropriate ways to view park wildlife. In the video, Delozier illustrates a 50-yard distance for safely observing bears. Failure to maintain a 50-yard distance from park wildlife is a federal offense. (You can view the video here: www.youtube.com/watch?v=qZ9GzIMGRMw&feature=youtu.be)

BEARS NEED PRIVACY, TOO!

DO YOU MIND?

View and photograph bears from a distance of at least 50 yards. Disturbing or approaching wildlife is a federal offense.

Reaching the park's millions of visitors with its critical messages can be challenging because the park has no entrance stations. This sign was designed for park restrooms, a place where nearly all visitors do stop.

Positive identification through DNA. When bear incidents occur in the park—including relatively rare attacks on humans—Stiver and his staff rely on scientific tools to help identify bears responsible for the incident. Among those tools is DNA sampling of evidence left behind, including bear saliva. According to Stiver, in an average year, 1 to 2 bears that have displayed overt aggression or predatory behavior toward humans must be euthanized, and DNA testing will help accurately identify the offending animals.

Aversive conditioning techniques. Stiver and his staff are conducting research on various measures to deter and drive off bears that have begun to exhibit habituation toward humans. A bear entering a crowded picnic area and feeding on human food or garbage would be a case in point. Among the more promising tools are paint-ball guns similar to those used by recreationists.

"The paintballs can accurately travel a relatively long distance, and the guns can fire multiple shots quickly," says Stiver. It's important to note that, while the paintballs do not harm the bears, they do frighten them. If the aversive conditioning is successful, the animals will learn to associate the act of approaching humans with the unpleasant experience of being pelted with paintballs. Over recent years, the park has secured funding to host numerous workshops on black bear aversive conditioning.

Tracking problem bears. GSMNP's nuisance bears often make forays beyond park boundaries and enter gateway communities, where they gain access to human food and garbage. GPS-equipped radio collars allow Stiver and his staff to track the movement of these troublesome bears and, in the process, to identify precisely where the animals are able to find food.

Equipped with the locations provided by the GPS collars, Stiver and his team can identify where within the park the bears may gain access to food or waste. When the GPS collars indicate that bears have located a food source outside the park, Stiver and his staff work with community leaders and business managers to secure these locations.

The GPS tracking project will run through 2018, and ultimately several dozen nuisance bears will be captured, anesthetized, and outfitted with the collars before being released.

Capture and relocation. When less intrusive measures fail to recondition a problem bear to fear and avoid humans, Stiver and his team capture them and release them, either into another area of the park or, with permission, into other managed areas, including national and state forests and other national parks. Because bears have strong homing instincts, captured bears are released at least 40 air miles from where they were captured.

The success of the park's bear management policies and visitor education has significantly reduced the need to capture and relocate problem bears. Between 1964 and 1976, the park captured and relocated an average of 28 bears per year. By contrast, according to Stiver, that number has been reduced to an average of 11 relocations per year, despite a bear population that has more than tripled since the 1970s.

Improved management of food waste. Working with a North Carolina-based product fabricator, the park developed a bear-proof dumpster that can withstand the repeated abuse that results when the large containers are emptied into a garbage truck.

The park has also provided cables at all backcountry campsites to safely hang and store food beyond the reach of bears and other scavenging animals. To date, the cables, when used correctly, have yet to be breached by a black bear.

CHAPTER 13
Deadly Derecho

One of the most violent and deadly storms ever to strike Great Smoky Mountains National Park (GSMNP) arrived on July 5, 2012, as visitor numbers peaked, campgrounds were filled to capacity, and thousands of vehicles coursed along park roads. Ultimately, the storm ravaged the park's extreme western region, causing fatalities and becoming a breaking story in the national news. With radios knocked out of service, limited phone coverage, and main roads choked off by fallen trees, the Park Service and its partnering agencies got creative in mobilizing a response.

July 5, 2012, arrived as most mid-summer days do in Great Smoky Mountains National Park, with the predawn cool giving way to steadily rising heat and humidity. Through the morning hours and into the early afternoon, the summer sun occasionally peeked out from behind a benign overcast, seemingly ideal weather conditions for spending a day in the mountains—provided park visitors didn't mind the crowds.

"The week of the July 4 holiday is typically one of the busiest weeks of the year in the park, if not the busiest," says Clayton Jordan, GSMNP chief ranger. Many visitors who had occupied sites in park campgrounds or rented cabins in Gatlinburg or Townsend in advance of the holiday planned to stay on through the weekend.

The Cades Cove Campground, the park's largest with 159 sites, was booked full, as were the campgrounds at Abrams Creek, Elkmont, and Smokemont. A steady influx of cars filled the parking lot in front of the

Cades Cove ranger station, and scores of other vehicles inched along the 11-mile Loop Road past preserved historic cabins and open meadows dotted with grazing deer.

Worrisome Weather

The week had begun with a heat wave, with temperatures soaring to a record 105 degrees in Knoxville on Sunday, July 1, and had hit 79 degrees at Le Conte Lodge for three days in a row. By July 4, temperatures had begun to moderate. The high in Cades Cove topped out at 87 degrees, and the high there the next day wouldn't make it out of the 70s.

By early afternoon on July 5, meteorologist Mary Black's colleagues at the National Weather Service (NWS) office in Morristown, Tennessee, were positioned at their computers, busily tracking the radar images of a system that had begun the night before as a collection of pop-up thunderstorms between the Ohio River Valley and the Great Lakes region. Though harmless enough individually, the storms had begun to organize and converge into a single squall line, a phenomenon known in meteorologist parlance as a mesoscale convection system.

Over the course of the day, the system had grown in size, gained intensity, and picked up speed as it moved, stretching more than 250 miles west to east, from Ohio into Virginia. While most storms track with the prevailing winds from the west, this one lumbered south, and the western section of GSMNP lay right in its path.

Just after 2:30 p.m., the storm edged south toward I-81 in southern Virginia. Within an hour, it arrived in Bristol and crossed into Tennessee. As it did, the Morristown NWS office fielded the first of the 79 weather-related incident reports it would receive over the next four hours, covering a geographic range of 40 Tennessee counties.[1]

According to Black, at 3:20 p.m., the NSW's Storm Prediction Center in Norman, Oklahoma, issued a severe thunderstorm watch for GSMNP and surrounding area. The initial watch, which extended from 7:20 to 11 p.m., seemed routine enough for the balmy South, a region that receives dozens of such alerts over the course of a typical summer.

---

1   The time stamps that chart the storm's approach and arrival in Great Smoky Mountains National Park differ by as much as a half hour among sources—including those of Great Smoky Mountains National Park dispatch, NOAA's National Climatic Data Center, and the local media that covered the event. The National Climatic Data Center's chronology reflects the time damage/incident reports were received, and those would necessarily lag behind the actual incident itself. Thus, time reference in this article should be interpreted as approximations.

While a severe thunderstorm *watch*, which advises that conditions are such that a storm might develop, is perhaps easy enough to shrug off, the more strident *warning* leaves little doubt; barring some unexpected and anomalous deliverance, the storm will arrive. Just over two and a half hours later, at 5:59 p.m., the NWS would escalate the severe thunderstorm watch to a warning for GSMNP, giving staff only moments to respond before the storm entered the park.

The storm had hit Union County at about 5:30, blasted through Knoxville a few minutes later, and soon ripped the roof off a commercial building in Sevierville, as it tore south. Just after 6 p.m., the storm reached Maryville.

At the time, Blount County Fire Chief Doug McClanahan was enjoying an evening meal with his family at TC's Grill, a burger joint on Old Niles Ferry Road. Within a few minutes McClanahan's pager would begin beeping, conveying the first of several emergency calls originating from inside the national park.

Two of McClanahan's firefighters, cousins Mike and Drew McClurg, had spent a lazy afternoon at Mike's home in the Top of the World community near the Foothills Parkway. The cousins had heard the severe weather warnings broadcast over radio and decided to head preemptively to Blount County Fire Station #8, situated on the swath of land between the Foothills Parkway and GSMNP.

Shortly after 6 p.m., the storm descended on GSMNP and began to uproot trees, turn fractured limbs into projectiles, and unleash persistent, straight-line winds gusting to at least 70 miles per hour (MPH)—just 4 MPH shy of hurricane force.

Ranger Jeff Filosa had completed his shift at Cades Cove and was heading toward Townsend on his way home. Filosa got as far as Townsend before wind gusts threatened to overturn his vehicle.

By then, the storm had acquired a new meteorological descriptor and one that, mercifully, weather forecasters rarely have to use in describing the atmospheric disturbances that strike East Tennessee. The savage storm was a derecho (pronounced deh-RAY-cho). The term may, for some, be difficult to pronounce or remember, but it describes an event that those involved would never forget. (For information on derecho formation and effects, see "The Perfectly Dreadful Storm" on page 178.)

THE PERFECTLY DREADFUL STORM

According to the National Oceanographic and Atmospheric Administration (NOAA), the parent organization of the National Weather Service, the weather phenomenon known as a derecho got its name from Gustavus Hinrichs, a professor of physics at the University of Iowa in the late 19th century.[2] Hinrichs and his colleagues no doubt knew a thing or two about wind; the university is located smack dab in the middle of so-called Tornado Alley.

Hinrichs chose the term derecho, the Spanish word for "straight" or "direct," to characterize the persistent straight-line winds that accompany these storms and to distinguish them from the cyclonic winds that accompany tornadoes. Hinrichs first used the term in a scholarly paper he published in 1888 in the American Meteorological Journal.

A derecho's intense winds result when rain-cooled air, denser than the surrounding warmer air of the storm front, creates a powerful downdraft, or downburst, that merges with and draws strength from existing strong, unidirectional winds on the earth's surface. The falling cooler air forces warmer, lighter air upward along the storm's leading edge, or gust front, spawning new thunderstorms, which subsequently produce more rain-cooled air and feed a cycle known as "forward propagation" or "downstream replication."

The storm's gust front is often characterized by a black, ominous shelf cloud, and many who witnessed the approach of the derecho that hit Great Smoky Mountains National Park on July 5, 2012, reported seeing just such a formation.

In the case of a derecho, an intensifying effect occurs as irregularly arranged downburst clusters advance ahead of the storm front. The line of storms that forms the front typically extends 250 miles or more. These downburst clusters, which measure about 60 miles from edge to edge, in turn create smaller, six-mile-wide downbursts that further create smaller-still microbursts, extremely powerful storm cells with intense, damaging winds that affect circumscribed areas usually less than a mile wide. Such microbursts accounted for the isolated zones of extreme damage that resulted from the July 2012 derecho that struck

2   For information on derechos, visit: http://www.spc.noaa.gov/misc/AbtDerechos/derechofacts.htm

Clockwise from top left: Chief Ranger Clayton Jordan and Ranger Helen McNutt, District Ranger Steve Kloster, and Ranger Kent Looney.

sections of Little River and Laurel Creek Roads, Cades Cove, and the Abrams Creek Campground in the park.

According to meteorologist Mary Black with the National Weather Service's Morristown office, derechos' intense straight-line winds push the center of the storm line forward, a phenomenon known as a bow echo, which imparts the shape of an inverted letter C to the advancing storm system.

Heavy rainfall also often accompanies derechos. Consider, for instance, that in the half hour after the derecho hit GSMNP, Cades Cove received 1.83 inches of rain. While predicting whether a line of thunderstorms will form into a derecho is notoriously difficult, says Black, tracking the storms once they've formed "is more straightforward because they are relatively long-lived and display distinct characteristics."

One passage on NOAA's web pages on derechos proves particularly prescient in describing the outcome that awaited GSMNP as the July 2012 storm approached:

"Because derechos are most common in the warm season, those involved in outdoor activities are most at risk. Campers or hikers in forested areas are vulnerable to being injured or killed by falling trees...Occupants of cars and trucks also are vulnerable to being hit by falling trees..."

Countdown to Chaos

In the minutes before the storm struck, at the Abrams Creek Campground, Chicagoans Alex Rudle and his fiancée Jenna Malone (they're now married) dozed in their tent at site number 9, adjacent to the gated Cooper Road Trail that leads a quarter mile to one of the park's more prized swimming holes on Abrams Creek.

Rachel Burkhart, 41, of Carryton, Tennessee, and a female friend shared the swimming hole with a family of five from Louisiana, including a 7-year-old girl, her parents, and grandparents.

Carole Cooper, from Knoxville, was staying with friends at a cabin near GSMNP and decided to drive them to Abrams Creek Campground, one of her favorite destinations in the park. In the coming hours, Cooper, and more important, her SUV, would play a critical—and lifesaving—role in the wake of the storm.

As the ranking park officer, Clayton Jordan remained in the headquarters building at Sugarlands directing NPS rescue operations until an interagency command could be established.

Meanwhile, dispatcher Randy Kelly manned the communications center, or, as he terms it, the park's "cerebral cortex," in the headquarters basement. Soon enough, the neural pathways of Kelly's cortex would spark to life. Over the next eight hours, he and his colleagues would field and dispatch nearly 300 calls, in some cases several per minute, from those stricken by the storm and those trying to rescue them. But as Kelly would soon discover, the storm would ultimately rob him and headquarters of a vital communications link. The derecho would knock out power to the radio repeater mounted atop Look Rock observation tower.

When the repeater is working properly it picks up and amplifies radio signals, allowing GSMNP personnel in the western end of the park to communicate with colleagues via their portable radios, regardless of their location. While short-distance line-of-sight communications would still be possible in the storm's wake, the communications link between Kelly and Jordan at headquarters and the rangers in the field would have been all but severed. Instead of the typically crisp, clear radio communiqués, Kelly would receive only garbled fragments.

"After the storm struck and the repeater went down, we really struggled with radio communications, which is part of the drama the incident generated," says Jordan. "The need for communications was critical, but we were getting only spotty, fragmented reports from the western end of the park, where most of the storm damage had occurred."

The early fragmented reports indicated that Cades Cove and Abrams Creek Campground had sustained extensive damage. But to the east of the Townsend "Wye"[3], along Little River Road, other storm-related dramas were playing out.

Scott and Ashley Hacker of Franklin, Tennessee, had parked their car along Little River Road west of Metcalf Bottoms and were teaching their 12-year-old son Noah to fly fish. Noah had just waded into the river and made his first cast when the storm hit. The Hackers quickly abandoned the fishing lesson, scrambled up the riverbank, and ran to their car. The family had managed to drive less than 100 yards when a tree fell on the vehicle, and one of its branches crashed through the sunroof. Noah, in the back seat, managed to duck in the nick of time. The branch tore his T-shirt, but he was otherwise unharmed. Nearby, a rock slide had struck another car, pinning the occupants inside. They were trapped but otherwise unhurt.

A short way down Little River Road, about two miles east of the Wye, motorcyclist Ralph Frazier wasn't so fortunate. Before the storm arrived, Frazier, 50, from Buford, Georgia, and his passenger had been exploring US 321/73 through Townsend on their Harley-Davidson motorcycle, accompanied by another couple, friends from back home, also on motorcycle. The couples had been riding together before deciding to return to their RV at a campsite in Wears Valley. Here, the couples split up.

Frazier's friends opted for the more direct route, following US 321 to Wears Valley, while Frazier and his passenger chose the longer, more scenic route through the park along Little River Road to Metcalf Bottoms and, from there, along Wear Gap Road back to their campsite. It would prove to be a fateful decision.

According to Frazier's passenger, rain had begun to fall so heavily that it was difficult to see the road. Frazier slowed to a crawl before deciding to head back toward Townsend. He never got the chance. As he executed the turn, branches began to fall on the road. A splintered section of tree about four inches in diameter hurtled through the air and struck Frazier directly on

---

3   The Townsend Wye refers to the T-junction where State Route 73 enters the park and splits east on Little River Road toward the Metcalf Bottoms Picnic Area and west on Laurel Creek Road toward Cades Cove.

the head, shattering his helmet and fracturing his skull. He never regained consciousness. Miraculously, his passenger, though momentarily trapped under the toppled motorcycle, sustained only minor injuries.

Frazier officially became the storm's first fatality, but another victim would join him soon enough.

The Roar of Jets

When the storm struck, Alex Rudle and Jenna Malone had been in their tent in the Abrams Creek Campground.

"In the snap of a finger, it went from a sunny, warm, and peaceful environment to almost complete darkness and a loud roar of what sounded like multiple jet planes flying directly over our heads," Rudle says. "Suddenly, the wind was gusting, trees were falling, and the rain was blowing sideways."

Those in the campground describe wind-borne tents rolling around like tumbleweeds. As the first gusts cut through the campground, a quarter mile down the Cooper Road Trail at the swimming hole, the family of five from Louisiana, along with Burkhart and her friend, at first instinctively scrambled out of the creek and up the bank to seek shelter. They soon surmised, though, that the tree-lined bank posed a greater risk than the creek itself, a tree-free zone measuring about 25 feet from shore to shore. All waded back into the water. It was a rational decision, no doubt, but it was the wrong one.

Seconds later, a 60-foot oak on the opposite bank, nearly two feet in diameter at chest height, popped its roots and crashed down on top of them, spanning the entire width of the creek. The 7-year-old girl, rendered unconscious by the impact, was pinned underwater near the shore.

The child's grandfather, the least injured of the seven, quickly set to work tying to free the entrapped child. By the time he managed to pull her from the water and carry her to the stream bank, she had stopped breathing. The child's mother had sustained multiple fractures of both arms, but despite her injuries, she managed to rescue breathe into the child and revive her.[4]

---

4   Reports on the incident offer conflicting accounts of who revived the child. Carole Cooper and Jenna Malone, who were on the scene immediately after the accident, and the official GSMNP incident summary suggest it was the mother, while several newspaper accounts indicate it was a by-stander. Privacy laws forbid the National Park from providing names and contact information for storm victims who survived their injuries, so the author was unable to contact them directly unless they were identified in published or posted media accounts. The names of those who died in the storm are public record.

The girl, who had sustained a fractured pelvis and broken arm, was now breathing and alert.

The child's father, who had taken the full impact of the tree while standing in the middle of the creek, was pinned and unable to move.

Immediately in the storm's wake, Rudle and Malone emerged from their tent and saw a woman running up the trail toward the campground, screaming for help and carrying the injured child in her arms. Malone surmises that the woman was the child's grandmother. As Malone helped the woman carry the child into the campground, Rudle sped down the trail toward the swimming hole. When he arrived, he confronted a grim scene.

The man still in the water was in exquisite pain, "moaning and groaning," according to Rudle, which prevented the man from being touched or moved. Medics would later determine that his injuries were severe and extensive: a punctured lung, nine broken ribs, and two fractured vertebrae in his back. His wife, from the shoreline, talked and sang to him in an effort to distract him from his suffering.

Rudle noted that the water lapped the man's chin and feared that if the rain persisted and the creek continued to rise, he would surely drown in place.

Unable to assist the man pinned in the river, Rudle turned his attention to Burkhart, who lay on the bank. At the time, she was being comforted by two other women.

"She was wheezing and breathing hard," he said. "You could see where the tree had struck her upper torso; the area was black and blue."

He talked to her and did his best to comfort her. "I asked her questions, I introduced myself, and at first there was some eye contact, and she was aware," he recalls, "but as time progressed, she became more and more distant and detached." [5]

Rudle soon noticed a "far-off gaze" in the woman's eyes as her breathing became less and less regular. Trained in CPR, Rudle began to perform the procedure on Burkhart but soon realized that she had died.

Back in the campground, Jenna and the grandmother carried the injured child to the bath house, the only hard-walled structure that wasn't locked up at the time.

"It was cold and raining, so we looked for a place to take the little girl

---

5   *The Knoxville News Sentinel* recorded an extensive video interview with Rudle and Malone the day after the storm: www.youtube.com/watch?v=c9JnFuAs-Zo. The author also interviewed the couple in researching this story.

to shelter her from the weather," Malone recalls. "The child was shivering, so we laid her on the floor and covered her with towels to keep her warm."

Meanwhile, three angels were about to arrive on the scene at Abrams Creek Campground, two in the form of Blount County firefighters. The other in the form of a middle-aged woman driving a Chevy Tahoe.

"Shelter in Place!"

The storm's arrival at Cades Cove had been just as abrupt and brutal. Just after 6 p.m., Ranger Kent Looney, inside the Cades Cove ranger station, heard dispatcher Randy Kelly relay the severe thunderstorm warning he had received from the National Weather Service. Within minutes, Jeff Filosa advanced the warning from the realm of conjecture to that of hard reality. From inside his wind-battered cruiser in Townsend, with trees toppling and branches flying all around him, Filosa keyed his radio and issued the system wide alert that the storm had arrived in Townsend, a mere 7 miles from Cades Cove. The storm, traveling at roughly 70 MPH, would close that distance in just over 5 minutes.

In the moments that followed, Looney ran out of the ranger station and confronted a scene of glaringly incongruous elements. Peering beyond the ridge to the north, Looney glimpsed an enormous black cloud mass that hugged the mountainside as it poured downslope and sped directly toward him. Meanwhile, the parking lot in front of the ranger station was filled with hundreds of carefree park visitors.

"Many of them were licking ice cream cones they had just purchased at the camp store," Looney recalls. All were seemingly unaware that a violent storm, borne by 70-MPH winds, was bearing down on them.

Without a moment to reflect or plan, Looney took action, screaming at the tops of his lungs, "Everyone shelter in place! There's a bad storm coming! Get in your cars!"

The more fortunate visitors had time to scatter to their vehicles, while others sought shelter in the ranger station and restrooms. Yet others were stranded out in the weather. Within minutes, the wind roared as trees toppled and branches and leaves ripped through the campground. The blast of wind momentarily pinned Looney against the sidewall of the ranger station.

"I didn't wait to see if the people heeded my warning," says Looney. "I was in crisis mode and was determined to do everything I could to respond."

His first thoughts turned to the line of Park Service patrol cars parked along the tree-lined drive leading to the ranger residence. Looney realized that if falling trees flattened the vehicles, he and his associates would be immobilized and unable to reach injured visitors. He had time enough to move only one car, that of Ranger Jamie Sanders.

It turned out to be a wise choice; immediately after Looney moved the car, a tree crashed down in the now-vacant parking slot.

Ranger Helen McNutt had ended her shift at the Cove and was preparing to head home when she heard the weather warning from Kelly at headquarters and the follow-on call from Filosa in Townsend. She immediately hopped into a patrol car and headed into the campground to advise visitors to take shelter. She was in the C loop of the campground when the first blast hit.

"I did a quick pass through of the campground," says McNutt. As she drove, she kept one eye on the road and the other on the chaos of falling limbs. "I remember looking up as I drove to see what might be coming down," she says.

After quickly scanning the campground loops and seeing no one injured or trapped under debris, she drove to where the campground entrance joined the end of the Loop Road.

"By then, we had received reports that Laurel Creek Road was blocked by fallen trees, which meant there was no way out," she says. "So at the intersection, I tried to stop traffic from trying to exit the park." She was able to stop some cars, but others had already streamed by.

As she waved vehicles to a stop, she encountered the first of several injuries that resulted—some directly, some indirectly—from the storm. A car pulled up with a shattered windshield. Inside, on the passenger side, sat a 50-year-old man. When the tree had struck the windshield, it sent shards of glass into his eyes.

According to McNutt, the brunt of the storm was over in five minutes. Then a torrential rain began to fall. As it did, the casualty list began to mount.

"All these reports of injuries came in at about the same time," says McNutt. An older woman experiencing chest pains suggestive of a heart attack arrived at the ranger station. A call came in of a man pinned under a large tree at the Methodist Church, about two and a half miles away along the Loop Road. The man had suffered a serious back injury. Shortly after, another report came in that a woman, 32 weeks pregnant, had begun to experience contractions.

Later, McNutt would respond to a report of domestic assault. Apparently, in the heat of an argument, fueled in part by the temporary entrapment occasioned by the storm, one of her campground guests had placed his hands around his wife's throat and throttled her as he lifted her off the ground. The rules of triage demanded that McNutt attend to the injured first, including the assault victim. Park law enforcement officials would deal with the abuser later. With roads blocked, McNutt knew he wasn't going anywhere.

Even the concessioners who operated the camp store soon lent their assistance. "The storm had knocked the power out, so after it got dark, a few of them stood with flashlights at the entrances to the restrooms, helping campers enter and exit," says McNutt.

McNutt, who, like all GSMNP park rangers, is a trained emergency medical technician (EMT), accessed the medical kit stored at the ranger station and administered the basic first aid necessary to stabilize her patients.[6] While she attended to those stricken at the campground, Ranger Marc Eckert, a park medic, drove to the Methodist Church to assist the man pinned under a tree. Eckert managed to free the injured man and place him on a backboard. At the time, neither McNutt nor Eckert could know that the more substantial help the victims needed was yet hours away.

The victims at the Abrams Creek Campground were, likewise, condemned to wait.

A Great Gift in a Large Package

Back at Abrams Creek, shortly after Alex Rudle had abandoned attempts to revive the now deceased Burkhart, he recalls seeing the first emergency responder arrive at the scene of the tree fall on the creek. Rudle's description of the man "as a really huge firefighter" almost certainly identifies him as Mike McClurg of the Blount County Fire Department.

By his own description, McClurg stands 6-foot-5-inches tall and weighs 300 pounds—"closer to 350 pounds if you count my bunker gear."

Just after the storm warning had been issued, Mike and his cousin Drew made their way to Blount County Fire Station #8, knowing that the distress calls would soon follow. They were at the station when the depart-

---

6   All GSMNP ranger stations and cruisers are equipped with first-aid supplies.

ment's radio crackled to life with the first of multiple calls that went out about the injured parties at the Abrams Creek Campground. Trained in rapid response, the two men quickly donned their protective bunker gear and climbed aboard a fire engine, which, unfortunately, was not equipped with the one tool they needed most: a chainsaw.

As they made their way from Maryville toward Abrams Creek, they began to encounter trees and limbs in the road; Mike managed to drive right over some of them as they coursed along Happy Valley Road and approached the entrance to the campground. There they confronted an insurmountable jumble of toppled trees blocking their path. Their motorized transit ended there; if they were going to reach the victims, they'd have to make their way on foot.

"At the campground entrance, there were hundreds, if not thousands, of trees on the ground, and all the power lines were hanging down," says Mike.

When they abandoned the fire engine, with its powerful onboard radio, Mike realized that they'd also be walking away from their only means of communicating with the outside world. Before they left the truck, they notified Blount County dispatch of the dire need for crews equipped with chainsaws.

From there, the cousins started walking—or rather climbing over and ducking under hundreds of trees that separated them from the injured parties in the campground. Mike led as Drew kept an eye on the drooping power lines which, for all the cousins knew, were still carrying live current.

"We probably had to cover less than a mile, but it felt like three," Mike recalls. "In the heat of the moment, it was difficult to gauge distance, but it felt like an eternity; we just never seemed to get any closer."

After more than a half hour of what Mike describes as "pretty rough going," he and Drew reached the campground at about 7 p.m. and were directed down the trail to the swimming hole.

Mike and Drew's boss, Blount County Fire Chief Doug McClanahan, arrived shortly behind them and assumed the role of incident command at the campground.

Within an hour, the Blount County highway department would arrive with a backhoe and crew of chainsaw operators. In the meantime, several residents of the nearby Happy Valley community had shown up with their own chainsaws and were doing their part to help.

Rescue workers gather at a makeshift command post at the Burgermaster Drive-In in Townsend.
Crews arrived to assist park visitors trapped in the Cades Cove area.

No Way Out (Or In)

Back at Cades Cove, Kent Looney realized that if visitors in the Cove couldn't make it out, that also meant that Rural Metro ambulances couldn't make it in, so he grabbed a chainsaw, a tank of gas, and safety gear and jumped in his cruiser. He planned to cut his way east on Laurel Creek Road toward Townsend, surmising correctly that crews in Townsend were doing likewise to close the gap that lay between.

As Looney exited the campground he pulled into the then vacant on-coming traffic lane on Laurel Creek Road and passed dozens of cars, their egress blocked, until he reached the first tangle of blowdowns. As he started to saw his way through, he soon discovered that he had help. More than a dozen burley men—many of them shirtless—had exited their idled vehicles and were trailing behind him, removing the sawn limbs as he cut.

"I felt like a pied piper," says Looney, who recalls that a couple of the volunteers who worked for a commercial tree service were a bit critical of his technique and insisted that he relinquish his saw to them. "No," he told them bluntly. "That's just not going to happen."

At the time, teams and equipment from the Townsend police and volunteer fire departments, Blount County highway and police departments, and Rural Metro Ambulance Service had assembled at a make-shift incident command post at the Burgermaster restaurant in Townsend. At the Wye, backhoes and teams of chainsaw operators soon divided into two forces, one heading east toward Metcalf Bottoms, the other moving west on Laurel Creek Road toward Looney and the Cove, clearing the roads as they moved.

Meanwhile, Tennessee District Ranger Steve Kloster was en route to Townsend and would soon assume the role of incident commander.

While at home and off the clock, Kloster had been watching the news, which included coverage of the breaking storm. Then his phone started ringing with calls from park headquarters. Kloster quickly dressed in his Park Service uniform and headed for Sugarlands. Once there, he grabbed a chainsaw, got behind the wheel of his cruiser, and headed toward Townsend along Little River Road. By then, word had reached him of a possible motorcycle fatality between The Sinks and Metcalf Bottoms. "At that point, things had really started to snowball," says Kloster. "Besides the incident with the motorcycle, we knew we had multiple injuries at Abrams Creek Campground and Cades Cove, but these people were cut off by fallen trees. We couldn't get in, and they couldn't get out. Never mind the fact that our radio system was down."

En route to Townsend along Little River Road, Kloster had driven past Metcalf Bottoms and cut through several large limbs sprawled across the road, but with the volume of downed trees, he quickly realized it was a lost cause for one man with a chainsaw. Jordan had dispatched a backhoe and chainsaw crew from Sugarlands, but they had yet to arrive.

"I knew that if I had tried to cut through all those trees, it would have taken me all night," says Kloster. Instead, he reversed course, cut through Metcalf Bottoms, and reached Townsend via Wears Valley Road. He arrived at the Burgermaster restaurant just after 7 p.m.

When he arrived, before he assumed command of incident response, his first order of business was to talk with Townsend Fire Chief Don Stallions, Blount County Rural Metro general manager Ron Parker, and a representative of the Blount County Highway Department and learn what they knew about those injured in the park and the mounting efforts to rescue them.

According to Kloster, it was a familiar and comfortable interagency working relationship.

"Incidents like this one require us to partner with agencies outside the National Park Service, and we have a long-term working relationship with the crews from Townsend and Blount County," says Kloster. "We know and respect each other, we've trained together, and that relationship makes a huge difference in responding to incidents like this."

But even absent an established working relationship, all of the agencies that massed at the incident command in Townsend would, as Jordan puts it, "all be trained to read from the same sheet of music" in mounting an orderly and unified response.

That sheet of music takes the form of the Incident Command System (ICS), an established paradigm for coordinating the collaborative emergency response efforts of federal, state, and local agencies. ICS clearly establishes a chain of command, assigns specific functions and tasks, and relies on a universal and well-understood system of communication codes and terminology. The National Park Service has predicated its emergency responses on the ICS system since the mid-1980s.

As Kloster supervised efforts to reach and rescue those injured in Cades Cove, events unfolding at the Abrams Creek Campground were proving even more desperate.

"OnStar, We Have a Problem"

In the campground bath house, Jenna and the grandmother struggled to keep the injured 7-year-old child warm and alert. As they tended to the child, Carole Cooper, in her Chevy Tahoe, arrived to offer assistance. With Cooper's appearance on the scene, the game was about to change.

According to Malone, Cooper pulled her Tahoe up to the bath house and Malone and the grandmother lay the shivering girl down in the back of the SUV, and Cooper turned on the heat. Cooper then drove to the clearing in front of the ranger station. With a critically injured child in her car and more injured parties in the creek, she felt the rising frustration—shared by many who were involved in the incident—of being cut off and isolated, with no means to call for help. Park radios weren't working, and Abrams is a notorious dead zone for cell phones.

Desperate and bereft of other options, Cooper reached up and, on a whim, pressed the emergency button on her OnStar console, fully expecting that the GM road assistance service would be as useless as her cell phone.

"Low and behold," says Cooper, "the emergency advisor came on."[7]

The voice of deliverance that issued through the OnStar speaker was that of Bryan Anta, a trained emergency medical dispatcher.

For the next three hours, OnStar would serve as a vital, life-saving nexus, linking Jordan and Kelly at GSMNP headquarters, along with Blount County emergency responders, to those stranded and injured in the Abrams Creek Campground.

Blount County Fire Chief McClanahan used the service to contact Rob Webb, then a supervisor with Rural Metro, and request a fleet of ambulances. McClanahan went one step further and attempted to call in a helicopter to evacuate the injured, but with weather conditions still unsettled, UT Medical Center's Lifestar crew determined that it was unsafe to fly.

By that point, McClanahan knew that the golden hour—the time period following a traumatic injury when medical intervention is most likely to save a life—was rapidly lapsing. "I was concerned that if we didn't quickly treat and evacuate the injured, we might have more fatalities on our hands," he says.

"For a time, OnStar and the Tahoe *were* the command center for this incident," says Ron Parker, then general manager of Blount County Rural Metro Ambulance Service.[8] Both Webb and Parker now work for Priority Ambulance Service in Blount County.

Motorcycle Medic

Upon his arrival at the Abrams Creek Campground, firefighter Mike McClurg had headed down to the swimming hole. Drew, who realized that the cousins lacked a motorized vehicle for transporting the injured, set out to acquire one.

According to Mike, a red pickup truck with a camper top had caught Drew's attention, and after informing the vehicle's owner that he was commandeering the truck in the name of the Blount County Fire Department, the owner graciously surrendered the keys.

The cousins now had a make-shift ambulance, but a locked gate

7   Cooper describes the incident in an online interview captured by CTIA Wireless Association and posted on YouTube: www.youtube.com/watch?v=z468JpT7ptU

8   Parker, McClanahan, Kloster, and Cooper appear in a documentary film produced by General Motors, the parent company of OnStar, that recounts the events of the evening of July 5, 2012. The video was intended for an internal GM audience and not released to the public, though GM provided the author with access to the video.

blocked the path from the campground down to the swimming hole on Abrams Creek. Drew summarily resolved that issue as well, snipping off the lock with a pair of bolt cutters. As he did, a regulation-obsessed camper advised him that doing so violated Park Service rules. Drew took little notice as he swung open the gate, and drove the truck down the Cooper Road Trail to the swimming hole to join his cousin.

Once at the swimming hole, Mike had initially moved to help the man pinned in the middle of the creek.

"All I could see of him was a nose, mouth, and hair," says Mike. Mike also noticed that the man's left ear had been all but severed from the side of his head.

As Mike entered the river, the man protested.

"He was screaming with pain," Mike recalls, "but he insisted that I go help the woman on the shore." Mike complied and performed CPR on the now-deceased Burkhart for 20 minutes before returning his attention to the man in the water.

By that time, Jim Patty, a captain with the Blount County Fire Department, had arrived and he and the two cousins worked to extricate the man. Freeing the severely injured man from the tree was one thing; transporting him to shore through water that was five feet deep was another.

As Mike and Drew began lifting limbs off the victim, Patty found an inflated child's inner tube that would answer nicely as a flotation device. Patty was able to place the inner tube under the man's back and rear, and within 20 minutes, they floated him to shore.

By that time, a backboard had materialized, though Mike is not sure where it came from, and they placed the man on the board and carried him to the commandeered truck.

As the McClurg cousins transported their patient to the ranger station, the Blount County road crews, with the help of private citizens equipped with chainsaws, had managed to cut a swath through the trees just wide enough for a motorcycle to pass. That narrow ingress provided all the access that the first-on-the-scene Rural Metro paramedic, later identified as Steve Mayes, needed to reach the victims. He arrived on scene just after 9 p.m. and immediately attended to the injured who had since been brought up from the creek.

Just past dark, at 9:44 p.m., with weather conditions improving, the Lifestar helicopter set down at an emergency landing zone created at the

Thanks to the hard work of Park Service and contracted clean up crews, roads that looked permanently impassable Thursday night were reopened within 48 hours. It was, afterall, the peak of summer vacation season in America's most-visited national park.

intersection of U.S. 129 and Happy Valley Road. Within minutes, the injured child and her father were en route to UT Medical Center. The child's injured mother would make the journey via ambulance.

Just over an hour later, medical care began to arrive at Cades Cove. The concerted efforts of Kent Looney working from the west and the Townsend and Blount County crews working from the east had cleared a single lane along Laurel Creek Road. At 10:46 p.m., GSMNP dispatch received the message that the caravan of Rural Metro ambulances was half way to the Cove. The ambulances arrived at the ranger station just over 10 minutes later. Shortly after, one of them reached Eckert attending to the man with the injured back at the Methodist Church.

With the arrival of the ambulances at Abrams Creek and Cades Cove, GSMNP staff could begin to relax a bit after hours of full-on crisis management, but they weren't in the clear just yet.

Confirming the Dead, Tending the Living

When the storm hit, Ranger Chuck Hester had been patrolling his district in the extreme eastern section of GSMNP, about as far from the site of the destruction as one could get and still be inside the park. The distance would be made all that much greater by the tangles of trees and branches that blocked the roads and impeded his efforts to reach his assigned destination, the Abrams Creek campground.

By the time Hester arrived at the campground, just after dark, Rural Metro paramedics were treating the injured, and the evacuation was underway. His first order of business involved attending to the deceased Burkhart. He interviewed witnesses, documented the circumstances surrounding her death, and positively confirmed her identity. GSMNP would bear the difficult responsibility of contacting her next of kin. Likewise, the park would also soon contact Ralph Frazier's family and convey to them news of his tragic death.

Next, Hester turned his attention to the living, and, as he did, a second communications miracle was about to occur. Shaken but uninjured campers, many of whose tents had been destroyed by the storm, began to gather at the ranger station. Hester knew that news of the storm had already begun to flash on TV screens across the country, including the mention of fatalities (national broadcast media, including CNN, would cover the story), and he knew that concerned loved ones back home eagerly awaited news.

With radio repeaters out, no cell phone coverage, and power lines down, Hester, like Carole Cooper a few hours earlier, succumbed to welling frustration. At the time, he may as well have been operating in the technological realm of the 19th century, as far as communications were concerned. And in this case, the 19th century answered the call.

As he walked past the ranger station, he peered in through the window and saw a landline telephone. Granted, the device has evolved considerably since Alexander Graham Bell was awarded his patent in 1876, but the system that turns speech into electrical pulses carried by copper wires hasn't changed all that much.

Hester entered the office, snatched the receiver off the hook, and placed it against his ear, certain it was an exercise in futility. Then…he heard the dial tone.

"I was not, in any way, expecting to hear that sound," he says. "I was dumbfounded. No power, no radio, but I had a dial tone!"

His first call went out to Jordan and Kelly at headquarters to confirm Burkhart's death and apprise them of the situation at the campground.

Next, he invited the campers, one by one, to make short calls home, to let their families know they were okay.

Later, Hester opened up the ranger station, which also serves as a

residence and has three bedrooms, and told the campers that anyone who
wished to could stay the night. Rudle and Malone took him up on his offer
and occupied one of the bedrooms. After the initial calls had gone home,
Hester also offered campers the luxury of longer calls, on the Park Service's
dime.

"I invited them to take all the time they need on the phone, but not
to call China or Japan," Hester says. "There's no telling what that phone bill
ran."

The Calm after the Storm
By 1 a.m., now July 6, back in the Cades Cove Campground, the fleet of
Rural Metro ambulances had transported out the last of the injured, and the
park staff reversed the flow on Laurel Creek Road, still down to only one
lane, allowing campers and sightseers to leave.

As the hundreds of cars streamed east, McNutt, Eckert, and Looney
made their way to campground loop C, site 74. They had some unfinished
business to attend to.

There, they slipped the handcuffs on a 58-year-old man and charged
him with assault for attempting to strangle his wife. The man pled guilty
and would pay a fine. At the time, his injured wife was receiving treatment
at Blount Memorial Hospital. With the man's arrest, the park's emergency
response shifted to sweeping the park's backcountry trails and campsites.
Surprisingly there were no injuries there.

The storm no doubt knocked the park staff back on its heels, but the
disruption was notably short lived. By Saturday—less than two days after the
derecho struck—park roads were clear and open, and, despite the two tragic
fatalities, all the others who had been harmed by the storm would eventually
recover from their injuries, at least the physical ones.

The derecho of July 5, 2012, for all its force and destruction, ultimately had little impact on the park east of Elkmont, and even the profound
damage it caused to the park's western end would resolve soon enough, in
part from the restorative powers of the natural world, in part from the toil of
men and women equipped with mechanized tools.

It's true that national parks and other wild areas are ever vulnerable to
Mother Nature's fury and, further, that natural disasters are beyond anyone's control. But our capacity to respond to them is not. In mobilizing the
life-saving response to the July 2012 storm, Jordan and his crew of rangers,

along with all the others who took part—professional partners and private citizens alike—demonstrated clearly that the worst of times can, and often do, inspire the best of human endeavors.

APPENDIX
Known Fatalities in Great Smoky Mountains National Park: 1931-2013

This report presents a running list of known fatalities that have occurred in Great Smoky Mountains National Park (GSMNP) between 1931
and 2013. The deaths are identified by date; cause; victim name, age, and
hometown (when available); and, in most cases, location of the fatality within GSMNP. In some cases, multiple causes contributed to the death (e.g., a
heart attack brought on by asthma, drowning caused by an auto accident or
fall, etc.). In such cases, the deaths are listed in multiple categories of cause
of death.

The master list is based on information gleaned from a number of
sources, including but not limited to: GSMNP monthly superintendents'
reports (1931-67) and later annual reports, files of official documents and
correspondence stored at the National Archives in College Park Maryland
and at GSMNP archives, official incident and park communications reports
provided by GSMNP, press releases issued by the park, published newspaper
reports, and internet searches (primarily for incidents dating from 2000 onward). Ancestry.com and Newspapers.com provided victim details that were,
in some cases, lacking or contradictory in the source reports, including full
names, ages and dates of birth, hometowns, official dates of death, and, in a
few cases, coroners' reports confirming date and cause of death.

In some incidents, searches were launched to locate missing persons
thought to be in the park but who were later found or recovered outside
the park boundary. A case in point is the fatal airplane crash of Teddy Ray

Jarnagin, 18, of Knoxville, TN (1955). Jarnagin's plane had been missing for several days, and Civil Air Patrol believed prevailing winds might have blown him off course and over the park. An intensive search for Jarnagin took place in the park, but Jarnagin's plane and body were later found on Walden's Ridge, well outside park boundaries. This and similar entries remain on the textual incident list, though the individual fatalities are not counted among the tally of deaths within the park.

In other cases, persons went missing within (or very near) the park but were never found. Cases in point include Dennis Martin (1969), Treeny Gibson (1976), Christopher Lee Cessna (2011), and Derek Leuking (2012). Because all were last seen in GSMNP or their vehicles were abandoned in the park, their presumptive deaths are counted on the master tally of fatalities in GSMNP.

In yet other instances, individuals who allegedly committed crimes outside the park but entered the park after the crimes had taken place are included in the textual master list of incidents. A case in point is William Bradford Bishop, who allegedly murdered five members of his family in Maryland in 1976. Bishop's abandoned station wagon was found near Elkmont, indicating that he did enter the park, though Bishop has never been found or brought to justice. Because of Bishop's connection with the park, this event remains on the textual incident list, but the deaths associated with Bishop are not counted on the master tally of fatalities in the park.

The list includes several deaths that occurred just outside park boundaries. The proximity of the deaths to the national park and, in some cases, the fact that some of the victims or participants had direct links to the park, warrants their inclusion. A case in point is an auto accident that occurred on June 2, 1934, in which a truck carrying a number of Civilian Conservation Corps (CCC) enrollees struck a civilian auto, killing one of the auto's occupants. The CCC enrollees in the truck were returning to the park after an unauthorized leave.

"A Partial listing of accidental deaths in the Smoky Mountains" in the book *Cades Cove: A Place in Appalachia*, by Gladys Oliver Burns, presents a list of deaths occurring in the park. Those incidents on the list that could be documented and confirmed through other sources are included in the master list and death tallies. Those that could not be confirmed were not added to the tallies but are appended to the end of the textual master list of deaths.

Because suicide deaths are particularly difficult for surviving family members and friends, the book's publisher has elected to present the initials, but not the full names, of suicide victims who died in the park. However, in instances where victims' names and the circumstances surrounding their deaths or disappearances appear in the book's text, the full names are retained in the appendix and index. A case in point is John Rudd, whose suicide death is described in chapter nine, "Star-crossed Lovers Part Ways on a Remote Mountain Ridge."

Murders, like suicide deaths, are emotionally difficult for family members and friends of the deceased, but, because murders and other violent crimes generally receive extensive media coverage, the appendix and index present the full names of homicide victims.

While this list is extensive, it should not be viewed as comprehensive or complete. There is no doubt that this inventory omits some deaths that have occurred in GSMNP but for which I discovered no records. Likewise, this list also should not be viewed as entirely accurate. In several cases, various sources provided conflicting information on spellings of names, ages, hometowns, location of deaths, causes of death, etc. In compiling this list, when possible, I cross-referenced reports from various sources to arrive at information that, based on the preponderance of evidence, appeared most likely to be correct. Ancestry.com and Newspapers.com were particularly useful in this regard.

I welcome any information that would help to correct errors and update the list to make it more comprehensive and accurate.

D.B.

Summary: All known deaths, deaths by cause, 1931–2013

Total number of deaths, all causes, 1931–2013 .... 470[1]

Deaths by cause:

Auto 132
Plane Crash 73
Drowning 61
Heart Attack 41
Suicide 37

       Male 29

       Female 8

Natural Causes 29
Motorcycle/Moped 21
Fall 18
Exposure/Hypothermia 14
Murder 14
Construction 13
Civilian Conservation Corps Activities 8
Tree Fall 8
Missing, Never Found, Presumed Dead 5
Unknown Causes 5
Lightning Strike 3
Livestock/Horse 3
Bicycle 2
Fire 2
Electrocution (non-lightning) 1
Explosives 1
Sudden Infant Death Syndrome 1
Animal Venom 1
Aspiration 1
Animal Attack 1
Asthma 1

---

1 The numbers of deaths by cause, if added together, will exceed the number of total deaths by all causes because many deaths were attributed to more than one cause (e.g., an auto accident that caused a vehicle to career into the river, where the victim(s) drowned; an individual who fell and sustained a head injury prior to falling into a waterway and drowning; an individual who experienced an asthma attack that triggered a fatal heart attack, etc.) In those cases, the individual deaths are counted among the totals for two or more causes of death.

Five Deadliest Years

1986 17
2003 16
1964 15
1946 15
1934 13

Five Deadliest Places

Newfound Gap Road (U.S. 441) Gatlinburg to Cherokee 68
Gatlinburg Spur (U.S. 441) Gatlinburg to Pigeon Forge 43
Appalachian Trail (including incidents within .5 mile of trail) 16
Little River Road (SR 73) 16
The Sinks 12

Multiple Deaths (3 or more) from Single Events

December 12, 1933: Fatal accident, construction. Multiple fatalities (3). Three men were killed and 3 injured in an accident at Newfound Gap. A crew of 1 foreman and 9 laborers was digging a trench for a toe wall when the slope slid, burying 3 men whose bodies were not extracted for 4 hours. The men were employed on the Newfound Gap-Clingmans Dome project under contract to the Arundel Corporation of Baltimore, Maryland. Killed were Robert Davis, foreman, Knoxville, TN; Edward Smiley, laborer, Bryson City, NC; and Robert Brooks, laborer, Bushnell, NC.

August 5, 1938: Flood. Fatal accident, drowning. Multiple fatalities (8). A cloudburst occurred along Webb Creek, near the boundary of the park, and swept away the home of Alfred Ball, killing Ball, his wife, their four children, and two visitors.

August 12, 1944: Fatal accident, plane crash. Multiple fatalities (3). On September 19, 1947, a group of hikers discovered the wreckage of a single-engine Beechcraft on Willy Tops Ridge in the Greenbrier section of the park. The plane had been missing for more than three years, having disappeared on August 12, 1944. The remains of three persons were recovered at the crash site (identities of the victims were not provided).

October 12, 1945: Fatal accident, plane crash. Multiple fatalities (6). GSMNP received confidential information from the Emergency Rescue Service of Nashville, TN, regarding a C-45 Army plane No. 3351, lost on October 5 while en route from St. Louis, MO, to Charlotte, NC. The wreck was found on October 12 in a dense wilderness area about 3,300 feet northeast of Mt. Sequoya and 1,200 feet south of the North Carolina state line. Killed in the crash were First Lt. William Robert Barton, pilot, Youngstown, OH; Staff Sgt. Raymond H. Kerkela, Minneapolis, MN; First Lt. Sam M. Lerner, Greensboro, NC; Staff Sgt. Hollis E. Broderick, Waltham, MA; Cpl. W.R. Hanes, Cleveland, OH; and Specialist (WAVE) Lena E. Allred, Charlotte, NC.

June 12, 1946: Fatal accident, plane crash. Multiple fatalities (12). Workers found an airplane engine on the side of the road near Clingmans Dome. The engine was from a B-29 that crashed into a mountain at 6,240 feet on the Tennessee side and tumbled end over end about 300 yards into North Carolina. All occupants of the plane, all U.S. Army personnel, were killed in the crash. The superintendent's report did not provide the number of dead, but an Associated Press article puts the number of fatalities at 12.

January 9, 1947: Fatal accident, plane crash, fire. Multiple fatalities (3). Members of the Smoky Mountain Hiking Club discovered the wreck-age of a Beechcraft airplane on Woolly Tops in the Greenbrier section of the park. The plane, assigned to the Oak Ridge, TN, Manhattan Project, had been missing since take-off from Knoxville on August 12, 1944. Civilian pilot E.A. Leonard, civilian co-pilot S. Parham, and civilian mechanic Reuben Johnson, had not been heard from since the plane disappeared and were presumed burned in the crash.

March 22, 1964: Fatal accident, plane crash. Heart attack, fatal. Multiple fatalities (7). Civil Air Patrol in Maryville called District Ranger Ward regarding a plane crash on the mountainside approximately 100 feet below Parson Bald. The plane, a BE-18 twin-engine Beechcraft, crashed on March 21 but was not reported lost until the 22nd because the pilot had not filed a flight plan. A Tennessee Highway patrol helicopter spotted the wreckage in the late afternoon of March 22 and reported that the plane had burned. Four adults and two children perished in the crash: J. Noble Miles, pilot; Mrs. Miles; Mr. and Mrs. John Fetto; and two nieces of the plane's owner, Joseph Fabick, ages 13 and 14, all of St. Louis, MO. A search party was sent to Parson Bald. At 2:30 a.m., as the search party neared the top, Frank Shults, a member of the party, died of an apparent heart attack. Shults' party brought out his body. Another crew set out and reached the wreckage at 12:22 p.m.

January 28, 1973: Fatal accident, plane crash. Multiple fatalities (3). Search for a light plane reported down in the Cades Cove area was hampered by heavy snowfall. Killed in the crash were pilot Peter Smith, Charleston, WV; Harry W. Adams Jr; and Carl T. Long, 50, San Marino, CA. J.W. Miller, 47, president of J.W. Miller and Associates of Charleston, WV, was the lone survivor. On January 24, 1974, a wrongful death suit was filed against the FAA by the children of crash victim Carl Long.

April 3, 1973: Fatal accident, plane crash. Multiple fatalities (4). Four were killed when a twin-engine Piper Aztec crashed on Mt. Le Conte. Killed were Thomas J. Suter, 39, Cincinnati, OH; John Brandt, 32, Crescent Springs, KY; Bonnie Lou Frasure, 18, South Shore, KY; Linda Picklesiner, 17, South Portsmouth, KY. An afghan hound on board survived the crash.

January 3, 1978: Fatal accident, plane crash, double. Multiple fatalities (9). Nine persons were killed in separate aircraft crashes. The first involved a twin-engine Cessna airplane, with five aboard (all were killed), and the second involved a search and rescue helicopter, with eight aboard, sent from Fort Campbell, KY, to the scene of the first crash. Four of the crewmembers aboard the helicopter survived.

May 24, 1992: Fatal accident, plane crash. Multiple fatalities (3). A Cessna 172 crashed near Tricorner Knob along the Appalachian Trail. A rescue team reached the crash site the following day. Killed in the crash were pilot Ronald Ward Baldwin, 27, Tami Dial, 23, and their 5-month-old daughter, Savannah Lorraine Baldwin, all from Rome, GA.

July 25, 1993: Fatal accident, auto. Multiple fatalities (4). An accident involving three vehicles, each carrying families of four, occurred on Newfound Gap Road (U.S. 441) about 5.5 miles north of Cherokee. Daniel Barnes, Candler, NC, the driver of a 1990 Ford Thunderbird, survived. His wife, Lisa Joyce Green Barnes, 37, and daughter Shannon Lear Barnes, 7, were pronounced dead at Cherokee Indian Health Service Hospital. The other daughter, Amber Melissa Barnes, 10, survived. Barnes, traveling south on U.S. 441, crossed the centerline and struck head-on a 1993 Ford Escort. Gregory Huddleston, 36, Morehead, KY, driver of the Escort, and his wife, Cejuana Huddleston, 36, were pronounced dead at the scene. Their two children survived, as did the four passengers in a Subaru sedan, the third car involved in the accident.

September 9, 1995: Fatal accident, auto. Multiple fatalities (3). Jimmy Wayne Lawson, 29, and his mother, Emily Jean Lawson, 57, of Beaufort County, VA, were killed in an auto accident on Newfound Gap Road (U.S. 441) near the Oconaluftee Visitor Center. Albert Lawson, 59, husband of

Emily Jean, died on September 20 at UT Medical Center of injuries sustained in the accident.

March 26, 2005: Fatal accident, auto. Multiple fatalities (5). A two-car collision on the Gatlinburg Spur of U.S. 441 resulted in five deaths. The dead included Myra Nelson, 63, her husband, George, 80, Myra's mother, Audrey Fentress, 84, all of Norfolk, VA, and Anthony Deitz, 69, and his wife, Betty, 69, both of Virginia Beach, VA. John M. Hall, 18, Lebanon, TN, and Steven A. Williams, 19, Murfreesboro, TN, were drag racing and caused the accident. Both men later pleaded guilty to one count each of second-degree murder and were sentenced to prison.

Known Deaths by All Causes, GSMNP 1931-2013

August 13, 1931: Fatal accident, auto. Fatal accident, construction. Joe Beck, an employee of the North Carolina State Highway Commission, died from injuries received by the overturning of a truck on the Newfound Gap Road (Highway 71) construction project.

January 11, 1933: Shooting, fatal. Murder. Charles Ogle, 22, Gatlinburg, TN, was killed from ambush while assisting a deputy game warden in locating a number of illegal game traps on Panther Creek near its junction with Mill Creek and inside the park area. At the time, the property was still owned by the state, having not yet been turned over to the federal government. Suspects Lee and Hubert Ownby, also residents of Gatlinburg, were arrested and placed in the Sevierville jail. At a preliminary hearing, they were bound over to court under a $5,000 bond each. The crime was reported to assistant Chief Ranger Dunn, who, accompanied by Bill Ramsey, West Ogle, Deputy Game Warden Minyard Connor, and several others, arrived on the scene shortly afterward. After the coroner arrived, Dunn removed the body to the home of relatives and was largely responsible for securing the evidence against the suspects.

July 17, 1933: Fatal accident, explosives. Fatal accident, Civilian Conservation Corps (CCC). The first fatal CCC accident in the park's 9 camps occurred when Will Fanchar, an enrolled local man, was fatally injured by a blast. Although Fanchar was 600 feet from the blast, around the bend of the creek, and behind a rock, he was struck by a rock fragment and killed.

July 25, 1933: Shooting, fatal. Murder. Jack Calhoun, 38, deputy state game warden, sole park leaseholder in the Twentymile District, and temporary National Park Service (NPS) fire guard, was shot and fatally wounded near his home in the park by his son, age 15. He was taken by friends to the Howard Henderson Hospital in Knoxville where he died early the following morning.

September 1, 1933: Fatal accident, CCC. Charles W. Maner, an enrolled CCC worker from Powell, TN, cut himself on the leg with an axe and later died. Immediately after the injury, a tourniquet was applied and loosened each 15 minutes. By the time Maner walked to camp, the wound had stopped bleeding. In dressing the wound, the Army doctor removed the clotted blood and bleeding started again. The young man rose to a sitting position and dropped back dead. Death was attributed to shock or heart failure.

December 12, 1933: Fatal accident, construction. Multiple fatalities (3). Three men were killed and 3 injured in an accident at Newfound Gap. A crew of 1 foreman and 9 laborers was digging a trench for a toe wall when the slope slid, burying 3 men whose bodies were not extracted for 4 hours. The men were employed on the Newfound Gap-Clingmans Dome project under contract to the Arundel Corporation of Baltimore, Maryland. Killed:

Robert Davis, foreman, Knoxville, TN
Edward Smiley, laborer, Bryson City, NC
Robert Brooks, laborer, Bushnell, NC
Injured:
James Breedlove, laborer, Almond City, NC
Grayson Gibson, laborer, Bryson City, NC
Jerome Blankenship, laborer, Bryson City, NC

December 30, 1933: Fatal accident, auto. Fatal accident, CCC. CCC worker Woodrow Boggs, Greensboro, NC, from Camp P-4, Smokemont, was killed on highway N.C. 112, when an Army CCC truck in which he was riding side-swiped a parked truck on the highway. Another passenger suffered a broken leg in the same incident.

January 22, 1934: Fatal accident, auto, fire, CCC. At 6:30 a.m., at a gasoline pump directly across the street from Assistant Chief Ranger Needham's office in Bryson City, NC, "occurred one of the worst tragedies Bryson City has ever witnessed." A bus transporting men to the CCC camps near Smokemont and to Newfound Gap was being fueled when the tank ignited. Sixteen men were seated in the bus at the time. The bus had only one door on the right side in front, and the flaming gas tank was under the right front seat, thus cutting off escape. The men were soon enveloped in flames but finally kicked the windows out and managed to crawl out, "all more or less roasted alive." Two of these men died from their burns the following day. Killed were C.W. Goodson of Bryson City, a local enrolled member of Camp P-5, and Riley Queen of Alarka, NC, who had been employed by the Arundel Corporation.

March 4, 1934: Fatal accident, auto. Mr. A.A. Wilson, Jasper, AL, was killed, Mr. R.W. Maddock, Knoxville, TN, suffered broken ribs and broken right shoulder, and Mrs. Maddock suffered broken ribs, left arm, and shoulder in an accident on the Newfound Gap Road (U.S. 441). The party was proceeding toward Newfound Gap. At a point about mid-way between Fighting Creek Junction and the Gap, the car struck a rock that heavy rains had dislodged, throwing the car to one side, off the road, and down a steep slope about 100 feet into the West Prong of Little Pigeon River. The car turned over 5 or 6 times before reaching the bottom of the slope.

April 1934: Fatal accident, construction. Three men were buried by a rock slide at a quarry on the Newfound Gap Road (U.S. 441) recon-struction project. Tennessee Foreman Elmer Dunn, Knoxville, and laborer Luther Bull, Elkmont, TN, were dead when dug out. Laborer E.J. Whaley, who was covered with rocks for several hours, was only slightly injured. This being the second fatal slide in the park, the Bureau of Public Roads called in a geologist for an investigation and report.

May 29, 1934: Fatal accident, auto. L.A. Enlow of Bryson City, NC, a locomotive engineer for the Southern Railroad, was killed when a car in which he and three friends were riding left the road and plunged over a cliff on Park Highway No. 1-B, about a mile north of Smokemont.

June 2, 1934: Fatal accident, auto. Fatal accident, CCC. About 1 a.m., a park CCC truck was involved in an accident just outside the park. An army truck and 3 park trucks filled with enrollees under the charge of an army officer were returning from Sylva, NC, where they had been on an unauthorized leave. The overhang of the body of the third truck in line demolished the body of a Ford driven by Shirley Spence of Knoxville, TN. The passengers in the Ford were J.R. Hooper, E.L. Thomas, and Oscar Tate, all of Knoxville. J.R. Hooper died about an hour after the accident.

June 19, 1934: Fatal accident, drowning. Burton Henry, 13, Maryville, TN, drowned at Abrams Falls in the Cades Cove area of the park.

July 8, 1934: Fatal accident, drowning. The body of Lewis Owl, a a member of the Eastern Band of Cherokee Indians, was found in the swimming hole at the confluence of the Left Fork and the Raven Fork of the Oconaluftee River. The discovery of Owl's clothes on the bank of the stream by CCC Project Superintendent F.C. Green led to a search by a party of his CCC enrollees, which resulted in discovery of the body. The condition of the body indicated that it had not been in the water for more than 24 hours, and there were no marks on it indicating foul play.

July 18, 1934: Fatal accident, auto. A Ford pickup carrying Charles B. Carter, Charles A. Murray Jr., and Buster Stevens, all of Knoxville, TN, ran off the road near the Appalachian Club in Elkmont. Stevens was driving the pickup, which belonged to Carter. Carter was fatally injured and died about one hour after reaching the Knoxville General Hospital where he was taken by CCC men in a park truck.

August 20, 1934: Fatal accident, tree fall. Fatal accident, CCC. CCC enrollee Charlie E. Lasater was killed while cutting a log off a downed tree.

September 8, 1934: Fatal accident, auto, CCC. At 12:10 a.m., CCC enrollee Archie Watkins, Raleigh, NC, was killed in a collision with a privately owned car just outside the park. Watkins was a member of an authorized leave party returning from the movies.

September 16, 1934: Fatal accident, construction. Fatal accident, explosives. Sam Hunter, 59, Marshall, NC, was fatally injured by a blast while at work for the Arundel Corporation on project 2A1, FP 142.8. He died a few days later in a Knoxville hospital. Hunter, a powder man, was attempting to set off a blast with an electric battery, which, due to a break in the line, did not detonate on the first attempt. Hunter went up the line to search for the break while his helper remained with the switch. He repaired the break and called down to his helper that it was fixed, but the helper did not understand the message and plunged the switch, causing the explosion.

October 17, 1937: Fatal accident, auto. Mr. E.L. Thomas of Knoxville, TN, was discovered dead in his car in the Little River about 1 mile above the Townsend entrance near the "Wye."[2] The car, a Pontiac sedan, had been traveling toward Elkmont on the afternoon of October 16 when the car left the road, turned over, and landed on its wheels in about 9 feet of water. The accident was not discovered until about 1 p.m. on October 17 by Mr. M.L. Clark, Louisville, KY, who had walked out to the edge of the stream. Thomas had leases on the property he sold to the park, which

---

2   The Townsend "Wye" describes the junction where Townsend Entrance Road meets Little River Road, leading east toward Sugarlands Visitors Center, and Laurel Creek Road, leading west toward Cades Cove.

included the orchard at Fighting Creek Gap and a cottage at Elkmont.

April 23, 1938: Dead body. Possible fatal accident, exposure/hypothermia. The body of Sue Grace Ingraham of Knoxville, TN, was found atop Mt. Le Conte. The body had been there since the previous November. The FBI aided in identifying the body.

June 12, 1938: Fatal accident, drowning. Katie Bradham, Maryville, TN, drowned in a deep hole at the Forks.

August 5, 1938: Flood. Fatal accident, drowning. Multiple fatalities (8). A cloudburst occurred along Webb Creek near the boundary of the park and swept away the home of Alfred Ball, killing Ball, his wife, their four children, and two visitors.

May 18, 1940: Fatal accident, motorcycle. The motorcycle operated by L.D. Byrd, with Iverson Thomason as passenger, collided with a CCC bus. Thomason was killed.

January 30, 1941: Fatal accident, exposure/hypothermia. The body of Tute Bright of Newport, TN, was found between NC 107 (today's Newfound Gap Road) and the Oconaluftee River. He had been dead a week and had died of exposure.

April 14, 1941: Fatal accident, exposure/hypothermia. The body of June Wolf (male), a member of the Eastern Band of Cherokee Indians, was found on Hyatt Ridge near Mount Hardison. Wolf had been missing since March 31.

May 17, 1941: Fatal accident, auto. Mr. W.F. Bridges, Asheville, NC, was killed and two others injured in an accident on NC 107 (today's Newfound Gap Road), about 1.5 miles above CCC Camp NP-5. The brakes failed on a Studebaker in which Bridges was riding, and the car plunged into a ditch.

April 5, 1942: Fatal accident, auto. J.M. Gass and Cline Wilkerson, both from Kingsport, were killed in a two-car accident.

July 2, 1943: Fatal accident, plane crash. A U.S. Army twin-engine plane crashed on Chilhowee Mountain in Happy Valley, just outside the park. The pilot (not named in the superintendent's report) was killed in the crash.

July 23, 1944: Fatal accident, drowning. Walter M. Clement, 17, Whittier, NC, drowned in the Oconaluftee River 0.9 miles below the Oconaluftee ranger station.

September 3, 1944: Fatal accident, auto. A Buick descending TN 71 (today's Newfound Gap Road) at a high rate of speed struck a car ascending the mountain 100 feet below the entrance to the Chimneys Campground and plunged over the bank and into the West Prong of the Little Pigeon River. John Wilson, 37, Knoxville, TN, a passenger in the Buick, died in the crash.

October 12, 1945: Fatal accident, plane crash. Multiple fatalities (6). GSMNP received confidential information from the Emergency Rescue Service of Nashville, TN, regarding a C-45 Army plane No. 3351, lost on October 5 while en route from St. Louis, MO, to Charlotte, NC. The wreck was found on October 12 in a dense wilderness area about 3,300 feet northeast of Mt. Sequoya and 1,200 feet south of the North Carolina state line. All six occupants of the C-45 were killed.

On October 17, 1945: An L-5 from Greenville Air Base sent to photograph the wreck of the C-45 crashed a short distance from the first crash site. Occupants of the L-5, Edward Aptt and J.R. Tettit, survived and hiked out.

On October 18, 1945: park rangers removed six bodies from the October 5 crash.

Killed in the crash:

First Lt. William Robert Barton, pilot, Youngstown, OH

Staff Sgt. Raymond H. Kerkela, Minneapolis, MN

First Lt. Sam M. Lerner, Greensboro, NC

Staff Sgt. Hollis E. Broderick, Waltham, MA

Cpl. W.R. Hanes, Cleveland, OH

Specialist (WAVE) Lena E. Allred, Charlotte, NC

October 15, 1945: Fatal accident, auto. Mrs. Charles L. Frederick, Grosse Point, MI, and Mrs. Robert Simmonds, Knoxville, TN, were killed in an accident that occurred on Little River Road (SR 73), two miles from park headquarters.

June 12, 1946: Fatal accident, plane crash. Multiple fatalities (12). Workers found an airplane engine on the side of the road near Clingmans Dome. The engine was from a B-29 that crashed into a mountain at 6,240 feet on the Tennessee side and tumbled end over end about 300 yards into North Carolina. All occupants of the plane, all U.S. Army personnel, were killed in the crash. The superintendent's report did not provide the number of dead, but an Associated Press article puts the number of fatalities at 12.

August 4, 1946: Fatal accident, lightning/electrocution. George

Hackman was killed when lightning struck the power line he was working on.

August 27, 1946: Suicide. S.R., Sevierville, TN, a leaseholder, committed suicide by hanging.

October 24, 1946: Fatal accident, auto. Mrs. Lewis King, mother-in-law of park warden Owenby, was thrown from a car and killed on Fighting Creek Gap Road.

February 23, 1947: Fatal accident, exposure/hypothermia. The car driven by Bonaventura Spink Cuniff and her sister, Dr. Urbana Spink, both from Indianapolis, IN, skidded off the road on the Little River Road (SR 73), 4 miles from the Townsend "Wye." At the time, 6 to 8 inches of snow lay on the ground and more was falling. The women started to walk toward Gatlinburg. On February 24, park snow-plow operators Ennis Ownby and John Dallard-Ownby found the women 7.5 miles from where they had left their car. Cuniff was dead and Spink was suffering from exposure.

August 7, 1947: Fatal accident, drowning. Rose Mary Mathias, 23, Frostburg, MD, died in a flash flood of the West Prong of the Little Pigeon River near the Chimneys parking area.

August 29, 1947: Fatal accident, auto. Filmore Wyatt, Lake Junaluska, NC, struck his head on a tree when the Jeep in which he was riding lost control on NC 107 (today's Newfound Gap Road) at the "Channel Change," one mile north of Smokemont, and left the road. Wyatt was pronounced dead on arrival at a hospital in Waynesville.

October 6, 1950: Fatal accident, drowning. Bridegroom George Michon, 23, of Yonkers, NY, drowned at The Sinks on the Little River when he attempted to photograph the rapids. His wife, an expert swimmer, tried to rescue him.

April 1, 1951: Fatal accident, plane crash. A National Guard P-51 Mustang crashed and exploded on the side of Hannah Mountain, 2 miles northeast of the Bunker Hill Lookout, killing Pilot Lt. Robert B. Hartman. The crash was discovered from the air on Thursday, April 5, and later confirmed by a ground party of service men. Parts of wrecked plane not buried were painted green.

July 6, 1952: Fatal accident, auto. Four-year-old Wayne Dixon of Clayton, GA, ran in front of a car driven by Norman Jeffreys of Burlington, NC, and was killed. The accident occurred about 4 miles west of Newfound Gap on the Clingmans Dome Road.

August 11, 1952: Fatal accident, auto. A Chevy sedan driven by Mrs. James Hodges of Gatlinburg, TN, plunged down a 250-foot bank 1 mile north of Newfound Gap. Kimsey Whaley of Gatlinburg was killed in the accident. Hodges was later charged with reckless driving.

May 24, 1953: Heart attack, fatal. Mr. Ashley Ownby of Cleveland, TN, suffered a fatal heart attack near the Millsap Picnic Area.

September 13, 1953: Fatal accident, auto. James A. Loveday, 50, Knoxville, TN, died from injuries sustained in an accident in the park just south of Gatlinburg.

July 27, 1954: Heart attack, fatal. Mr. L.B. Smith of Savannah, GA, died of a heart attack in the Clingmans Dome parking area.

October 7, 1954: Fatal accident, auto. Agnes Wichmann, Parma, OH, died in a car wreck on Newfound Gap Road (U.S. 441). The driver lost control of the vehicle, and it plunged into an 8-foot ravine. Passenger Anna Meier, of Parma, was seriously injured.

October 24, 1954: Fatal accident, auto. Two cars collided on the Foothills Parkway. Donnie Reagan, 7, was killed and the other passengers injured. A manslaughter charge was brought against one of the drivers.

December 16, 1954: Fatal accident, auto. Dewan Amos King, 24, Gatlinburg, TN, died of contusions of the brain, chest, and abdomen as a result of an accident on Newfound Gap Road (U.S. 441) when his car ran off the road and struck a tree.

January 30, 1955: Fatal accident, drowning. Ranger Messer accompanied by Clint Green found the body of Jess Williams, who had drowned in Fontana Lake on August 1, 1954.

February 11, 1955: Fatal accident, plane crash (occurred outside the park). Personnel from the U.S. Air Force and the Civil Air Patrol searched in the park for the missing four-seater plane piloted by Teddy Ray Jarnagin, 18, Knoxville, TN. Jarnagin was en route from Knoxville to Atlanta when his plane disappeared. A Civil Air Patrol spokesman said that high winds could have blown Jarnagin off course and into the Smoky Mountains. Jarnagin's body was found next to his crashed plane on Walden's Ridge after a 12-day search. According to a newspaper account, Jarnagin had aspired to serve as a flying missionary.

March 21, 1955: Fatal accident, auto. Lt. Orin Dayton, U.S. Air Force, died from injuries sustained in a jeep accident on Clingmans Dome Road. Dayton was part of a group from the 729th Aircraft Control and

214 INTO THE MIST

Warning Command of the 507th Tactical Control Group, from Sumter, SC, that was conducting radar tests at the Forney Ridge parking area from March 14-31. The group was camped at the Smokemont Campground.

January 15, 1956: Accidental death, exposure/hypothermia. Mr. C. H. Lindsley of Asheville, NC, reported to rangers that he had found the body of a man at the Pecks Corner shelter site on the night of January 14. He also discovered that the shelter had been destroyed by fire. Rangers Ealy, Rolen, and Rogers went to the site and identified the body of Edwin Windell Wolf, of Cherokee, NC. Evidence suggests that the deceased had accidentally set the shelter on fire. After the shelter was destroyed, Wolf apparently went to sleep and died from exposure. He had no camping permit for the shelter. The body was removed, examined by the Swain County Coroner, and claimed by the father of the deceased, Jim Wolf.

June 6, 1956: Fatal accident, drowning. Donald Charles Wright, 19, Knoxville, TN, drowned in the Little River near the upper end of Metcalf Bottoms after slipping from a rocky ledge and falling into deep water. According to witnesses, Wright rose to the surface twice and called for help. The other members of his party, like Wright, were nonswimmers and were unable to offer assistance.

March 12, 1956: Heart attack, fatal. Ray E. York, 56, Detroit, MI, suffered a fatal heart attack at the Upper Walker Prong Bridge 14 miles south of park headquarters.

July 1, 1956: Fatal accident, auto. William Isaac Hollis, 20, Dothan, AL, died of a fractured skull sustained in auto accident on Little River Road (SR 73).

August 16, 1956: Fatal accident, auto. Joyce Van Hook, 7, of Canton, NC, died as result of injuries sustained when hit by an auto operated by Dorothy T. Schiefelbein of McFarland, WI. The accident occurred on Newfound Gap Road (U.S. 441) near Towstring Road.

August 16, 1956: Fatal accident, drowning. Walter Jack Walker, 6, Cherokee, NC, drowned while swimming in the Oconaluftee River near the Oconaluftee Ranger Station.

July 4, 1957: Heart attack, fatal. Fatal accident, drowning. Robert Irwin, 17, Knoxville, TN, suffered a fatal heart attack and drowned while swimming in the Little River in the park.

October 1957: Murder. Willie Standingdeer was murdered and his body was dragged into the park. (No additional details provided.)

July 4, 1958: Fatal accident, auto. Barbara Jean Murphy, 17, Cleveland, TN, was killed in an accident near the Smokemont entrance. Barbara's husband, Jimmy, 19, died in December, presumably from injuries sustained in the accident.

March 19, 1959: Fatal accident, auto. Mrs. Ivan Poteet of Lebanon, OH, died as result of injuries received in car-bus collision on Newfound Gap Road (U.S. 441).

July 1, 1959: Fatal accident, plane crash. NPS and U.S. Air Force personnel searched the Abrams Creek district for a missing plane. Residents in Happy Valley reported seeing an explosion in the vicinity of Polecat Ridge on the previous evening. Searchers found an F-102 jet fighter completely demolished and scattered over 5 acres. Pilot, Lt. Russell Peterson from 71st Fighter Interceptor Squadron, Selfridge AFB, Michigan, died in the crash.

August 28, 1959: Fatal accident, construction. Ralph King, 22, an employee of Southern Roadway Company, subcontractor of Ray D. Bolander Co., contractor on the Newfound Gap Road (U.S. 441) construction job, was killed when a boom fell on him on the North Carolina section of the road.

May 9, 1960: Human remains, dead body. Death, natural causes. The remains of Henry Clinton Barlow, 45, Clemmons, NC, were found 300 yards inside the park boundary near the mouth of Chambers Creek on Fontana Lake. Barlow had been reported missing from his fishing camp. His death was attributed to natural causes. Barlow's body had been ravaged by wild animals. According to a report in the *Knoxville Journal*, the search of Barlow's camp turned up a buried pistol and a wallet containing $2,200. (Barlow's age at his death and the dates of his birth and death are inconsistent as listed on his tombstone, death certificate, and draft registration. This entry reflects the birth and death dates that appear on Barlow's tombstone.)

July 27, 1960: Fatal accident, auto. Princella Gale Effler, 18, Maryville, TN, died as result of injuries sustained in auto accident on the Gatlinburg Spur of U.S. 441, which connects Gatlinburg and Pigeon Forge.

October 24, 1960: Heart attack, fatal. Mrs. Ethel LaJule Bunde, Swanton, OH, suffered a fatal heart attack on the Clingmans Dome Trail.

December 25, 1960: Suicide. F.J.D., Kitty Hawk, NC, 47, wrecked his Jeep pickup along the Little River Road (SR 73) about 1 mile east of the Townsend "Wye" and later fatally shot himself in the head. He had left a note.

May 6, 1961: Fatal accident, fall. Charles Smith Sample, 14, Maryville, TN, died as a result of a 150-foot fall from the rock cliffs above the Buckeye Nature Trail. Sample had been hiking with his family at the time of the fall.

August 22, 1961: Fatal accident, construction. De Vine Brackins, 19, an employee of the Southern Roadway Corporation of Sevierville, TN, was killed when his truck overturned on an embankment on the Foothills Parkway, section 8G1.

November 7, 1961: Fatal accident, auto. Glenda Irene Qualls, Knoxville, TN, died as a result of a one-car accident above the Chimneys Campground on Newfound Gap Road (U.S. 441).

March 25, 1962: Fatal accident, auto. Ronald Cates, 19, Sevierville, TN, died as result of injuries sustained in an auto accident on Newfound Gap Road (U.S. 441) at park headquarters.

March 25, 1962: Dead body. No cause of death provided. Remains of a human body were found by two park visitors in the vicinity of the Buckeye Nature Trail. After three searches, the major portions of the body were recovered and sent to FBI lab for assistance in identification. No further details provided.

May 8, 1962: Fatal accident, auto. Cranston Casey, Pacific Palisades, CA, died on May 13 of injuries sustained in a May 8 auto accident in the park. Location not provided.

July 14, 1962: Fatal accident, drowning. Albert Mills, 18, Union Mills, NC, drowned in the Oconaluftee River approximately 50 feet north of the Blue Ridge Parkway bridge near the junction of the Parkway with Newfound Gap Road (U.S. 441). Mills was with a group from the Young Men's Civic Club of Union Mills.

July 22, 1962: Asthma attack, fatal. Heart attack, fatal. Beatrice Leonard, 49, Maryville, TN, suffered a fatal heart attack induced by asthma in the Cades Cove Campground.

July 28, 1962: Fatal accident, fall. Louise Ann Barber, 14, Knoxville, TN, fell 50 feet to her death from the top of Ramsey Cascades.

August 12, 1962: Heart attack, fatal. Scoutmaster W. R. Gilkeson, 57, Chattanooga, TN, died on the Appalachian Trail between Cosby Knob and Tricorner Knob. Gilkeson was co-leader of a group from Explorer Troop 2015.

October 13, 1962: Heart attack, fatal. William C. Wayland, Knoxville, TN, died of an apparent heart attack in the Cades Cove Picnic Area.

November 14, 1962: Fatal accident, plane crash. A U.S. Air Force plane carrying two officers, missing since November 10 and presumed to have crashed, was sighted by a Civil Air Patrol observer plane near Inadu Knob in the eastern district of the park on November 13. Search parties reached the wreckage early on November 14. The bodies of Brig. Gen. John I. Lerom and Capt. Ludwig Gesund were brought out to Cosby and later taken to Donaldson Air Force Base, SC.

July 10, 1963: Fatal accident, auto. Beverly T. Witcher (male), 76, Greenville, SC, died as result of injuries sustained in an auto accident near the Oconaluftee Ranger Station on Newfound Gap Road (U.S. 441).

March 3, 1964: Fatal accident, plane crash/incident. It was reported that a U.S. Air Force plane had lost its door and that an airman was also lost between Mt. Le Conte and Mt. Guyot. A seat and seat belt from the plane were found in the Glades area (outside the park near Gatlinburg) along with other equipment, and a parachute was found on Gilliland Creek. The body of Airman 2/C Gary D. Back was found on March 5 just outside the park a short distance from the Greenbrier Motel on the north side of State Road 73.

March 22, 1964: Fatal accident, plane crash. Heart attack, fatal. Multiple fatalities (7). Civil Air Patrol in Maryville called District Ranger Ward regarding a plane crash on the mountainside approximately 100 feet below Parson Bald. The plane, a BE-18 twin-engine Beechcraft, crashed on March 21 but was not reported lost until the 22nd because the pilot had not filed a flight plan. A Tennessee Highway patrol helicopter spotted the wreckage in the late afternoon of March 22 and reported that the plane had burned. Four adults and two children perished in the crash: J. Noble Miles, pilot; Mrs. Miles; Mr. and Mrs. John Fetto; and two nieces of the plane's owner, Joseph Fabick, ages 13 and 14, all of St. Louis, MO. A search party was sent to Parson Bald. At 2:30 a.m., as the search party neared the top, Frank Shults, a member of the party, died of an apparent heart attack. Shults' party brought out his body. Another crew set out and reached the wreckage 12:22 p.m.

May 17, 1964: Fatal accident, livestock. Manny Moore, 35, Hartford, TN, died in a Newport hospital from injuries sustained in an accident on the Walnut Bottoms truck trail. He was driving a mule-drawn 2-wheel cart down a steep grade when the tongue broke and the mules bolted, dragging Moore for 804 feet. At the time of the accident, 7 men and 1 child rode in the cart, which contained the party's camping gear. Passengers David Clark and Nick Price, both from Hartford, were injured in the accident.

May 19, 1964: Fatal accident, auto. Lee N. Johnson Jr., Gatlinburg, TN, was killed on the northbound lane of Gatlinburg Spur of U.S. 441.

June 6, 1964: Fatal accident, plane crash. A Piper Comanche crashed about 100 yards from the fire road in the Little Cataloochee section of the park. The wreckage was discovered on the following day by two men attending the Little Cataloochee homecoming. The plane's occupants, both killed, were Walter C. Bowsman, 44, and his mother, Margaret W. Bowsman, 87, of Elgin, IL.

June 14, 1964: Fatal accident, drowning. Darlene Riden, 12, of Maryville, TN, drowned while swimming in the Little River at the Townsend "Wye." Riden, a nonswimmer, was wading toward an island in the river when she slipped and fell and was carried away by the current.

September 5, 1964: Fatal accident, auto. An auto fatality occurred on the northbound lane of the Gatlinburg Spur of U.S. 441. The car was driven by Donald Wayne Sexton of Sevierville, who was killed. Eleven one-car and eight two-car accidents occurred during the month, resulting in 1 fatality, 8 personal injuries, and property damage estimated at $11,157.

October 11, 1964: Heart attack, fatal. Jesse James Hallum, 46, Cleveland, TN, died as result of a heart attack suffered near Sugarlands Visitor Center.

December 30, 1964: Heart attack, fatal. Dr. Lea Callaway, 53, Maryville, TN, died of a heart attack while hiking the Appalachian Trail 1.5 miles north of Newfound Gap. Calloway and his party were en route to the LeConte lodge.

March 13, 1965: Fatal accident, auto. Barbara Ann Talley, 21, Franklin, NC, was killed in an accident that occurred on Newfound Gap Road (U.S. 441) near the entrance to Smokemont Campground. Excessive speed was believed to have been the cause of the accident.

April 25, 1965: Fatal accident, auto. Joe P. Cole, 69, Gatlinburg, TN, was killed when his car left Newfound Gap Road (U.S. 441) at the Chimneys Campground and collided head-on with the bridge across the West Prong of the Little Pigeon River.

June 5, 1965: Heart attack, fatal. Dan Myers, 77, Walland, TN, died en route to the hospital after suffering a heart attack at the Primitive Baptist Church in Cades Cove.

June 13, 1965: Fatal accident, auto. Roy Van Thorn, 36, Grand Rapids, MI, was killed when he lost control of his tractor-trailer on the North

Carolina side of Newfound Gap Road (U.S. 441) and crashed into a vertical rock face. Commercial vehicles were allowed on the road at the time. The brakes on Thorn's truck had failed prior to the accident.

June 16, 1965: Fatal accident, auto. Jerry L. Cloyd, 16, and Jerry D. Rauhuff, 16, both of Sevier County, TN, died from injuries sustained in an accident near the junction of the Gatlinburg Bypass and the Gatlinburg Spur of U.S. 441. Cloyd's mother, Barbara, and stepfather, Von Teaster, were both park employees.

June 1965: Heart attack, fatal. Two heart attacks were suffered by visitors, one resulted in death (no additional details appear in the superintendent's report).

July 14, 1965: Heart attack, fatal. Stewart Rogers, 59, Hobart, IN, died of an apparent heart attack in the Elkmont Campground.

August 29, 1965: Heart attack, fatal. An elderly woman suffered a fatal heart attack while sitting in a car parked at Luftee Overlook on Clingmans Dome Road (superintendent's report does not provide the victim's name).

October 31, 1965: Heart attack, fatal. Cleo Clifton Liles, 50, Durham, NC, died of a heart attack at the Forney Ridge parking area.

November 16, 1965: Fatal accident, auto. Human remains. While painting guard posts along the new stretch of Newfound Gap Road south of Newfound Gap, truck driver Dan Lambert spotted a car over the bank at a deep cut. An investigation indicated that the vehicle had been wrecked and abandoned. The vehicle was registered to a Lewis Alexander Swink, 39, Lincolntown, NC, and contact with police there revealed that Mr. Swink was last heard from in Knoxville on September 27. An intensive search of the general area resulted in the discovery of Swink's billfold, a belt and bits of clothing, and bone fragments. The bone fragments were sent to the FBI laboratory in Washington for identification. Swink's death certificate indicates date of death as September 27, 1965, and cause of death a fractured skull resulting from an automobile accident. The certificate also indicates that Swink's body had been "devoured by animals."

February 10, 1966: Heart attack, fatal. NPS forestry technician Roy C. Whaley died of an apparent heart attack near the Sugarlands Visitor Center while returning from a field assignment in Cades Cove.

February 12, 1966: Suicide. L.T., 17, Maryville, TN, committed suicide at the Walland entrance to the Foothills Parkway.

August 20, 1966: Fatal accident, drowning. Richard A. Stansberry, 18, Knoxville, TN, drowned in Little River near the Townsend "Wye" while trying to test his SCUBA equipment. The search and recovery were carried out by rangers, Tremont Job Corps personnel and corpsmen, and the Blount County rescue squad. The body was recovered the following morning and sent to Blount Memorial Hospital where the coroner ruled death by drowning with a blow to the head as a contributing factor. The stream was running high at the time of the incident.

October 13, 1966: Heart attack, fatal. Otto Strasser, 62, Iowa City, IA, suffered a fatal heart attack in the Smokemont Campground.

October 30, 1966: Fatal accident, auto. Lloyd H. Green, 44, Sevierville, TN, was killed on SR 73/U.S. 321, where the highway forms the park boundary, when he pulled out from a service station into the path of an oncoming car.

December 11, 1966: Fatal accident, auto. James Lillard Smith, 18, Knoxville, TN, apparently went to sleep behind the wheel, left the road, and struck a tree on SR 73 2.6 miles west of the U.S. 441-SR 73 junction. Lillard died of injuries from the accident. Passenger Steve Craig Dyer, 18, Knoxville, was seriously injured.

March 11, 1967: Fatal accident, auto. Fatal accident, drowning. At about 10:30 p.m., a car driven by James A. Ray, 22, Pigeon Forge, TN, went out of control and careened into the West Prong of the Little Pigeon River on the Gatlinburg Spur of U.S. 441. Death was attributed to drowning when Ray apparently attempted to leave the vehicle and fell into the river. The body was recovered at 5 a.m. the following morning in a pool of water approximately 15 to 20 feet deep about 75 feet from the vehicle.

April 10, 1967: Fatal accident, auto. A car driven by William H. Owle, Cherokee, NC, pulled from the Big Cove road into the path of a northbound Trailways bus on Newfound Gap Road (U.S. 441). Owle was killed and two passengers in the car were hospitalized.

May 28, 1967: Fatal accident, auto. A vehicle driven by Thomas K. Field, 22, Putnam Valley, NY, failed to negotiate a sharp curve on Newfound Gap Road (U.S. 441) in front of park headquarters and crashed into a group of trees. Field was dead on arrival at Baptist Hospital in Knoxville.

October 13, 1968: Fatal accident, plane crash. A Cessna 190 crashed near the Spruce Mountain lookout tower, 700 feet north of Horse Creek Gap. Pilot Thomas Johnstone Crawford, 64, Bainbridge, GA, the plane's only occupant, died in the crash.

November 12, 1968: Fatal accident, exposure/hypothermia. Two unnamed 19-year-old men died of exposure just outside the park in Townsend, TN, after being lost for 30 hours during a hunting trip. Heavy snow and freezing rain contributed to the men's deaths. A third member of the hunting party managed to walk to safety.

February 12, 1969: Fatal accident, plane crash. A Cessna 182 aircraft, piloted by John C. Koppert, 44, Columbus, OH, disappeared over the park during a flight from Knoxville, TN, to Asheville, NC. Over a year later, on May 24, 1970, a Civil Air Patrol pilot spotted the wreckage of Koppert's plane in the park on Mt. Chapman, at an elevation of 6,160 feet. A search party recovered Koppert's remains on May 29.

June 14, 1969: Missing, not found. Members of the Martin family gathered in Spence Field for an annual Father's Day celebration. At about 4:30 in the afternoon, Dennis Martin, 6, who was playing with a group of other boys, disappeared. An extensive search failed to find any trace of him. He has never been found and is presumed dead.

August 12, 1969: Fatal accident, plane crash, helicopter. A helicopter piloted by Gene Henry, 30, Knoxville, TN, crashed near a parking area south of Indian Gap. Henry, who was killed in the crash, was the helicopter's only occupant.

October 29, 1969: Heart attack, fatal. Robert James Bathe, 54, McMinnville, TN, died of a heart attack while hiking on the Appalachian Trail near the Icewater Spring Shelter.

February 18, 1970: Fatal accident, hypothermia/exposure. After an intensive 11-day search, a team of GSMNP rangers and others located the body of Explorer Scout Geoff Hague, 16, Morristown, TN, about a half-mile from the junction of the Appalachian and Boulevard trails in the park. Two days earlier, the search team had located Hague's pack, extra clothing, and food on a boulder near where the body was later found. According to members of Hague's hiking party, the scout was last seen on February 8 at the trail junction. On Sunday, February 15, the Reverend Billy Graham held a prayer service in Gatlinburg, TN, for the missing hiker.

April 30, 1970: Fatal accident, auto. A car driven by Dennis A. Trentham, 19, Sevierville, TN, went out of control on the Gatlinburg Spur of U.S. 441, near Gatlinburg, resulting in the death of one passenger, Carol Ann Cardwell, 16, Sevierville.

August 12, 1971: Fatal accident, fall. Larry E. Cebuhar, 23, of Peo-

ria, IL, was on his honeymoon in GSMNP when he slipped on wet moss
and fell 80 feet to his death from the top of Ramsey Cascades.

August 22, 1972: Fatal accident, drowning. The body of John
Childers, 59, Whittier, NC, a park employee, was pulled from 200 feet of
water near the Fontana boat dock. Childers and five other park employees
were thrown from a barge loaded with heavy equipment after the steel craft
struck the wake left by a passing pleasure boat.

March 14, 1973: Fatal accident, tree fall. Michael Anthony Ward, 5,
Cherokee, NC, was killed when a basswood tree fell on him and his grandmother near the Luftee Overlook on Clingmans Dome Road.

April 3, 1973: Fatal accident, plane crash. Multiple fatalities (4).
Four were killed when a twin-engine Piper Aztec crashed on Mt. Le Conte.
Killed were Thomas J. Suter, 39, Cincinnati, OH; John Brandt, 32, Crescent
Springs, KY; Bonnie Lou Frasure, 18, South Shore, KY; Linda Picklesiner,
17, South Portsmouth, KY. An afghan hound on board survived the crash.

May 28, 1973: Fatal accident, drowning. William Lawrence Bridge,
19, DeSoto, MO, drowned when his canoe capsized in deep, swift water
near the Townsend "Wye."

June 16, 1973: Fatal accident, drowning. Alexander S. Moffatt, 20,
Tampa, FL, drowned while trying to cross rain-swollen Forney Creek. He
was swept downstream and lodged under a log.

June 23, 1973: Fatal accident, auto. Tracy M. Clay, 8, Absecon, NJ,
was killed when a camper van overturned on her on Old NC 284 (Cove
Creek Road) in Haywood County, NC.

July 13, 1973: Fatal accident, auto. Larry Steve Loveday, 19, Sevierville, TN, was killed when his car went off a curve on the Gatlinburg Spur
of U.S. 441 near Pigeon Forge.

July 20, 1973: Fatal accident, drowning, fall. Malcolm McAtee, 20,
Memphis, TN, drowned at Abrams Creek when he apparently slipped from
a rock and plunged into a deep pool.

August 2, 1973: Heart attack, fatal. Margaret Scott, 47, St. Peters-
burg, FL, slumped over in her parked car after returning to it after a short
hike on Trillium Gap Trail. She was later pronounced dead.

October 7, 1973: Dead body. Murder. At about noon, a park vis-
itor discovered a duffel bag containing the nude body of a woman along
Clingmans Dome Road. The body was later identified as that of Janet Gail
Carter, 24, Hueytown, AL. Carter apparently died of suffocation. An article

in the October 31, 1973, edition of *The Anniston* (AL) *Star*, reports that Carter's daughter, Christina, 3, had been reported missing in September and had not been found. The child's father, Lindsay Carter, expressed fear that his daughter was also dead. According to the article, Lindsay and Janet were recently divorced.

November 2, 1973: Fatal accident, plane crash. Photographer Jimmy Yett, 28, Sevierville, TN, was aboard a Cessna 150 piloted by Jack Roberts (no age provided), also of Sevierville, when the plane crashed about 2 miles from SR 73 near Noisy Creek in the Greenbrier section of the park. Roberts' and Yett's bodies were recovered early the following morning.

July 10, 1974: Fatal accident, auto. Richard L. Taliaferro, 24, Hixson, TN, died in an auto accident on the Gatlinburg Spur of U.S. 441.

August 15, 1974: Fatal accident, fall. John A. Salvaggio (no age or hometown provided) died after a fall from Ramsey Cascades.

December 1, 1974: Fatal accident, aspiration. Richard H. Roach, 17, Knoxville, TN, son of a Knoxville police officer, died of aspiration in the Cades Cove Campground after consuming potted meat, crackers, and soft drinks. His two companions were treated for exposure.

March 9, 1975: Lost hiker, dead body. Fatal accident, exposure/hypothermia. Search began for lost hiker Mark Hanson, 20, a student at Eastern Kentucky University. His body was found on March 17 near Tri-Corner Knob Shelter. Hanson and his hiking companion became separated in a late-winter snowstorm.

April 27, 1975: Fatal accident, auto/motorcycle. Robert E. Lewis, 21, Hendersonville (record does not specify whether Lewis was from Hendersonville TN or NC), was killed when he lost control of his motorcycle and crashed into a guardrail on Newfound Gap Road (U.S. 441).

March 1, 1976: Murder, multiple victims (occurred outside the park). William Bradford Bishop, a foreign service officer with the U.S. State Department, is suspected of murdering five family members in their Bethesda, MD, home on or about March 1. Bishop's 1974 Chevrolet station wagon was later found abandoned near the Elkmont Campground at the Jakes Creek Trailhead. Bishop has never been captured, though he is still on the FBI's most-wanted list.

April 1, 1976: Heart attack, fatal. Boy Scout Troup Leader A. Leon Smith, 55, Thomaston, GA, collapsed and died on the trail to Mt. Sterling.

June 4, 1976: Fatal accident, drowning. Gregory Michael Kirk, 15,

Seymour, TN, drowned while tubing the Little River. His leg became trapped in debris.

June 26, 1976: Fatal accident, drowning. Troy Titlow, 22, Dalton, GA, drowned while tubing the Little River below Townsend "Wye."

August 14, 1976: Dead body. Murder. Shooting. A body was found partly submerged in Rabbit Creek, near the Parson Branch Road in the Cades Cove area. The victim had been shot once in the left temple and apparently dragged into the creek. Over a month later, the body was identified as that of Emily Phyllis Moore, of Nashville, IN, 52. Leslie Standifer, Scottsburg, IN, 44, was later charged with murder and convicted.

October 8, 1976: Missing, not found. Trenny Gibson, 16, high school student from Knoxville, TN, was reported missing from school trip to Clingmans Dome. She was never found and is presumed dead.

May 20, 1977: Fatal accident, drowning, broken neck. Donald Eugene Manis, 27, Knoxville, TN, was killed when he dove into Little River near Long Arm Bridge and struck his head on a rock, which broke his neck.

May 28, 1977: Fatal accident, fall. Newlywed Bryan Zugelder, 21, Dayton, OH, died when he fell 80 feet from Ramsey Cascades into a pool at the bottom of the falls.

June 23, 1977: Fatal accident, drowning, blow to head. Jay Kragt, 11, Crystal, MN, died after slipping in the creek at the Elkmont Campground and hitting his head on a rock. He was revived briefly but died later.

June 27, 1977: Fatal accident, drowning. Shirley Bolin, 29, Knoxville, TN, drowned in the rain-swollen Little River about 3 miles above the Townsend "Wye."

October 21, 1977: Heart attack, fatal. William Shepard, 49, Centerville, TN, died of a heart attack while hiking on the Abrams Falls Trail in the Cades Cove area of the park.

December 1, 1977: Fatal accident, plane crash. Thomas Shrewsbury, 34, was piloting a Cessna 172 en route to Detroit, MI, from Blairsville, GA. On board the plane were the pilot's three children, Laura, 12, Jeff, 10, and Jennifer, 8. The plane crashed in the park 2.5 miles east of Gregory Bald. Thomas and Laura were killed in the crash. The two other children, who were seriously injured but survived, were extracted from the crash site by a U.S. Army helicopter and transferred to a medical helicopter on Gregory Bald. From there, they were flown to an area hospital.

January 3, 1978: Fatal accident, plane crash, double. Multiple fatalities (9). Nine persons were killed in separate aircraft crashes. The first involved a twin-engine Cessna airplane, with five aboard (all were killed), and the second involved a search and rescue helicopter, with eight aboard, sent from Fort Campbell, KY, to the scene of the first crash. Four of the crewmembers aboard the helicopter survived, including two NPS rangers. However, one of the rangers, Dave Harbin, died much later, potentially from complications related to a blood transfusion received at the time of the accident.

Killed in the crash of the Cessna:

Fred Philip, 27, pilot; his parents Thomas Hartley, 43, and Elaine; brother Tim, 10; and Fred's girlfriend, Marla Yates, 22, all from Chicago, IL.

Killed in the helicopter:

Capt. John L. Dunnavant, Pilot, 26, Lynnville, TN

Lt. Col. Ray Maynard, 62, Knoxville, TN

Capt. Terrance K. Woolever, 31, Mount Pleasant, MI

Sgt. Floyd Smith, 27, Greenville, MS

June 11, 1978: Fatal accident, fall. Tommy King, 20, Sevierville, TN, and friends were walking north on Newfound Gap Road (U.S. 441), near the Alum Cave Trail, at 4 a.m. An oncoming car startled them, and King fell 14 feet onto river rock below. King died of his injuries.

December 23, 1978: Murder. Shooting. The body of Kenneth Landon Taylor, 40, Strawberry Plains, TN, was found in woods 20 feet from the Foothills Parkway east. Taylor had been shot three times in the head. According to a February 14, 1981, article in the *New York Times*, two armed men in ski masks burst into the Newport, TN, home of Taylor's widow, Evelyn, bound and gagged her and a business partner, and kidnapped her 6-year-old son and demanded $200,000 ransom. The boy was later found unharmed. The article notes that Kenneth Taylor was in the "amusement machine business" and that, as of the time of the article's publication, the FBI had made no arrests in his murder.

August 29, 1979: Suicide. Three backpackers discovered the body of T.H.R., 41, Charleston, SC, on the Appalachian Trail near Clingmans Dome. Suicide by drug overdose was the suspected cause of death. Pills were found on his person.

January 25, 1980: Suicide. The body of A.D.M., 19, Knoxville, TN, was discovered slumped in his vehicle in an overlook parking area above the Chimneys area on Newfound Gap Road (U.S. 441). He died of an apparent self-inflicted gunshot wound.

May 16, 1980: Fatal accident, auto/motorcycle. Stanley P. Warren, 21, Dillsboro, NC, died when he lost control of his motorcycle 0.2 mile south of the Alum Cave Trail parking area on Newfound Gap Road (U.S. 441) and struck a rock.

July 10, 1980: Fatal accident, lightning strike, electrocution. Roger L. McGlone, 32, Maysville, OH, and Jeffrey S. Powell, 19, Saline, MI, were killed when lightning struck the Double Spring Gap Shelter on the Appalachian Trail. The wire mesh bunks conducted the current from the lightning and electrocuted the victims. The lightning splintered a tree approximately 20 feet from the shelter. Shortly after the first strike that killed McGlone and Powell, a second strike hit the shelter, shocking, but not harming, the other 6 occupants of the shelter.

March 7, 1981: Fatal accident, auto. Donna McMichen Heard, 19, Acworth, GA, was a passenger in a car driven by her husband eastbound on Little River Road (SR 73) about a mile east of Metcalf Bottoms Picnic Area. The car crossed into the westbound lane, struck a large tree, went over the bank, and came to rest with its rear in the river. Donna died of her injuries, and her husband, who told investigators that he believed that he had fallen asleep at the wheel, suffered head and face lacerations, possible fractured ribs, and fractured right arm and leg.

March 29, 1981: Fatal accident, auto/motorcycle. Donald R. Smith, Morristown, TN, 20, died when he crashed his motorcycle while traveling at a high rate of speed northbound on the Gatlinburg Spur of U.S. 441, one mile south of Pigeon Forge.

March 29–April 1, 1981: Suicide. Newlyweds Janet Andrea Rudd, 18, (the incident report lists her city of residence as Tampa, FL, but newspaper accounts variously place her home in Sarasota and Coral Gables, FL), and John Patrick Rudd, 19, (the incident report first lists his home as Sarasota and later as Coral Gables, FL), had entered the park with the intent to carry out a suicide pact. At 7:15 p.m. on March 29, Janet arrived at the Abrams Creek Ranger Station and related a story about a planned honeymoon/double suicide. Janet had a slash on her wrist. On April 1, after a search, rangers discovered the couples' campsite about a half mile south of Scott Gap, and John's body was discovered about 2 miles from the campsite and about 2 miles from the Abrams Creek ranger station. John had bled to death after slashing his wrist. Janet's wound was not life threatening. The couple had married in secret on March 2.

April 15, 1981: Fatal accident, auto/motorcycle. Karl B. Luzader, 17, (no hometown listed) was fatally injured in a motorcycle accident on Cherokee Orchard Road. Luzader had been traveling northbound on Cherokee Orchard, .3 miles from the Junglebrook parking area, when he left the road at a curve and crashed.

April 22, 1981: Fatal accident, auto. Jack R. Thomas, 44, Candler, NC, was a passenger in a car driven by Thomas Betterton II, Charlotte, NC, and headed northbound on Newfound Gap Road (U.S. 441). At 1.3 miles north of the TN/NC state line the car skidded on a curve, left the roadway, and fell down a steep embankment. Thomas was pronounced dead on arrival at the Sevier County Medical Center.

July 10–December 8, 1981: Dead body. Murder. Human remains of a male were found on July 10 along Walker Prong, on the south flank of Mt. Le Conte, about 1.5 miles from Newfound Gap. The man may have been dead for as long as two months. The body was later identified as that of Albert Brian Hunt, 20, a college student from Arcadia, FL. Hunt was last seen on April 29. Hunt's car was found on May 4 abandoned near Lawrenceville, GA. Robert Elton Taylor, 29, a North Carolina native living in Lawrenceville, was charged with the theft of the car. Taylor and Freddie Ray Staton Jr. were later charged with robbery, interstate transport of a stolen motor vehicle, and Hunt's murder. Hunt had been bludgeoned to death.

August 15, 1981: Fatal accident, auto. Jeffrey W. Sheppard, 18, Knoxville, TN, a passenger in a car driven by Jonathan S. Olandt, 18, Concord, TN, was killed when the car crossed the centerline of Little River Road (SR 73) 3.6 miles east of the Townsend "Wye," struck a large rock, and landed in the river. The driver and a backseat passenger were injured but survived.

September 25, 1981: Missing not found. Thelma Pauline Melton, 58, Jacksonville, FL, was hiking on the Deep Creek Trail with two friends when she went missing. She was never found and is presumed dead.

February 28, 1982: Fatal accident, exposure/hypothermia. Backpackers arrived at Newfound Gap and reported to rangers that hiker John E. Hernholm, 29, Memphis, TN, was having difficulty in the backcountry. The hikers had been traveling with Hernholm, but Hernholm, who was partially paralyzed on one side, was moving at a slower pace. The hikers had left Hernholm at Charlies Bunion and continued on to the Pecks Corner Shelter. Hernholm never arrived. On March 1, a ranger on horseback discovered Hernholm's body on the Hughes Ridge Trail about .25

mile south of Pecks Corner. More than a foot of snow lay on the ground at Pecks Corner.

July 31, 1982: Fatal accident, drowning. David E. Rayson, 19, Knoxville, TN, had been wading in the Little River at The Sinks. He strayed into waist-deep water, lost his footing, and disappeared below the water's surface. The river was about 5 feet above its normal level at the time. On August 1, rangers and the Blount County rescue squad recovered Rayson's body 1.5 miles downstream of where he had last been seen.

August 22, 1982: Fatal accident, auto. James Todd Ogle, 18, Elkmont, TN, a passenger in a Jeep driven by Jack Maples, died when the Jeep left the road while headed southbound on the Gatlinburg Spur of U.S. 441.

December 21, 1982: Murder. The body of Randy R. Morgan, 21, was discovered on Gnatty Branch Road just inside the boundary of the Foothills Parkway, off the Gatlinburg Spur of U.S. 441 in Pigeon Forge. Morgan had been killed by a shotgun blast to the lower chest.

August 2, 1983: Fatal accident, drowning, blunt force trauma. Family members of Olivia A. Granat, 34, Abita Springs, LA, located Granat's body in Cole Branch along Newfound Gap Road (U.S. 441) south of the Chimneys Picnic Area. Granat, who had been missing since Saturday, July 30, had been staying at a hotel in Pigeon Forge with her 17-year-old son. She had gone out Saturday night, after 11 p.m., to listen to music at a bar in Gatlinburg and left her son alone in the hotel room. She never returned. Granat's rental car was found parked in a pulloff on Newfound Gap Road .3 miles south of the loop. Granat's rental car showed signs of impact, and rangers later documented four areas of damage along the road that were likely caused by Granat's car. The death was ruled accidental.

August 10, 1983: Fatal accident, auto/motorcycle. Curtis Lyle Talbot Jr., 37, Sevier County, TN, died on the scene after a motorcycle accident on the Gatlinburg Spur of U.S. 441 at Beech Branch.

January 5, 1984: Fatal accident, plane crash. A U.S. Air Force RF-4C Phantom jet crashed and exploded in the park on Inadu Knob, killing pilot Capt. David F. Greggs, 28, Montgomery, AL, and navigator Capt. Scott A. Miller, 32, Irving, TX. The aircraft was returning to Shaw Air Force Base, near Sumter, SC, at the time of the crash. Miller's body was recovered shortly after the accident. Greggs' body was recovered on January 13. The plane crashed at approximately 5,800 feet, just 100 feet or so short of clearing the ridge.

March 2, 1984: Accidental death, exposure/hypothermia. Searchers discovered the body of hiker John Eric Mink, 25, Dunkirk, IN, on the Appalachian Trail about 1.5 miles west of Silers Bald. Mink's parents had notified the park on March 1 that their son was overdue from a three-day, two-night hike in the park. Cause of death was hypothermia from exposure to extreme winter conditions. Snow had reached a depth of three feet on the day rangers believe Mink died, February 29, 1984, a leap year.

March 4, 1984: Fatal accident, auto. Robert Dockery (no date of birth or home address appears in the incident report) was driving a red Oldsmobile Cutlass eastward on Laurel Creek Road, 0.25 mile east of the tunnel, when he lost control of the vehicle and crashed into a tree. According to one of Dockery's passengers, Dockery had been driving at a high rate of speed just before the crash. The impact killed Dockery and injured his two passengers.

June 15, 1984: Fatal accident, auto. Joyce B. Ferguson, 51, Philadelphia, TN, died as a result of injuries she sustained in an auto accident that occurred on Little River Road (SR 73), 1.25 miles west of the intersection with Elkmont Road. Joyce was a passenger in a VW Rabbit driven by her husband, Robert Ferguson. Robert was driving east on Little River Road toward Gatlinburg when he crossed the double-yellow line and struck an oncoming vehicle head on. According to the incident report, Robert stated that he believed he had fallen asleep at the wheel.

August 10, 1984: Fatal accident, drowning. Randall Smith, 29, Hattiesburg, MS, was swept into Raven Fork near Enloe Creek campsite #47 while trying to cross the creek at high water. Smith, co-leader of a Methodist Church group, was helping two young men from his group evacuate the campsite, about 4 miles northeast of the Smokemont Campground, after having been harassed by a bear. While crossing the creek, Smith was swept away. Searchers found his body in Raven Fork about 0.5 mile from the park boundary.

August 22, 1984: Heart attack, fatal. Nathaniel M. Mann, 73, Aiken, SC, suffered a heart attack in the parking lot at The Sinks. Bystanders administered CPR, but Mann did not regain consciousness. He was pronounced dead on arrival at the Sevier County Medical Center.

December 29, 1984: Murder. Skeletal remains. Park visitors from Madisonville, TN, discovered skeletal remains near the Tipton-Oliver cabin on the Cades Cove Loop Road. The remains were later identified as those of Rosalind (Rosalyn, according to Social Security records) Goodman, 35, Memphis, TN. Goodman had been missing since going on a camping trip to the park in late September. William and Rebecca Jo Hewlett were arrested in Gulfport, MS, on December 19, 1988, and William later confessed to Goodman's murder. Goodman had camped with the couple at the Cades Cove Campground. At the time of the arrest, William Hewlett, who had been on the run for 11 years as a parole violator, was on the U.S. Marshall Service's top-15 most-wanted list and was also wanted in West Virginia and Florida for sexual assault. Dr. William Bass, University of Tennessee (UT) forensic anthropologist, confirmed Goodman's identity through dental records.

July 19, 1985: Fatal accident, drowning. Daniel L. Johnson, 36, Cullowhee, NC, drowned in Raven Fork downstream of the Raven Fork Bridge near the confluence with the Oconaluftee River. Johnson had been tubing with friends. When one of the friends fell from his tube, Johnson tried to assist him and drowned in the attempt.

October 26, 1985: Accidental death, tree fall, construction. George W. Anderson, 60, Corbin, KY, an employee of Whayne Supply Company, had been servicing Caterpillar heavy construction equipment on a construction site at an unopened section of the Foothills Parkway. At the time, employees of a construction company based in London, KY, were clearing trees on the parkway right-of-way. Anderson was hauling cut wood to his truck when a hanging tree cut earlier fell and struck him on top of his head. Anderson died of his injuries.

January 5, 1986: Heart attack, fatal. Gerald Arthur Burbage, 66, Cincinnati, OH, died of a fatal heart attack while driving southbound on Newfound Gap Road (U.S. 441) just south of the Ford Harry parking area.

January 18, 1986: Fatal accident, auto. Fatal accident, drowning. James McNeel, 20, Birmingham, AL, and Anthony Grisdale, 19, Talladega, AL, were killed when their Datsun 280Z left the road about 3.5 miles east of the Townsend "Wye" on Little River Road (SR 73). The car careened down a 20-foot cliff and landed on its top in the creek. Grisdale was driving at the time of the accident.

February 8, 1986: Fatal accident, auto. David R. Noland, 26, Sevierville, TN, died in a single-vehicle accident while traveling south on the Gatlinburg Spur of U.S. 441. Noland, a passenger in the 1985 Ford pickup truck driven by Richard E. Mason, Noland's brother-in-law, died when the vehicle veered off the right side of the road and grazed a rock outcropping.

March 31, 1986: Murder, strangulation. The body of Donna Sue Bookout, 19, Maryville, TN, was discovered 35 feet off the side of Chilhowee Mountain below Butterfly Gap Road near the Foothills Parkway west. Bookout's 1978 Ford Pinto was located downhill from her body. James Amos Parker, 21, Greenback, TN, confessed to strangling Bookout with her brassier before he drove Bookout's Pinto, with the body inside, off the road. Bookout was pregnant at the time of her death. On April 29, 1987, Parker was convicted and sentenced for the murder strangulation death of Bookout.

May 13, 1986: Fatal accident, auto. Kathleen S. McCarty, 40, Corryton, TN, was a passenger in a Corvette driven by Charles Spradlin of Garland, TX, when the auto left the road northbound on the Gatlinburg Spur of U.S. 441 near Little Smoky Road. McCarty's right leg was severed in the accident and she died of blood loss.

May 19, 1986: Heart attack, fatal. Raymond L. Mills, 58, died of a fatal heart attack while a passenger in a car traveling from Cherokee, NC, to Knoxville, TN, on Newfound Gap Road (U.S. 441) near Walker Prong.

June 14, 1986: Fatal accident, auto. Alberta Knoerr, 71, Louisville, KY, died in a two-car accident on Newfound Gap Road (U.S. 441) near the park boundary with Cherokee, NC. Robert Richard, Knoxville, TN, was driving a 1972 Chevrolet pickup that crossed the road and struck a Buick driven by Daniel W. Clark. There were eight passengers in Clark's car, including Knoerr and two minor children who were sitting on the laps of adult passengers. Knoerr was pronounced dead at the scene.

June 17, 1986: Heart attack, fatal. Lester Furgess (no age or hometown provided) died of a heart attack near the tower on Clingmans Dome.

June 19, 1986: Fatal accident, auto. Cecil P. Faulkner Jr., Sevierville, TN, 31, was traveling northbound on the Gatlinburg Spur of U.S. 441 when he lost control of his CJ5 Jeep. The vehicle rolled twice, at which time Faulkner's head struck the pavement, killing him.

July 7, 1986: Fatal accident, auto. Emert R. Ownby, 38, Gatlinburg, TN, was traveling south on the Gatlinburg Spur of U.S. 441 when he lost control of his Ford tow truck. The truck went off the left side of the road and into the river. Ownby was thrown from the vehicle when it struck a gum tree and was found on the opposite side of the river.

July 27, 1986: Fatal accident, auto. Victim pregnant. Baby delivered but later died. Joyce A. Yoakum, 29, Knoxville, TN, and her unborn child died when the 1985 Buick driven by Joyce's husband, Ernest Yoakum, crashed while headed north on the Gatlinburg Spur of U.S. 441. Yoakum lost control of the car near the Rock Wall Curve.

August 13, 1986: Suicide. B.A.O., 19, Oak Ridge, TN, died at the UT Medical Center from a self-inflicted gunshot wound. He shot himself in a roadside turnout on Little River Road (SR 73) west of Elkmont.

August 19, 1986: Death, natural causes. Andrew Weyland, 75, Hackettstown, NJ, died during the night in his camper in Cades Cove Campground. The death was attributed to natural causes. Weyland had a history of heart problems and had recently undergone open-heart surgery.

October 5, 1986: Fatal accident, auto. John Stambaugh Jr., 23, Knoxville, TN, died in a single-car accident on Little River Road (SR 73) two miles west of Sugarlands Visitor Center.

October 18, 1986: Fatal accident, auto. Douglas Stone, 20, of Arab, AL, was killed in a single-car accident on the Gatlinburg Spur of U.S. 441 .1 mile north of the tunnel. Stone was a passenger in a Corvette driven by Russell Bobo.

March 8, 1987: Fatal accident, auto. Stephen L. Hodge, 23, and Ella Louise Robertson, 22, both from Morristown, TN, were killed when their Toyota Celica, driven by Hodge, hit the rock face at the entrance to a tunnel on the Gatlinburg Spur of U.S. 441. Hodge was traveling north at a high rate of speed at the time of the accident. The car burst into flames, and both occupants were killed.

June 10, 1987: Suicide. T.C.L., 28, Burlington, WI, died of carbon monoxide poisoning in a van parked atop Webb Overlook on Newfound Gap Road (U.S. 441). The van's exhaust system had been "adapted so that the exhaust came into the vehicle."

June 29, 1987: Heart attack, fatal. Raquel Rubert, 55, Miami, FL, was traveling in a van from Cades Cove toward Tremont when Rubert suffered an apparent heart attack. At the Laurel Creek Road at Tremont, a passenger in the van flagged down ranger Lawrence Robinson, who was unable to revive Rubert.

July 22, 1987: Fatal accident, auto/motorcycle. Benjamin K. Kuykendal, 60, (hometown not listed), was driving north on the Gatlinburg Spur of U.S. 441, near the by-pass junction, at a high rate of speed when he lost control of his Honda motorcycle and crashed into a guardrail. He was pronounced dead at the scene.

November 4, 1987: Fatal accident, drowning. Alvin N. McCarter, 80, (no hometown listed) drowned while fishing in the Pigeon River in the

Flat Branch area along the Gatlinburg Spur of U.S. 441. McCarter's body was found in 12 feet of water in a large pool 200 yards north of the Husky Grove Bridge.

January 9, 1988: Suicide. The body of R.B.W., 30, Maryville, TN, was found off the Cades Cove Loop Road on the Anthony Creek Trail, about a mile and a half beyond the entrance gate. He died of a self-inflicted gunshot wound to the head.

April 28, 1988: Suicide. Rangers located the vehicle of W.L.P., 31, Harvey, LA, at the Sugarlands Mountain Trailhead parking lot at Fighting Creek Gap on Little River Road (SR 73). P., a pharmacist, had sent his wife a letter indicating his intent to commit suicide. Rangers found his body in the backcountry about 0.3 mile south of the parking lot. The TBI toxicology report indicated that he died of a fatal self-induced overdose of the barbiturate pentobarbital.

August 3, 1988: Fatal accident, fall. Todd Remer, 15, Utica, MI, slipped while climbing on Charlies Bunion and fell approximately 600 feet to his death. The helicopter sent to help recover the body crashed while landing near a fueling station at the Gatlinburg-Pigeon Forge Airport. Rangers Holland and Brewer were injured and received U.S. Department of Interior Valor Awards.

August 13, 1988: Fatal accident, bicycle. Roma Strickland, a minor female from Maryville, TN, was fatally injured from a fall from her bicycle at the base of a hill in the Look Rock picnic area. Most of the incident report is too faint to be read.

June 5, 1989: Fatal accident, auto. A truck driven by Phillip W. Turner, 20, a private first class in the U.S. Marine Corps and stationed at Bangor, WA, naval base, veered off the right side of the northbound Gatlinburg Spur of U.S. 441 and struck a rock outcropping. Turner's passenger, Kevin N. Ramsey, 19, Piney Flats, TN, had been vomiting out the passenger window at the time. The impact fractured Ramsey's skull and broke his neck, and he died of his injuries.

June 13, 1989: Fatal accident, fall. Eve Jones, 70, Midville, GA, a staff person for a group of mentally challenged adults, fell approximately 10 feet on a short-cut [unofficial] trail near the restrooms at Newfound Gap and struck her head on the paved trail below. Jones, who had been attempting to stop one of her clients who had wandered down the short-cut trail, died of her injury.

July 5, 1989: Fatal accident, tree fall. Roy F. Autery, 40, Saraland, AL, died of massive head injury when a tree fell on his car on Newfound Gap Road (U.S. 441),approximately 1.5 miles north of Cherokee, NC. The passenger in Autery's car was unharmed.

October 16, 1989: Accidental death, Sudden Infant Death Syndrome. Parents of a 9-month-old boy discovered that he was not breathing and did not have a pulse. The family, from Zackery, LA, were camping in the Balsam Mountain Campground, and the parents had been seated by a campfire after putting the boy and his brother to bed in their tent. The mother found the child unresponsive the next morning. The autopsy attributed no foul play to the child's death and indicated that the probable cause was Sudden Infant Death Syndrome.

January 19, 1990: Fatal accident, auto. Annette Shultz, 22, Cosby, TN, was killed when the car in which she was traveling failed to negotiate a curve and flipped over about 200 yards south of intersection with SR 32 on the entrance road to Cosby. She was not wearing a seatbelt and was thrown from the car.

April 8, 1990: Fatal accident, auto. Wanda F. Treadway, 22, Sevierville, TN, was killed when the car she was traveling in, heading north on Gatlinburg Spur of U.S. 441 between the bypass and Little Smoky Road, struck several trees.

June 30, 1990: Fatal accident, bicycle. Robert A. Cooper, 49, Gatlinburg, TN, was riding a bicycle when he struck a deer about 0.5 mile west of Sparks Lane on the Cades Cove Loop Road. The collision caused Cooper to tumble from the bicycle and strike his head on the pavement. Cooper was flown by Lifestar to UT Medical Center. He died on the morning of July 1 of head injuries sustained in the accident. According to newspaper accounts, rangers investigating the incident found deer fur in the brakes of Cooper's bicycle.

November 27, 1990: Fatal accident, auto. Dead body. Park officials found remains of William Dewayne Farris, 37, Maryville, TN, in his pickup truck off the edge of the Foothills Parkway near Cosby. Farris, who had been missing since July 4, was the apparent victim of a vehicle accident that went undetected until November 27. Farris was last seen at Cherokee Lake. The truck went off a steep embankment near the parkway's first overlook, and a 10-inch diameter poplar fell across the truck and flattened it.

December 19, 1990: Suicide. Maintenance workers discovered the body of R.H.T., 35, Gulfport, MS, on a bluff overlooking the river near the parking area at The Sinks. His pickup truck was parked nearby. He died of a self-inflicted gunshot wound. Suicide notes were found with the body.

January 29, 1991: Fatal accident, plane crash. Wreckage of a small Cessna missing since January 27 was located four miles west of Clingmans Dome off Welch Ridge Trail, 0.5 mile south of the Appalachian Trail. Pilot Barron Ivan Vernon, 50, Sylva, NC, was killed in the crash.

March 14, 1991: Fatal accident, auto. Dale Edward Morgan, 36, Sevierville, TN, was killed in a one-car crash on the northbound Gatlinburg Spur of U.S. 441 just south of Pigeon Forge. A passenger was thrown from the car but survived.

April 28, 1991: Fatal accident, auto. Carl Hill, 72, Abington, VA, was injured in a crash on Newfound Gap Road (U.S. 441) 2 miles from Gatlinburg and heading toward Cherokee. Hill died later at UT Medical Center, but his wife survived.

July 8, 1991: Heart attack, fatal. Robert J. Moser, 55, Knoxville, TN, collapsed while hiking, about 0.5 mile from Rainbow Falls.

November 11, 1991: Fatal accident, auto. A group of foreign students attending Maryville College, Maryville, TN, and traveling east on the Foothills Parkway crashed near Walland when the driver lost control of the car. Ms. Merce Villarroga-Rafals, 22, Barcelona, Spain, died when she, along with five others, were ejected from the vehicle.

January 2, 1992: Heart attack, fatal. Earnest M. Luallen, 69, Knoxville, TN, collapsed and died at Arch Rock on the Alum Cave Trail.

January 29, 1992: Suicide. Rangers spotted a white pickup parked in the Metcalf Bottoms Picnic Area that had been there overnight. Inside they found the body of P.W., 51, Harrogate, TN. She died from a self-inflicted gunshot wound probably in combination with ingesting or injecting a toxic substance.

March 25, 1992: Fatal accident, auto. Heart attack, fatal. Arthur Hanks, 66, Portland, IN, was driving, and his wife, Edwina, 66, a passenger, in a vehicle headed south on Newfound Gap Road (U.S. 441) 200 yards north of the Alum Cave Trail parking area on the Tennessee side of the park. Their car was struck head-on by a northbound vehicle driven by Vivek Jaikamal, 24, a college student from Columbus, OH. Edwina was pronounced dead at scene. Arthur died of cardiac arrest in the ambulance.

April 26, 1992: Fatal accident, plane crash. A twin-engine Cessna

310 en route from Cartersville, GA, to Greenville, TN, crashed in the park near Clingmans Dome. Killed in the crash was pilot Mark Williams, 33, Cartersville. Severe weather conditions, including 9 inches of snow at the crash site, delayed recovery of Williams' body until Tuesday, April 28.

March 28–April 4, 1993: Fatal accident, fall. Missing person. Dead body. Brad Lavies, 13, Adamsville, AL, became separated from his family while hiking the Rainbow Falls Trail. Searchers found Lavies' body at the base of a 100-foot bluff on April 4. Lavies had died of massive head injuries that resulted from the fall.

April 11, 1993: Fatal accident, drowning. The body of Junior Rae Grooms, 50, Hartford, TN, was discovered in Big Creek. A group of horseback riders located the body about 2.5 miles up the Big Creek Trail from Big Creek Campground. Grooms had been fishing.

May 22, 1993: Fatal accident, auto. Backseat passenger William Horace Shackleford, 78, Rome, GA, died of trauma and blood loss after a head-on collision near the Camp Two Bridge on the Little River Road (SR 73) between the Townsend "Wye" and the Metcalf Bottoms Picnic Area. The driver of the other car, John Sheffey, 45, Sevierville, crossed the center line and struck Shackleford's car.

June 5, 1993: Fatal accident, drowning. Dead body. The body of Corey Washington, 16, Dalzell, SC, a resident of the Oconaluftee Job Corps Civilian Conservation Center, was found in the Oconaluftee River. Washington's body was found face down in 4 inches of water just downstream from a swimming hole and rope swing, about 1 mile above the Oconaluftee Visitor Center.

July 16, 1993: Heart attack, fatal. Joseph F. Nelson Jr., 52, Berwick, LA, suffered a fatal heart attack while camping at the Balsam Mountain Campground.

July 21, 1993: Fatal accident, auto. Ranger Cathy Nelson encountered a man and a woman along the west shoulder of Newfound Gap Road (U.S. 441), just south of the Mingus Mill intersection. The woman, Connie L. Morgan, 34, Huber Heights, OH, had no pulse, was not breathing, and had blood on her face. Her husband, Wayne Morgan, 40, claimed that he and his wife had been arguing and that his wife jumped out of the truck as it was moving, and the right rear tire ran over her. Morgan was pronounced dead at the scene.

July 25, 1993: Fatal accident, auto. Multiple fatalities (4). An accident involving three vehicles, each carrying families of four, occurred on Newfound Gap Road (U.S. 441) about 5.5 miles north of Cherokee. Daniel Barnes, Candler, NC, the driver of a 1990 Ford Thunderbird, survived. His wife, Lisa Joyce Green Barnes, 37, and daughter Shannon Lear Barnes, 7, were pronounced dead at Cherokee Indian Health Service Hospital. The other daughter, Amber Melissa Barnes, 10, survived. Barnes, traveling south on U.S. 441, crossed the centerline and struck head-on a 1993 Ford Escort. Gregory Huddleston, 36, Moorehead, KY, driver of the Escort, and his wife, Cejuana Huddleston, 36, were pronounced dead at the scene. Their two children survived, as did the four passengers in a Subaru sedan, the third car involved in the accident.

September 3, 1993: Suicide. Criminal investigation. R.B.J., 38, Morristown, TN, was found in his Mercedes Benz in the Newfound Gap parking area with a self-inflicted gunshot wound to the head. He was transported by ambulance to Sugarlands Visitor Center, where Lifestar picked him up and transported him to UT Medical Center. He died later that day. According to the National Park Service incident report, J. was under investigation by the Jefferson County Sheriff's Department over the alleged theft of property from United Parcel Service in Morristown, where he worked. Notes and cassette tapes in the car were connected to the suicide.

January 30, 1994: Suicide. An extensive four-day search located the body of R.S., 45, Memphis, TN, 2,000 feet off the Sugarland Mountain Trail near Catron Branch. His car was located about three-quarters of a mile away at the Laurel Falls trailhead. Two empty pill bottles and a can of scent remover used by hunters were found about 50 yards from the body. S. had a history of depression.

March 28, 1994: Fatal accident, drowning. A body was discovered in Newt Prong, a tributary which crosses Jakes Creek Trail. Rangers believed it was the body of missing backpacker William (Billy) Diefenbach, 19, Savannah, GA. That identity was later confirmed. Rain had swollen the usually shallow creek to about 25 feet wide and 2-3 feet deep.

May 18, 1994: Fatal accident, auto. Stolen, invalid driver's license. A one-car accident about 0.5 mile south of Gatlinburg on Newfound Gap Road (U.S. 441) claimed the life of a man who was initially unidentified. The victim carried a stolen driver's license from Yakima, WA. A hand-written note on the report indicates the victim was David Allan Spreitler, 31, Harrison County, MS. Spreitler had an extensive criminal record, mainly drug possession and vehicle theft, in multiple states. He was wanted in Key West, FL, for probation violation. Spreitler died from blood loss.

June 16, 1994: Suicide. The body of S.J., 42, Wilmington, NC, was found in the woods a short distance from Overlook #9 on Foothills Parkway West, just above Butterfly Gap Road. She died of a single self-inflicted gunshot wound from a single-shot .410 shotgun, which was found between her legs.

August 17, 1994: Suicide. The body of an unidentified woman was found dead of a self-inflicted gunshot wound in a car parked at an overlook on the Foothills Parkway. The car was registered in Wilmington, NC, but it was unclear if the woman was the car's owner.

August 18, 1994: Fatal accident, auto. Patti Jean Szuber, 22, Royal Oak, MI, a passenger, was injured and later died of injuries sustained in an auto accident on the north-bound side of the Gatlinburg Spur of U.S. 441. The driver, Todd Douglas Herbst, 24, Royal Oak, MI, survived. Patti Szuber's heart was flown from UT Medical Center to Michigan, where it was successfully transplanted into her father, Chester Szuber, 58, who suffered heart problems and had been on the transplant waiting list for four years.

September 16, 1994: Fatal accident, fall. Charlotte L. Marshall, 69, Knoxville, TN, died of injuries sustained in a fall at Abrams Creek.

November 5, 1994: Fatal accident, auto. Thomas Loveday, 21, Dandridge, TN, son of a Tennessee police officer, died in a single-vehicle accident on the northbound lane of Newfound Gap Road (U.S. 441) about 15 miles south of Gatlinburg. Loveday was pronounced dead at UT Medical Center.

November 7, 1994: Murder. Brett Rae, 25, Sevierville, was charged with the first degree murder of Kelly Joe Lovera, 33, Sevierville, TN. The two lived in the same apartment complex. Lovera's body was found in a jeep that had run off the side of the Gatlinburg bypass near the Upper Overlook. The murder took place in Sevierville and Lovera's wife was also charged in the crime. Rae and Lovera's wife tried to cover up the crime by pushing the car off the side of the park road.

December 29, 1994: Suicide. The body of M.J.G., 42, Knoxville, TN, was found a short distance off the north side of the Appalachian Trail about a 10-minute hike east of the Newfound Gap parking area. His death was caused by a self-inflicted overdose of drugs. Drug related material was found at the scene. A suicide note was found at G.'s apartment.

January 19, 1995: Fatal accident, auto. Calvin Davis, 22, Augusta, GA, was fatally injured when his 18-wheeler drove off the shoulder of Newfound Gap Road (U.S. 441) and flipped onto its top about 7 miles north of Cherokee, NC. Jacqueline Dukes, 16, Augusta, GA, a passenger, survived the accident. Large trucks and other commercial vehicles are not allowed on park roads.

February 12, 1995: Fatal accident, plane crash. Dr. Edward M. Malone, 56, Concord, TN, died when his twin-engine Beechcraft airplane crashed near Cove Mountain. Malone's body was found inside the charred wreckage.

February 21, 1995: Suicide (witnessed by park ranger). Park Ranger Jeff Carlisle approached a vehicle parked near the Primitive Baptist Church on the Cades Cove Loop Road as he prepared to close the road for the night. Inside the vehicle were a 15-year-old girl (the minor's name appeared in the newspaper but is not reprinted here), and J.B., 18, both of Knoxville, TN, who apparently had forged a suicide pact. When Carlisle approached the vehicle to speak to the occupants, he noticed a gun in the back of the car. Carlisle returned to his cruiser to get a flashlight and approached the rear of the vehicle and attempted to open the rear door to remove the weapon. The girl grabbed the 12-gauge shotgun and fatally wounded herself.

July 23, 1995: Fatal accident, drowning. Matthew DeShone, 10, Antioch, TN, drowned in the Little River while wading at The Sinks.

November 12, 1995: Fatal accident, exposure/hypothermia. Thomas Ruchinski, 34, a resident of Pennsylvania, died of exposure on the Appalachian Trail near Pecks Corner.

June 3, 1996: Fatal accident, auto/motorcycle. Gary G. Paulis, 44, Boca Raton, FL, died in a motorcycle accident on Newfound Gap Road (U.S. 441) near the Chimneys Picnic Area.

August 25, 1996: Fatal accident, animal venom. Charles Berry, 51, Maryville, TN, died of respiratory failure after being stung by yellow jackets while fishing in the Tremont section of the park.

September 2, 1996: Fatal accident, horse. Jerry Taylor, 39, Hartford, TN, was killed when he and his horse fell 25 feet from a bridge on the Big Creek Trail into the river about 2.3 miles from the trailhead.

September 6, 1996: Fatal accident, auto. Michael Chad Bickle, 25, Pigeon Forge, TN, died in a one-car accident on the northbound Gatlinburg Spur of U.S. 441 about 1.5 miles north of the tunnel.

October 31, 1996: Suicide. The body of F.W.H., 38, Maryville, TN, was found on overlook No. 11 on the Foothills Parkway. He died of a self-inflicted gunshot wound. H.'s truck was parked nearby.

November 28, 1996: Suicide. C.S.W., 40, of Carrollton, TX, spoke briefly to two hikers at the Mount Le Conte Shelter before she walked to the rear of the shelter and shot herself. She had a suicide note in her possession.

May 21, 1997: Fatal accident, auto. Timothy M. Rollings, 27, Johnson City, TN, died when the car he was riding in hit an embankment and flipped over on the northbound Gatlinburg Spur of U.S. 441 just south of the tunnel.

July 23, 1997: Fatal accident, drowning. Daniel Bruce Hampton, 19, Decatur, TN, drowned while fishing in the Abrams Creek area of the park.

September 27, 1997: Fatal accident, drowning. Paul Edward Perry, 39, Knoxville, dived into the pool at the base of Abrams Falls, struck his head on an underwater object, and drowned.

October 10, 1997: Fatal accident, drowning. Sharon Bochsler (no age or hometown provided) drowned in Abrams Creek.

October 25, 1997: Fatal accident, auto. Todd B. Dykes, 19, Monroe County, TN, died in an auto accident on the Foothills Parkway west.

December 1, 1997: Fatal accident, plane crash. Jeffrey Mann, 35, New Berlin, WI, died when his small plane crashed 0.5 mile east of the Russell Field Shelter along the Appalachian Trail. Rescue personnel reached the crash site on December 2.

April 4, 1998: Heart attack, fatal. Leonard Branam, 74, Sevierville, TN, died of a heart attack on the Ramsey Cascades Trail.

April 19, 1998: Fatal accident, drowning. B.J. Allen, 18, Summerville, SC, drowned 1.5 miles west (downriver) from The Sinks in Little River Gorge when he tried to swim across the flooding waterway.

October 10, 1998: Heart attack, fatal. Richard J. Callahan, 71, Rockford, MI, died of a heart attack in the Smokemont Campground.

December 23, 1998: Fatal accident, drowning. Edward L. Green, 45, Silva, NC, drowned in the Raven Fork of the Oconaluftee River near the park boundary.

December 29, 1998: Suicide. C.A.M., 60, Jefferson City, TN, died of a self-inflicted gunshot wound on the Cades Cove Loop Road.

April 3, 1999: Death, natural causes. Nathan R. Polnisch, 32, Salisbury, NC, died of natural causes in the Big Creek Campground.

May 5, 1999: Fatal accident, plane crash. Frank Thomas (no age or hometown provided) died in a plane crash east of the Jenkins Ridge Trail in North Carolina.

June 3, 1999: Death, natural causes. Sam Kinley Jr., 66, Johnson City, TN, died of natural causes on the AT near Double Spring Gap.

July 4, 1999: Death, natural causes. Alan B. Tarpley, 53, St. Albans, GA, died of natural causes on the Trillium Gap Trail.

July 8, 1999: Fatal accident, drowning. Amanda Carole Smith, 17, Knoxville, TN, drowned while tubing on Little River, near The Sinks, 2 miles from Meigs Falls.

July 16, 1999: Fatal accident, drowning. Mary C. Ward, 80, Statesville, NC, drowned in the Deep Creek section of the park.

July 16, 1999: Death, natural causes. Wendell J. Breining, 76, Harrison, OH, died of natural causes on the Gatlinburg Bypass.

August 1, 1999: Fatal accident, drowning. David K. Boots (no age or hometown provided) was pulled from the water at The Sinks. He died later at the hospital.

September 1, 1999: Fatal accident, construction. James Gregory Ivey, 37, Sevierville, TN, an employee of Charles Blalock and Sons, was killed when the backhoe he was operating slid down a slope and rolled onto its side. Ivey left the cab, and the backhoe landed on top of him. The accident occurred 9 miles east of the junction of U.S. 321 and the Foothills Parkway on a section of bridge along the unopened parkway.

October 5, 1999: Possible suicide. C.L.N., 42, Knoxville, TN, was found dead on Snake Den Ridge. Her death was ruled a possible suicide. No additional details provided.

November 5, 1999: Death, natural causes. Howard Ward, 71, Cincinnati, OH, died of natural causes near the Chimney Tops.

December 29, 1999: Fatal accident, auto. Betty Jean Waldrop, 67, Oconee, SC, died in an accident on Newfound Gap Road (U.S. 441) 1 mile south of Alum Cave.

February 10, 2000: Suicide. The body of E.M.E., 46, Maryville, was found 15 feet from an overlook on the Foothills Parkway. He died of an apparent self-inflicted gunshot wound. The body was found near a vehicle parked at the third overlook on the southern section of the Foothills Parkway about 15 miles south of the intersection with East Lamar Alexander Parkway.

March 23, 2000: Fatal accident, fall. Walter Reid (no age or hometown provided) died after hitting his head on the pavement at an overlook on the Gatlinburg Bypass.

April 26, 2000: Fatal accident, auto. Matthew Jackson Lynch, 21, Sevierville, died in an auto accident while traveling northbound on the Gatlinburg Spur of U.S. 441 at the entrance to the tunnel.

May 21, 2000: Fatal accident, bear mauling. Glenda Ann Bradley, 50, Cosby, TN, a teacher at Jones Cove Elementary School, was attacked by two bears and killed approximately 2 miles up Little River Trail from its trailhead in Elkmont. Bradley was hiking with her former husband, Ralph Hill, 52, also of Cosby, who was fishing at the time of the attack.

June 5, 2000: Fatal accident, auto. Chanda Miller, 10, Knoxville, TN, was killed when the car in which she and her family were traveling was involved in a two-car accident on Newfound Gap Road (U.S. 441) near the Collins Creek Picnic Area on the North Carolina side of the park. Karen Ward, 30, Blue Ridge, GA, was headed northbound and crossed the centerline, hitting the Millers' car. Chanda Miller was a passenger in back seat.

June 23, 2000: Fatal accident, auto. Taxi driver Robert Clayton Owensby, 82, Gatlinburg, TN, died in an accident while transporting individuals on Newfound Gap Road (U.S. 441) southbound at the Chimneys parking area.

June 24, 2000: Death, natural causes. Charles L. Stivers, 56, (no hometown provided), died of natural causes near the Middle Prong of the Little Pigeon River.

July 31, 2000: Fatal accident, auto. Cynthia Ann Willis, 50, Maryville, TN, was killed in a one-car crash on the Foothills Parkway west, six miles from the intersection with U.S. 321 at Walland. Willis' cocker spaniel-mix dog survived the accident.

August 16, 2000: Fatal accident, construction, electrocution. Robert Bonnetau, 30, Canadian, a project supervisor of Florida-based PCL, Inc., was killed while testing an electrical device on a failed piece of construction equipment used to form concrete. The accident occurred during construction on one of the 10 planned bridges at the Missing Link section on the western end of the Foothills Parkway. The section of parkway was closed for construction.

September 5, 2000: Suicide. K.C.L., 32, Wymore, NE, died of an apparent suicide on the Abrams Falls Trail.

October 14, 2000: Death, natural causes. Sergei Aldakimov, 69, Medford, NJ, died of natural causes near the Clingmans Dome Tower.

October 28, 2000: Fatal accident, auto. This marked the third fatality associated with construction of the section on the Foothills Parkway between Walland and Wears Valley. Donald Eli Howell, 35, Jefferson City, TN, an employee of PCL, Inc., was killed in a one-car crash as he traveled west on the unfinished roadway and failed to negotiate a left curve about a half mile from the barrier gate.

December 21, 2000: Dead body, exposure/hypothermia. Two hikers discovered the body of Cyril Jaroslav Janda, 43, Chapel Hill, NC, on the Alum Cave Trail just below Arch Rock, about 1.3 miles from the trailhead on Newfound Gap Road (U.S. 441). Jaroslav began his hike late and was caught out after dark. Temperatures dropped to around zero at 4,400 feet, where his body was found. He was wearing cotton clothes and only a light jacket.

March 15–16, 2001: Fatal accident, auto. Two park visitors flying a kite off the stone retaining wall along Newfound Gap Road (U.S. 441) discovered a wrecked vehicle at the base of a slope. The body of Rose Marie Wallace, 43, Knoxville, TN, was found inside the vehicle. The vehicle was located off the west side of U.S. 441, about 100 yards north of where the Appalachian Trail crosses the road at Newfound Gap.

April 29, 2001: Fatal accident, auto. A three-car accident led to the death of Mr. J.L. Ramsey, 51, Sevierville, TN. The head-on wreck occurred on Newfound Gap Road (U.S. 441) about .75 mile north of the Smokemont Campground.

May 12, 2001: Fatal accident, auto. Jeff Ray Grooms, 31, Cosby, TN, died in a single-car accident on the northbound Gatlinburg Spur of U.S. 441 south of Beech Branch. Grooms was a passenger in the car.

May 16, 2001: Fatal accident, auto. Ben M. Sanchez (no age or hometown provided) was involved in an accident on the Gatlinburg Spur of U.S. 441. Sanchez died on May 18.

July 3, 2001: Fatal accident, tree fall. Joetta K. Bidle, 45, Beavercreek, OH, was struck on the head by a tree while hiking on the Middle Prong Trail. She died from her injury on July 4, 2001.

October 23, 2001: Heart attack, fatal. William G. Mount, 71, Atlanta, GA, died of an apparent heart attack near the Look Rock Tower.

December 3, 2001: Fatal accident, auto. Keith L. Huskey, 28, Gatlinburg, TN, died in a single-car crash while traveling southbound on the Gatlinburg Spur of U.S. 441.

December 9, 2001: Heart attack, fatal. Clifford Rowe, 65, Lexington, SC, died of an apparent heart attack on the Gatlinburg Spur of U.S. 441 near Gum Stand Road.

April 8, 2002: Suicide. S.L.P., 36, Blount County, TN, died of an apparent suicide near the junction of U.S. 129 and Foothills Parkway. No additional details provided.

April 23, 2002: Suicide. C.R.W. (no age or hometown provided) died of an apparent suicide along Meigs Creek near Little River Road.

February 3, 2003: Fatal accident, auto. Claude Vernon Conley, 66, Virginia Beach, VA, was killed when he lost control of his vehicle while traveling eastbound on the Little River Road (SR 73) 3.5 miles from the Townsend "Wye."

March 27, 2003: Fatal accident, plane crash. Charles Woodson, 42, Seymour, TN, died when his Cessna 172 crashed about 1 mile east of Clingmans Dome and about 40 yards south of the Appalachian Trail.

March 29, 2003: Suicide. D.R.S., 54, Swain County, NC, died of an apparent suicide on Lakeview Drive along the north shore of Fontana Lake.

May 5, 2003: Suicide. J.A.G., 21, Maryville, TN, died of an apparent suicide on Laurel Creek Road near the Tremont Bridge.

May 9, 2003: Murder. Dead body. The body of Sandy A. Jeffers, 25, Maryville, was found near the Look Rock Tower on the Foothills Parkway. On Saturday, May 10, Aaron L. Skeen, 20, was charged with first-degree murder, rape, kidnapping, and burglary in connection with Jeffers' death. Jeffers, who was scheduled to graduate from UT the day after her body was discovered, had been abducted on Tuesday, May 6, from her apartment in Maryville.

May 26, 2003: Death, natural causes. Rita Gamble, 55, Knoxville, TN, died of natural causes in the Look Rock Campground.

June 16, 2003: Death, natural causes. Osbin L. Ervin, 64, Carbondale, IL, died of natural causes on the Trillium Gap Trail.

July 5, 2003: Death, natural causes. David E. Gunter, 53, Newport, TN, died of natural causes in the Cosby Campground.

July 19, 2003: Fatal accident, drowning. Fatal accident, fall. Wesley Riddle, 15, Canton, NC, drowned at The Sinks after he struck his head on rocks above a 10-foot waterfall and was swept over the drop and into the stream.

July 28, 2003: Fatal accident, auto/motorcycle. Jason Craig Graves, 17, Montevelo, AL, was killed when he lost control of his rental moped and crossed directly into the path of an oncoming car about 1 mile east of the Metcalf Bottoms Picnic Area.

August 5, 2003: Fatal accident, auto/motorcycle. Debbie Lawson, 48, Kingsport, TN, was killed in a head-on collision between the rental motor scooter she was riding and two motorcycles on Little River Road (SR 73) 3.3 miles east of the Townsend "Wye."

August 21, 2003: Fatal accident, auto. Oscar Lizarralde, 38, Greenwood, SC, died as a result of an auto accident on Little River Road (SR 73) on the Camp 2 Bridge.

October 1, 2003: Death, natural causes. George D. Janak, 67, Houston, TX, died of natural causes on Newfound Gap Road (U.S. 441) near the intersection with Clingmans Dome Road.

October 19, 2003: Death, natural causes. John W. Heid, 55, Maryville, TN, died of natural causes on the Clingmans Dome Trail.

November 8, 2003: Death, natural causes. James P. Hood, 45, Maryville, TN, died of natural causes at the Clingmans Dome Tower.

November 22, 2003: Death, natural causes. James S. Demorest, 61, Hohenwald, TN, died of natural causes on the Whiteoak Branch Trail near Fontana Lake.

March 12, 2004: Fatal accident, auto. Ralph Larry Thomas, 56, Pigeon Forge, TN, was killed in a two-car head-on collision on the Gatlinburg Spur of U.S. 441 just a few feet from the Gatlinburg City boundary.

March 18, 2004: Suicide. The body of R.P.M., 27, Bristol, VA, was found in the Little River, 1.5 miles east of the Townsend "Wye." The body had a puncture wound to the chest. It was later determined that M.'s death was the result of a self-inflicted gunshot wound. Kayakers discovered his body floating face down in the river.

April 10, 2004: Heart attack, fatal. Oliver F. Furst, 68, Kodak, TN, died of an apparent heart attack in the Cades Cove Campground.

April 22, 2004: Heart attack, fatal. Park employee Ricky Campbell, 50, Newport, TN, collapsed while working to clear trees from the Snake Den Ridge Trail. His co-workers began CPR, but Campbell could not be revived.

April 30, 2004: Fatal accident, drowning. Christopher Drinkard, 12, a seventh-grade student on a field trip from Vine Middle Magnet School in

Knoxville, TN, fell and drowned below Abrams Falls. In January 2005, the death was ruled an accident.

June 8, 2004: Murder. Suicide. Rangers received a call from the Blue Ridge Parkway to be on the lookout for John Brian Peck, 27, Wilmington, NC, wanted for first-degree murder of his ex-girlfriend on June 4. Rangers encountered a man believed to be Peck at Newfound Gap parking area. Peck was later seen traveling south on Newfound Gap Road (U.S. 441). Rangers set up two roadblocks on U.S. 441: one near Collins Creek Picnic Area, about 7 miles north of Cherokee, and the second at the junction of U.S. 441 and Clingmans Dome Road. Peck approached the roadblock near Collins Creek but turned around. Peck fired toward the officers at the roadblock. Rangers gave chase over 4 miles, at which point Peck's vehicle lights disappeared. Authorities found Peck's vehicle at the base of a 60-foot embankment. Peck, whose body was found on a rock in the creek near his vehicle, died from a self-inflicted gunshot wound.

September 12, 2004: Fatal accident, auto/motorcycle. Matt Green, 29, Hickory, NC, and Lea Smith, Morganton, NC, died when Green lost control of his motorcycle and swerved into the oncoming lane on Newfound Gap Road (U.S. 441) 7 miles north of Cherokee. Smith was a passenger on Green's motorcycle. The two had been attending the annual Cherokee Survivors Motorcycle Rally and Concert.

September 26, 2004: Fatal accident, auto/motorcycle. James Lionel House, 53, and Sara Carol House, 53, both from Buford, GA, were traveling westbound on Foothills Parkway when a van driven by Jeffery Scott Jennings, 43, Maryville, TN, crashed head on into the Houses' Honda Goldwing. James and Sara died from injuries sustained in the accident. According to a June 22, 2006, newspaper account in the *The Gainesville Times*, Jennings pleaded guilty to two counts of manslaughter in the Houses' deaths.

October 2, 2004: Fatal accident, auto. Margaret S. Britt, 53, Maryville, TN, died in a head-on collision on Newfound Gap Road (U.S. 441) about 4 miles south of Sugarlands Visitor Center.

October 15, 2004: Heart attack, fatal. Marion G. Baskins, 70, Murfreesboro, TN, died of an apparent heart attack on the Rainbow Falls Trail.

October 25, 2004: Heart attack, fatal. Ray I. Bridges (no age or hometown provided) died of an apparent heart attack on the Roaring Fork Motor Nature Trail.

January 16, 2005: Fatal accident, auto. Angel Jennifer Schutze, 30,

Sevierville, TN, was killed in a single-car wreck on the Gatlinburg Spur of U.S. 441 near Little Smoky Road.

March 26, 2005: Fatal accident, auto. Multiple fatalities (5). A two-car collision on the Gatlinburg Spur of U.S. 441 resulted in five deaths. The dead included Myra Nelson, 63, her husband, George, 80, Myra's mother, Audrey Fentress, 84, all of Norfolk, VA, and Anthony Deitz, 69, and his wife, Betty, 69, both of Virginia Beach, VA. John M. Hall, 18, Lebanon, TN, and Steven A. Williams, 19, Murfreesboro, TN, were drag racing and caused the accident. Both men later pled guilty to one count each of second-degree murder and were sentenced to prison.

April 15, 2005: Fatal accident, horse. Mark D. Hutchins, Bardstown, KY, tried to mount his horse near the Middle Prong Trailhead at the end of the Tremont Road but fell off. His brother led Mark's horse back to the trailer, at which time Mark tried to mount his brother's horse. The horse reared and Hutchins fell off, hitting his head on the ground. The horse fell partially on top of him. Hutchins was flown by Lifestar to UT Medical Center, where he died on April 17, after suffering irreversible brain damage.

May 29, 2005: Heart attack, fatal. John M. Bolinger, 55 (no hometown provided), died of an apparent heart attack on the Alum Cave Trail.

July 29, 2005: Fatal accident, fall. Donald Thralls, 72, Phoenix, AZ, walked with his 4-year-old grandson to the rocky banks of the Little River. Thralls slipped and fell, striking his head on rocks and then tumbled into the river. He had suffered a severe open-skull fracture and neck injuries. He died later at UT Medical Center after being transported there by Lifestar.

September 8, 2005: Fatal accident, auto/motorcycle. Lester K. Jones, 65, Blaine, TN, was traveling westbound on Foothills Parkway west past the Look Rock Overlook when he lost control of his motorcycle, ran off the road, and struck a culvert. He was thrown 35 feet and died of his injuries.

October 18, 2005: Death, natural causes. Wilbur A. Lauber, 83, Decatur, IL, died of natural causes near Smokemont.

October 28, 2005: Heart attack, fatal. Kenneth W. Garland, 70, Bluff City, TN, died of an apparent heart attack on the southern section of Newfound Gap Road (U.S. 441).

January 15, 2006: Dead body. Murder. The body of Tamara Susan Seay, 17, Cherokee, NC, was found off Tom Branch Road by a church group hiking in the Deep Creek area of the park. On January 20, park rangers, FBI, and Cherokee police arrested Terrence Roach, 20, of Cherokee in connection with the murder. He was later charged with the crime. Seay had been shot.

February 6, 2006: Fatal accident, auto. Arnold V. Kovin Jr., 54, Cullowhee, NC, died in a single-car accident 4 miles north of Cherokee, along Newfound Gap Road (U.S. 441). Kovin was a park employee.

March 31, 2006: Death, natural causes. Paul W. Nix, 65, Huntingdon, TN, died of natural causes at the Mt. Collins Shelter.

April 5, 2006: Death, natural causes. Stephen P. Hunsaker, 60, Princeton, KY, died of natural causes near the Walker Sisters Cabin in the Little Greenbrier section of the park.

April 24, 2006: Suicide. C.G.G., 43, Blount County, TN, died on the western section of Foothills Parkway. Park communications records indicate that she committed suicide.

May 9, 2006: Fatal accident, auto/motorcycle. Hugh Scully, 68, and Thomas Mock Jr., 59, both of Long Beach, MS, died from injuries sustained in a motorcycle accident on Little River Road (SR 73) about 4.5 miles east of the junction with the Townsend "Wye."

May 21, 2006: Dead body. Murder. The body of Steven Lynn Davis, 25, Maryville, TN, was found at the Abrams Creek Campground. Davis had been stabbed. William Joseph Moyers Jr., 42, Alcoa, TN, was charged with second-degree murder.

July 2, 2006: Fatal accident, drowning. Vivek Kumaralingham, 26, Manchester, CT, originally from India, was swimming at the base of Abrams Falls and drowned as he swam underwater toward the base of the falls. His body was recovered the following day.

July 15, 2006: No cause of death provided. Michael K. Ballew, 56, Knoxville, TN, died of undisclosed causes in the Deep Creek section of the park.

July 15, 2006: No cause of death provided. Robert B. Rudasill (no age or hometown provided) died of undisclosed causes on Newfound Gap Road (U.S. 441) near the Morton Overlook.

July 27, 2006: Death, natural causes. Gabriel J. Michelena, 59, Miami, FL, died of natural causes in the Deep Creek section of the park.

March 11, 2007: No cause of death provided. Ronald S. Neff, 35, Townsend, TN, died of unknown causes near Happy Valley Road.

April 6, 2007: Death, natural causes. Richard S. Dubbuison Sr., 52, Gulfport, Mississippi, died of natural causes on the Chimney Tops Trail.

April 15, 2007: Fatal accident, auto. Terry Lee Fox, 45, Gatlinburg, TN, was involved in a single-car accident when his car struck a guard rail on the left side of the Gatlinburg Spur of U.S. 441 in the turn lane of the left-hand exit to Flat Branch Road. The car sustained only minor damage. EMS had to break into the car to reach Fox, who was unresponsive. Fox was later pronounced dead. Given the minor damage to the car, rangers investigated the possibility that a medical condition may have caused the accident and death.

June 4, 2007: Fatal accident, drowning. Joshua Roberson, 24, Maryville, TN, drowned in the Little River at The Sinks. Roberson had slipped on rocks above the waterfall, was carried over the falls, and dropped 12 feet amid plunging water.

July 17, 2007: Death, natural causes. Edward B. Johnson, 60, Knoxville, TN, died of natural causes near Backcountry Camp Site #37.

September 11, 2007: Death, natural causes. Albert H. Brigance, 74, died of natural causes at the lodge on Mt. Le Conte. Brigance was a noted author and special education expert.

December 21, 2007: Death, natural causes. Monie A. Sneed, 73, Black Mountain, NC, died of natural causes on the Big Fork Ridge Trail in the Cataloochee section of the park.

February 24-25, 2008: Fatal accident, auto. Fatal accident, drowning. Officials recovered the body of Matthew Johnson, 24, Toccoa, GA, from a vehicle submerged in the Little River about 4 miles east of the Townsend "Wye." During the middle of the night of February 24-25, Johnson had been traveling east on Little River Road (SR 73) and failed to negotiate a right-hand turn. His car plummeted 25 feet into the river.

May 23, 2008: Fatal accident, auto. Charles Priest (no age or hometown provided) died following an auto accident on Newfound Gap Road (U.S. 441).

July 4, 2008: Death, natural causes. Harry E. Lewis, 67, Talbott, TN, died of natural causes on the Little River Trail.

August 26, 2008: Fatal accident, drowning. Kayaking death. The body of kayaker Isaac Ludwig, 27, Hartford, TN, was discovered in a section of the West Prong of the Little Pigeon River on August 27. Ludwig was part of a group of kayakers who planned to paddle from the Chimney Tops Trailhead to the Chimneys Picnic Area, a distance of 1-2 miles, during an episode of very high water. The three entered the water on Tuesday, August

26. Ludwig's two companions quickly returned to shore after determining that the current was too swift, but Ludwig continued on.

November 8, 2008: Fatal accident, fall. Jeremy Frye, 25, Knoxville, TN, fell 25-30 feet from the top of Grotto Falls along the Trillium Gap Trail a few miles south of Gatlinburg. He sustained leg, back, and head injuries. Frye died of his injuries on December 3, 2008.

November 26, 2008: Death, natural causes. Curtis Severson Jr., 66, Cordova, TN, died of natural causes on the Rainbow Falls Trail.

February 3, 2009: Suicide. M.R.D., 62, Maryville, TN, died of apparent suicide near Crib Gap Trail on Laurel Creek Road.

March 8, 2009: Death, natural causes. John D. Reid, 65, Bryson City, NC, died of natural causes on the Juney Whank Falls Trail in the Deep Creek area of the park.

April 10, 2009: Fatal accident, fall. Robert Lyons, 73, Louisville, KY, took a 20-foot fall down a steep slope while hiking with his wife a few hundred yards up the Chestnut Top Trail, en route to Schoolhouse Gap. Lyons was able to walk down the trail to the side of the park's Townsend entrance road, where rescue personnel found him sitting up. Lyons was conscious but reported back pain. Lyons was flown by Lifestar air ambulance to UT Medical Center, where he later died of blunt trauma to the chest.

April 23, 2009: Fatal accident, auto. Patricia Louise Mendenhall, 81, Middletown, OH, was injured in an accident that occurred northbound on the Gatlinburg Spur of U.S. 441 at Legion Field Bridge. Mendenhall died of her injuries on April 25.

May 17, 2009: Death, natural causes. Howell Lee Davidson III, 57, Sevierville, Tennessee, collapsed and died of natural causes while hiking the Chimney Tops Trail.

May 24, 2009: Fatal accident, drowning. Nublan Zaki Norhadi, 20, Malaysia, a student at Pennsylvania State University, drowned in the pool at the base of Abrams Falls. His body was recovered on May 25.

July 17, 2009: Fatal accident, motorcycle/RV. Raymond Joseph Vosika, 73, Chipley, FL, was killed when he lost control of his motorcycle, crossed the centerline, and struck an RV driven by Wayne Smith, 65, Westminster, SC.

August 9, 2009: Fatal accident, auto. James Michael Broderick, 61, Gatlinburg, TN, died in a single-car accident while traveling north on the Gatlinburg Spur of U.S. 441.

August 19, 2009: Fatal accident, auto/motorcycle. Driver Charles

Earl Bolt, 55, and his passenger, his wife, Diane K. Bolt, 55, Belton, SC, were killed when their motorcycle was hit head-on by a mid-sized SUV on Newfound Gap Road (U.S. 441) about 2 miles south of the NC/TN line at Newfound Gap. A third vehicle was also involved. The SUV driver, Clyde L. Grubbs, 74, Cincinnati, OH, was later charged with two criminal counts in connection with the accident. According to reports, Grubbs was traveling south on Newfound Gap Road when he crossed the centerline, sideswiped a second car, and struck the two motorcyclists.

October 7, 2009: Fatal accident, auto. Tommy Rogers, 50, Maryville, TN, was pronounced dead at the scene of single-vehicle accident on the Foothills Parkway west, 1 mile from the junction with U.S. 321.

December 21, 2009: Fatal accident, drowning. Cindy Hill, 45, Columbia, MD, was hiking with her husband when she slipped on a rock and fell into the Middle Prong of the Little Pigeon River in the Greenbrier section of the park. She was later pronounced dead at the hospital.

January 24, 2010: Fatal accident, tree fall. Tonya Renee Eichler, 39, Sevierville, TN, was killed by trees felled by 70 MPH winds while in a car headed north on Newfound Gap Road (U.S. 441) near the Chimneys Picnic Area. Driver Jody Simonds, Sevierville, and his juvenile daughter, were also in the car. Simonds and his daughter were treated and released from the hospital.

April 15, 2010: Fatal accident, auto. Israel Chavez, 26, Kodak, TN, died in a single-car accident that occurred on the northbound Gatlinburg Spur of U.S. 441, just north of the King Branch interchange. Chavez, the passenger, was thrown from the car when the vehicle struck a rock wall.

May 8, 2010: Dead body. Death, unknown causes. Ross Sabin Enderle, 26, Pontiac, MI, died during the night in the Icewater Spring shelter while on a two-night backpacking trip. Preliminary reports indicated no foul play.

May 18, 2010: Fatal accident, auto/motorcycle. Shazad Haider, 37, Huntley, IL, was killed when he crashed his motorcycle into a rock wall on Little River Road (SR 73) about 1 mile from Townsend.

July 27, 2010: Fatal accident, auto. Paul J. Rodgers, 47, Knoxville, TN, was killed in a single-car wreck on the Laurel Creek Road about 5.5 miles from the Townsend "Wye."

September 1, 2010: Fatal accident, auto. Judith Christoff died from injuries sustained in an accident on Little River Road (SR 73). No additional details available.

October 19, 2010: Crime. Suicide. Pigeon Forge PD K-9 units located the body of M.C., 45, Lebanon, TN, about 20 feet inside the park boundary on the south bank of Dudley Creek, which runs along the south side of U.S. 321. The police had been searching for C. in connection with the alleged rape of his wife at a rental cabin in Gatlinburg. He died of an apparently intentional drug overdose.

November 17, 2010: Fatal accident, auto. Carolyn M. Decker, 50, Woodstock, GA, was ejected from the Jeep she was driving and was found 40 feet from the vehicle, which was 10 feet off the road and resting on its top. She was pronounced dead at the scene.

May 18, 2011: Missing not found. Possible suicide. An intensive week-long search failed to locate Christopher Lee Cessna, 45, of Cary, NC, who had been missing in the park since April 27. Park personnel learned that Cessna was missing when they located and identified his car, left in the Newfound Gap parking area. Cessna had been reported to be depressed, and a handgun he owned could not be found at his residence. The park scaled back the search on May 25. Presumed dead.

May 24, 2011: Suicide. Search teams with dogs located a body believed to be that of D.H., 58, Largo, FL, 250 yards from H.'s vehicle, which had been parked for nearly a week in a pullout along Newfound Gap Road (U.S. 441) 0.6 mile from the Smokemont Campground. Medical examiners determined that H. died of a self-inflicted gunshot wound.

June 16, 2011: Fatal accident, auto. James Childre, 45, Knoxville, died from injuries sustained in an accident on Little River Road (SR 73).

July 11, 2011: Fatal accident, drowning. The body of Dick Chijioke, 34, Plano, TX, was recovered from the Little River at the Townsend "Wye." Chijioke, a nonswimmer, was tubing with his family when the rental tube tipped and he fell into a 12-foot-deep pool.

July 30, 2011: Fatal accident, drowning. Amber Rose Mirisola, 17, Mount Dora, FL, was swept over a 15-foot waterfall while wading across the Little River at The Sinks. She became entrapped at the base of the falls in chest-deep water. Visitors formed a human chain to reach her, but their efforts to free her failed.

January 16, 2012: Fatal accident, fall. John Rollings fell at the Dan Lawson Place on the Cades Cove Loop Road and later died. No additional details provided.

March 17, 2012: Missing not found. Possible suicide. An intensive search began for Derek Joseph Lueking, 24, Louisville, TN, who was reported missing by coworkers and family members on Thursday, March 15. Lueking's white Ford Escape was located Saturday, March 17, at Newfound Gap parking area. Rangers found recently purchased backpacking gear and a note in the car. The search was scaled back on March 23, 2012. Lueking has not been found and is presumed dead.

March 20, 2012: Missing, later found. Suspected suicide. The park began an intensive search for M.G.C., 23, Nashville, TN, who was staying temporarily in Gatlinburg. Officials found Cocchini's car parked at a quiet walkway along Newfound Gap Road (U.S. 441) about 1 mile south of the Sugarlands Visitor Center. C.'s remains were discovered August 19, 2012, near Sugarlands and close to where rangers had found his abandoned vehicle.

July 5, 2012: Fatal accident, tree fall. Storm damage. Two people were killed by falling trees when a violent thunderstorm struck the park. Ralph Frazier, 50, Buford, GA, was struck on the head by a falling limb as he drove his motorcycle on Little River Road near the Townsend "Wye" and died at the scene. Rachel Burkhart, 41, Corryton, TN, was killed by a falling tree in Abrams Creek near the Abrams Creek Campground. Several other individuals were injured, including a 7-year-old girl who was struck by the same tree that killed Burkhart. The girl was unconscious and not breathing when pulled from the water but was later resuscitated. The storm forced the closure of sections of the Cades Cove Loop Road, Laurel Creek Road, and Little River Road (SR 73). Downed trees made many park trails impassable.

September 8, 2012. Fatal accident, fall. Justin D. Pheasant, 22, Cherokee, NC, died as a result of injuries sustained in a fall near the park boundary in North Carolina.

October 13, 2012: Fatal accident, auto. Joseph Madden, 34, Pittman Center, TN, was killed in a two-car crash along the northbound Gatlinburg Spur of U.S. 441. Preliminary reports indicate that Madden may have been attempting to cross the northbound Spur from Westgate when a westbound vehicle driven by Nicholas Swaggerty, 19, Kodak, TN, collided with his pickup. Madden was pronounced dead at the LeConte Medical Center in Sevierville. Through a deal with federal prosecutors, Swaggerty, who was speeding at the time of the accident, later pleaded guilty to three misdemeanors rather than a felony. On October 6, 2014, a federal judge sentenced Swaggerty to 500 hours of community service in GSMNP.

January 15, 2013: Fatal accident, auto. Tracy Marie Anderson, 34,

Morrice, MI, was killed in a collision with an NPS vehicle on Newfound Gap Road (U.S. 441) in North Carolina. According to reports, Anderson had crossed the center line.

January 16, 2013: Fatal accident, exposure/hypothermia. The body of Richard H. Lemarr, 50, Knoxville, TN, was found in the Tricorner Knob Shelter on the Appalachian Trail. Lemarr had begun a 30-mile hike from Newfound Gap to Davenport Gap on Saturday, January 12, and had been reported past due. Lemarr's death was attributed to exposure/hypothermia.

March 11, 2013: Fatal accident, drowning. Steve Senior, 65, Bridgenorth, Ontario, became trapped above The Sinks when his canoe capsized. Senior, who had been underwater for 30 minutes, was unresponsive when rescued but later had spontaneous heartbeats and respiration. He died later of his injuries at Blount Memorial Hospital.

August 9, 2013: Fatal accident, auto. James E. Bigmeat Jr., 44, Cherokee, NC, was killed in a single-car accident while traveling northbound on Newfound Gap Road (U.S. 441) in front of park headquarters. Bigmeat's Ford Explorer struck a tree. Bigmeat's passenger, Angie Murphy, 34, Cherokee, survived the wreck.

December 19, 2013: Fatal accident, auto. Possible drowning. Frank T. Lohmann, 83, Maryville, TN, died in a two-car accident on Little River Road (SR 73) about 3 miles east of the Townsend "Wye." Lohmann's vehicle plunged down a 30-foot bank and wound up upside down in the river.

"A Partial listing of accidental deaths in the Smoky Mountains," from *Cades Cove: A Place in Appalachia***, by Gladys Oliver Burns.**

Incidents from Burns' list not found or confirmed by superintendents' reports, press releases, newspaper clippings, morning reports, or other sources:

January 1971: Fatal accident, fall. Charles Lindsey was killed in a fall on Alum Cave Trail.

September 30, 1972: Fatal accident, bicycle. Joann Hannah bled to death after a bicycle accident.

September 28, 1980: Fatal accident, auto/motorcycle. Donna Walker was killed in motorcycle accident heading north on the Gatlinburg Spur of U.S. 441.

October 12, 1980: Fatal accident, auto/motorcycle. John Frye was killed in motorcycle accident heading north on the Gatlinburg Spur of U.S. 441.

July 18, 1981: Fatal accident, drowning. David Smith drowned while tubing Raven Fork.

ACKNOWLEDGMENTS

Over the past decade, editor Steve Kemp, of Great Smoky Mountains Association (GSMA), publisher of this book, has handed me some of the more engaging assignments of my career for his gracefully designed and executed magazine *Smokies Life*. Steve likewise guided my efforts in researching and writing this book, which began with his concept for the structure it might assume and the content it might present. Steve consistently offered thoughtful critique and, in the process, revealed editorial instincts that are among the best I've encountered. I regard my professional relationship with Steve among the more fruitful, challenging, and enjoyable I've experienced in my nearly 40 years as a journalist.

Literary agent Giles Anderson's considerable expertise in the business end of book publishing has, for nearly 15 years, allowed me to focus my energies entirely on the creative process. I'm beyond grateful to have Giles in my corner.

On my frequent visits to park headquarters, the offices were always bustling with the level of activity required to operate the United States' most-visited national park. Yet all of the staffers, including those at the top tier of the management hierarchy, always seemed to find time to respond to my questions and direct me to valuable resources. Deputy Superintendent Clayton Jordan, then acting superintendent, engaged on the front end in discussions about the shape and form this book would take and the range of incidents it would address.

Clay also played a pivotal role in providing information and helping to structure the narrative for "Deadly Derecho," the chapter on the deadly storm that struck the park in 2012. Chief Ranger Steve Kloster's institutional knowledge of Great Smoky Mountains National Park (GSMNP), particularly in terms of emergency response and public health and safety, is unrivaled. Steve was also involved in early scoping meetings for this book, and, through the research process, he contributed significant information and background details for several chapters, including the one on the storm of 2012.

Public affairs officer Dana Soehn shared generously of her office space and her time in locating reports and other essential documents, all while responding to an unceasing barrage of phone calls and emails requests, many from the media, for information on events and incidents occurring in the park. Dana also provided thoughtful review of "When Bears Attack," the chapter on the first and only fatal attack by a black bear on a human in park history. Dana's associate, Brent Everitt, was likewise always willing to do what he could to support my efforts.

Kent Cave, who recently retired as GSMNP's interpretive media branch chief, possesses an encyclopedic knowledge of park history, artifacts, and interpretive resources. Over many years, I've leaned heavily on Kent's extensive knowledge, and he's never failed to direct me to the crucial information I've needed to help tell the park's story. Kent continued in that role through production of this book and assisted Steve with the book's editing.

Emergency dispatchers Randy Kelly and Dan Lawler spent significant time to locate official park incident reports on events tracing back over more than 40 years. Most of the information contained in this book is based on details those reports provided. Other park rangers, present and past, including Kent Looney, Helen McNutt, Jack Pipenbring, and Bob Wightman, contributed essential information for some of the book's chapters.

Bill Sorrell provided summaries of deaths by cause compiled by park staff. Bob Wightman also graciously agreed to read and review the entire manuscript and, in the process, provided many useful and important details. Bob also helped document several dozen deaths.

Compiling the details of the incidents presented in this book required considerable digging, and many individuals assisted mightily with the shovel work. Mike Aday, GSMNP librarian-archivist, spent countless hours searching for archival documents, pointing to digitized online resources, and providing the author with stacks and stacks of requested photocopies. John McDade, former GSMNP museum curator, also helped locate pertinent documents and materials.

Former GSMNP ranger Dwight McCarter and Jeff Wadley, a member of the Civil Air Patrol, compiled an extensive database of aircraft crashes in the park, which provided essential detail for the fatalities list contained in this book's appendix.

Bill Stiver, GSMNP supervisory wildlife biologist, likewise made a considerable contribution to the chapter on the fatal bear attack, particularly in providing information on the park's on-going science-based strategy for managing its bear population.

Anyone who has perused the beautifully designed pages of *Smokies Life* magazine recognizes GSMA's Karen Key as one of our region's finest graphic artists. Karen lent that same artistic excellence to the design of this book.

This is the second of my books to feature stunning cover art provided by landscape and wildlife photographer Bill Lea, who has spent decades capturing the park's natural beauty.

University of Tennessee (UT) Associate Professor Ken Wise, an expert on GSMNP history and author of books on the park, has, over many years, guided me to particularly rare or difficult-to-find resources on park history.

UT College of Law professors Lucy Jewel and Gary Pulsinelli provided invaluable guidance and advice on issues related to copyright law, fair use, and privacy protection. Jewel in particular took time to review copy and respond to specific questions that arose during the writing process.

Ray Garrett, UT physics professor emeritus, reviewed "The Deadliest Night in the Smokies' Deadliest Place," the chapter on the fatal car crash on the Pigeon Forge-Gatlinburg Spur in 2005, with particular attention given to the discussion of Sir Isaac Newton's laws of motion. And Mike Pelton, black-bear expert and professor emeritus of UT's Department of Forestry, Wildlife, and Fisheries, provided important information for "When Bears Attack."

GSMA associates who staff the park's visitor centers play an essential role in responding to questions and directing visitors to resources—including books and other media—that will help them gain the most from their time in the park.

GSMNP volunteer Raymond Palmer helped me build the list of known fatalities in the park by directing me to "A Partial Listing of Accidental Deaths in the Smoky Mountains," which is included as an appendix in the book *Cades Cove: A Place in Appalachia*, by Gladys Oliver Burns.

My father, Ronald Brill, has been the first to review nearly every word

I've written since I launched my writing career several decades ago. His thoughtful critique has helped weed out countless typographical blunders and grammatical missteps, but even more valuable were his suggestions pertaining to phrasing, word choice, and story organization and structure. Had Dad not been an advertising executive, he would have made a fine editor.

My wife, Belinda, has patiently abided my frequent preoccupation with story lines I'm crafting in my head and, like my father, has read nearly every word that appears in this book. Her insight is always constructive and beneficial, and her nurturing and companionship are essential to me in more ways than I can count. My daughters, Challen and Logan, sustain me always through their compassionate and loving presence in my life.

Photography credits: Bill Lea—cover, 4, 22, 59, 152, 165, 263; Great Smoky Mountains National Park Archives—19, 26, 143, 159; NPS Photos—37 (all), 72, 119 (all), 123, 179 (District Ranger Steve Kloster); Gary Wilson—54, 193; Courtesy of David Brill—262; Courtesy of Eric Johnson—67; Courtesy Frank Norton—114; Courtesy of *Knoxville News Sentinel*—188; David Luttrell—179 (Chief Ranger Clayton Jordan and Ranger Helen McNutt and Ranger Kent Looney)

ABOUT
THE AUTHOR

David Brill's articles on science, ecology, the environment, business, health, fitness, parenting, and adventure-travel have appeared in more than 25 national and regional magazines, including *National Geographic Traveler* and *Men's Health*. Brill has written extensively for and about Great Smoky Mountains National Park for nearly 20 years and has been a regular contributor to *Smokies Life* magazine since the publication's launch in 2007.

Brill has published four nonfiction books. *As Far as the Eye Can See: Reflections of an Appalachian Trail Hiker* (UT Press-Appalachian Trail Conservancy, 2013) is a collection of essays based on his six-month, 2,100-mile trek of the Appalachian Trail, from Georgia to Maine. The book, originally published in 1990, is now in its fourth edition, seventh printing.

A Separate Place: A Father's Reflection on Building a Home and Renewing a Family (Plume, 2001), chronicles the author's efforts to rekindle a connection to the natural and spiritual world by retreating to a 600-square foot cabin in the Cumberland Mountains of Tennessee.

Desire and Ice: Searching for Perspective atop Denali (National Geographic Adventure Press, 2002) recounts the ascent of eight amateur mountaineers to the top of Denali (Mt. McKinley), at 20,320 feet, the highest peak in North America and one of the coldest mountains on Earth. The book features the images of National Geographic photographer Bill Hatcher.

Cumberland Odyssey: A Journey in Pictures and Words along Tennessee's Cumberland Trail and Plateau (Mountain Trail Press, 2010) explores the natural and cultural history of the Cumberland Plateau and features Brill's essays

and the nature photography of Bill Campbell.

Brill, his wife, Belinda, their dog, Zebulon, and two cats, Elle and Tater Tot, live in a cabin in Morgan County, Tennessee.

INDEX